Strength Through Peace

The Ideas and People of Nonviolence

Center for Tea...

Edited by ...

The *Center for Teaching Peace*, a non-profit founded in 1985, works to assist students, faculties, parents, administrators, school boards, legislatures, churches, courts, prisons and any other person or group seeking to decrease violence and increase peace through education.

Strength Through Peace is another of the Center's publications. Earlier ones include *Solutions to Violence, All of One Peace: Essays on Nonviolence, A Teacher's Manual* and *Keeping Faith, Keeping On*.

In addition, the Center conducts a home study correspondence course. A newsletter is sent regularly to Center members and friends.

The *Center for Teaching Peace*
4501 Van Ness St.
Washington DC 20016

(202) 537-1372

Dedication

To all practitioners of active nonviolence, whose numbers are larger than they think and whose work more fruitful than they know. Peace is not only possible but inevitable.

Acknowledgements

There's an old Irish saying—and it usually is—that goes like this: the trouble with a good idea is that it soon degenerates into hard work.

The degeneracy behind this book belongs to Mav McCarthy whose brain power, slogging power and staying power were essential throughout the long days of formatting, editing, correcting and moving the copy. Her mentor, Lili Robins, is owed a debt for being Mav's tender guide to the world of graphics and computers.

As publisher, the *Center for Teaching Peace* has been generously backed by a range of financial supporters: the Helen Sperry Lea Foundation, the Florence and John Schumann Foundation, the Morris and Gwendolyn Cafritz Foundation, the Olender Foundation, the Streisand Foundation, the Public Welfare Foundation, the Peace Development Fund, The Washington Post Company, Sargent Shriver, Linda Smith, Polly Steinway, Kathy Hessler, John Stohrm and many others of spirited nature.

The staff at the Media Center at American University and Balmar Printing offered invaluable counsel.

Finally, large thanks to those friends—students, teachers, peace builders, lovers of long shots, uphill pushers of stones—who offered suggestions on which essays to include in this anthology. For them, nonviolence and pacifism are adventures, not mere beliefs.

Introduction

One problem with reading a lot, which I do, is wanting to tell others what I've read, which I'm doing now. The essays here are ones I've saved over the years, some found in the back shelves of musty, small-town bookstores, others clipped from newspapers amid the daily fare of war and gore.

Speaking of bookstores, one of my hangouts is Second Story Books in Bethesda, Md., not far from the public high school where I have been teaching courses on nonviolence since 1988. Second Story offers discounts that get bibliophiles salivating. Sagging shelf after sagging shelf brims with thousands of books on wars—from biographies of militarists, dictators, fuhrers and assorted fugelmen, to accounts of ancient and modern battles used as school texts to prep the next generation for its wars.

I asked the manager, how about a peace shelf? Kindly entrepreneur that he was, he smiled: "Not likely." It wouldn't be profitable: peaceniks browse more than they buy.

Another manager came along a few years later and I tried again—with better luck. The store now has a peace shelf. The expected is there—Gandhi biographies, collections by Linus Pauling, King anthologies—along with an occasional rare find like a Michael True or John Dear book on nonviolence.

The peace shelf is growing, I'm happy to report. Peace folks are actually buying—no, splurging—on gems like Michael Nagler's "America Without Violence."

An excerpt from that classic is the first essay here. Ones that follow in 12 chapters explain, advocate, defend, cherish, and honor the varicolored idea of strength through peace. The essays provide the intellectual tools to build a moral structure in which the mind and heart can win inner peace and begin working for outer peace in the community and among governments.

So read on. And while waiting for the bookstores to install peace shelves, start stacking your own at home. Begin with this one!

Colman McCarthy

Contents

5   Is Gandhi Right?

6   Okay, But What About Hitler?

7   Pacifism or Warism

8   The Vietnam War Is Not Over

1

Active Nonviolence

I would say that I'm a nonviolent soldier. In place of weapons of violence, you have to use your mind, your heart, your sense of humor, every faculty available to you …because no one has the right to take the life of another human being.

Joan Baez

I despair to see so many radicals turn to violence as a proof of their militancy and commitment. It is heart-breaking to see all the old mistakes being made all over again. The usual pattern seems to be that people give nonviolence two weeks to solve their problem …and then decide it has "failed." Then they go on with violence for the next hundred years …and it seems never to "fail" and be rejected.

Ted Roszak

At the Core of Nonviolence
by Michael Nagler

Gandhi said, "Non-violence is the greatest force man has ever been endowed with." It is in all likelihood the most positive force in the universe. Without it, as Kropotkin realized when he discovered the "mutual aid factor" in evolution, all social progress would have stopped long ago and "human society could not be maintained for even one single generation." It is this power that we have to understand by turning inside out some of our preconceptions and by looking for what is there: not the negation of something else but the thing itself.

Here it is best to look to the people who have actually used nonviolence. One of them, of course, was George Fox. The year that Cromwell died, 1658, was one of great tribulation for Fox and the Society of Friends. "Great stirs were in the nation, the minds of the people being unsettled," and many Friends, too, were tempted to fly to arms to defend themselves or to take advantage of the chaos to advance their positions. Fox sent out a ringing epistle to warn them of the dangers of such a move and inspired them to:

> Stand in the fear and dread of the Lord God; His power, life, light, seed and wisdom, by which ye may take away the occasion of wars, and so know a kingdom which hath no end, *and fight for that with spiritual weapons*, which takes away the occasion of the carnal, and there gather men to war, as many as ye can, and set up as many as ye can with these weapons.

What exactly are "spiritual weapons"? He was simply referring to the power of love. "Love has more power," said Saint Teresa somewhere, "than a besieging army." Similarly, the Buddha described a "true brahmin" as one who "fears neither jail nor death: He has the power of love no army can defeat." But the love they are speaking of is rather different from the love we speak of when we describe, for example, the love of one person for another, which is a wonderful thing, but which has never prevailed against the power of wars. The love that Fox, Saint Teresa, and others are alluding to is love for all. It is the commitment to expand our circles of compassion outward without limit. It starts as the love we are familiar with but becomes qualitatively different: This kind of love makes us unsatisfied to love only this person or another; it means we cannot bear the alienation of being for one party against another, as though we were divided against ourselves. When we think of loving the people in an oppressed country whom we have never seen—and their oppressors—we realize that this love requires an immense unification of individual drives and predilections and could well generate within us a greater than individual force. "My life is an indivisible whole," said Gandhi, and "all of my actions have their rise in my insatiable love of mankind."

One example of how this kind of love can work comes from an eyewitness account of a great civil rights breakthrough that occurred in Birmingham, Alabama, in 1964. That was the year a major civil rights march found its way blocked by the city's police and firemen. Everything Martin Luther King and his followers had worked for was put to the test in this confrontation, and this is what happened:

> "We're going to win our freedom," a Negro leader said at a mass meeting in Birmingham last year, "and as we do it we're going to set our white brothers free." A short while later, when the Negroes faced a barricade of police dogs, clubs and fire hoses, they "became spiritually intoxicated," as another leader described it. "This was sensed by the police and firemen and it began to have an effect on them .... I don't know what happened to me .... I got up from my knees and said to the cops: `We're not turning back. We haven't done anything wrong. All we want is our freedom. How do you feel doing these things?'" The Negroes started advancing and Sheriff Bull Connor shouted: "Turn on the water!" But the firemen did not respond. Again he gave the order and nothing happened. Some observers claim chat they saw firemen crying. Whatever happened, the Negroes went through the lives .... Until now this mood of outgoing empathetic nonviolence has been rarely achieved in this country. It was only part of the story in

Birmingham, where in the end a more cautious tokenism gripped the cop leaders. But it is the due to the potential power of nonviolence.

This is not an isolated occurrence in the annals of nonviolence. British police fell back before a slowly advancing band of unarmed demonstrators crossing a field in India because even when the latter were beaten to the ground they stood up and kept advancing with smiles on their faces. "You just can't hit a chap who smiles at you like that," the police would say later.

The force of this love, as Martin Luther King said, is "passive physically, but strongly active spiritually"; that is, "while the nonviolent resister is passive in the sense that he is not physically aggressive toward his opponent, his mind and his emotions are constantly active," constantly seeking to persuade the opposition. These "spiritual weapons" do what guns and armies only pretend to do, they defend us.

What is more, as the examples quoted above show, they can bring about the kind of great social changes on which stability and true security depend.

Although they can be used for social changes, these "spiritual weapons" do not arise from society. As we have seen before, they are brought into play when the individual contacts more love for all within.

Nonviolence, then, seeks lasting gains, not a rapid "win"; it always wants improved relations with the opposing party, never its submission. It operates by persuasion, not coercion. Shortly after William Penn was attracted to George Fox's way of life he asked Fox if he had to stop wearing a sword. Fox's answer was something like, "Wear thy sword as long as thou canst." He wanted Penn to outgrow the need for a sword and renounce it of his own free will. In the same way Gandhi never urged people to leave military service just to gratify him or anyone else; rather, he suggested they think the problem through and come to their own conclusions. "Error" was less to be shunned than insincerity. Fox and Gandhi strove constantly to move people's hearts but not to move them against their will. They wanted to educate their will, to free it from the compulsions of anger and fear, to help them get in touch with a deeper and wiser will inside themselves. Love, like gravity, works by bending the space around it so that the other's will moves into that new space. One is naturally and steadily drawn into the new position rather than shoved into it from behind. Although selfless love seems to operate slowly, it operates irresistibly, and what it gains is permanent.

Gandhi always insisted that he had not invented anything, that there was no such thing as "Gandhism," and that truth and nonviolence were as "old as the hills." He was just a scientist, an experimenter; what he experimented with was the truth and what he discovered was its practical application, love for all. The problem is that although truth, love, and nonviolence are as "old as the hills," although they have been silently at work in the life process since before there were Homo Sapiens, we human beings on the whole are at a primitive stage of understanding and developing them.

The tinkerers who preceded Gandhi, the Marconis and Edisons of this field, had to use rather picturesque language in their attempts to describe what kinds of forces love and its opposite really are. Ballou referred to "phrenomagnetic fluid" (or "vibes," in the lingo of our day). Emerson, slightly after him, said, people "imagine that they communicate their virtue and vice only by overt actions, and do not see that virtue and vice emit a breath every moment." In a sermon given in 1906 in Europe, Rabbi Aaron Tamaret used the most picturesque language of all:

> Good actions set good waves moving in the air, and a man performing good acts soon purifies the air which surrounds him. Evil actions poison the atmosphere, and a man's evil acts pollute the air until finally he himself breathes the poisonous vapors .... Were the eye able to perceive it, we should see that when a man raises his fist against another man, the air surrounding him is filled with waving fists; that when a man raises a foot to kick another man, the air registers feet raised high and aimed at him.

These writers were groping for images to describe an unseen force that is working in human affairs the way gravity or electricity is silently working in the world of matter. Nonviolence, as Kropotkin pointed out, is working to keep societies from falling apart as surely as electricity is holding proton and electron together in the atomic nucleus and gravity is keeping you and me from flying off the surface of the planet. In fact, we could call love for all, or nonviolence, a spiritual force of gravity. Though the attraction may seem weak at times, though it may even turn inside out and become repulsion, there is a force in the heart of every sentient creature that draws all life together spiritually. Gandhi did not invent but only discovered this force, in just the way that Sir Isaac Newton discovered the law of gravity. Both these pioneers made their epochal discoveries not by looking beyond the bounds of ordinary experience but by looking at ordinary experience in a new way. Hundreds of men and women had been hit by falling apples; millions have been subjected to indignities like being ejected from a railroad carriage. An occasional genius can use such common experiences to discover a law of gravity-or a law of love.

from "America Without Violence:
Why Violence Persists and How You Can Stop It."
1982. Island Press, Box 38, Covelo, CA 95428

6

Those Troublesome Pacifists
by Caroline Moorehead

Pacifism is basically the most lonely of beliefs, held for the most part in private, and sustained in isolation, often in the face of powerful opposition . . . .To profess this faith, people have fasted, marched, survived long winters of extreme discomfort protesting at the gates of military bases, and been arrested more times than it is possible to record. Some have risked the death penalty rather than alter their views; some have indeed died for it. A few, their health and spirit broken by punishment, have gone mad. There is a stubbornness, and obduracy about pacifism that can be infuriating; it can also be heroic, admirable.

Behind the tactics of nonviolence lies the clearest pacifist philosophy.

Pacifist belief relies on a notion of personal morality. Conscientious objectors, who embody this sense of responsibility, form a crucial element in pacifist ideology, though they became important only with the advent of conscription in Europe at the end of the 18th century.

The exact point where pacifist rejection of war begins has varied from century to century and group to group and continues to vary today. At its most extreme, pacifism can mean complete dissociation from society and all its violent tenets, like the Huttrite communities of the 16th century; it can mean refusing to kill animals as well as men, and rejecting, like the Anabaptists, the whole structure of government, along with the machinery of war, as basically violent in character; it can mean absolute non-violence for oneself, but no strictures on those who have not seen the light (some Buddhists); it can mean the refusal to condone or be involved in one war, but not all wars, as in the case of American pacifists in the war between the states. In between come those who protest against war, in whatever form it appears, but not against self-defence; and those who refuse to fight, not because they are against fighting, but because they do not believe that the state has any right to order them to do so. Most common in the 20th century Western world have been those who have opposed war from rationalist, humanitarian reasons, rather than purely religious ones, men rejecting not government itself, but only the use by governments of what they consider unnecessary violence, and who have tried at the same time to integrate pacifism into the order of the world. Such people often see themselves as disciples of the great teachers of non-violence, Thoreau, Garrison, Tolstoy and Gandhi, all of whom argued that the techniques of non-resistance are ultimately more effective than, as well as ethically superior to, violence. It is the very diversity of these beliefs and the complexity of their origins that has made the task of the Tribunals set up to pass judgment on those who hold them during times of war so very hard.

Pacifism, in the narrow sense of the rejection of war by an individual, is rather less than 2,000 years old. Before the Christians, as Peter Brock shows in Pacifism in Europe to 1914, there is no record of a soldier refusing to take part in war on grounds of conscience; and right up until the early 18th century Western pacifism was a concern only of those who belonged firmly inside the Christian teachings.

Though a number of sayings have been attributed to Jesus which collectively suggest rejection of violence—"all they that take the sword shall perish with the sword"; "blessed are the peacemakers: for they shall be called the children of God"—no pronouncement is in fact to be found in the Gospels concerning the rightness or wrongness of military service. Christian scholars agree that Jesus preached a philosophy of nonviolence; where they disagree is over what precisely it meant and whether it was intended to cover all circumstances and all times.

Many of the early church fathers condemned war, and two of them, Tertullian and Origen, stated unequivocally that Christ's words were incompatible with war. By the 4th century, though official church sayings continued to be anti-military in tone, soldiering had become an accepted profession for Christians, Constantine having accommodated the Church to the necessities of warfare. It was under the sign of the cross that his army defeated that of his imperial rival, Maxentius, and a Christian emperor was to become the protector of the persecuted sect: at a price. In 314, two years after Constantine's victory at the Milvian Bridge outside Rome, a Church synod in Arles declared: "Concerning those who lay down their arms in time of peace: let them be excluded from communion." Those with conscientious scruples were to be tolerated in time of war but not in time of peace. Soon, they acquired a patron saint, in the form of St. Maximilianus. Early in the 5th century, St. Augustine of Hippo produced his theory of a Just War—that a war fought for a just cause, with a right intention, declared by lawful authority, conducted within certain strict moral limits and only in the very last resort, could be justified—which, alongside the notion of the Holy War, was to become medieval Christianity's stand on war and peace. With the barbarian invasions, pacifism among the Christians vanished, and reappeared only later and then among more obscure sects and not as an extension of the Reformation, which repudiated the state and all its laws and turned instead to higher dictates. The Anabaptists, too, moved and took new roots and new positions. In north-west Germany and the Netherlands, they were influenced by a former Catholic priest called Menno Simons, founder of the Mennonites, who announced his desire to build up a new congregation of Christians "without spot or wrinkle" and celebrated only the kingdom of the spirit. Manichaeism flourished for a time in the Balkans, emerging also in Italy, and later in France where, known as Albigensians, its numerous supporters were eventually crushed by Simon de Montfort. The 15th century saw the Waldensians in Lyons, preaching Christian obedience and the literal following of the Sermon on the Mount, and a number of Bohemian sects rejecting non-violence.

In England, there were also the Quakers. George Fox, a Leicestershire shoemaker, preached the need to return to what he saw as the spiritual teachings of Christ. Fox repudiated "carnal weapons", and by 1652 was writing, "The peacemaker hath the Kingdom and is in it". Persecuted, condemned as traitors and reviled, it was not until the end of the 17th century that the Quakers emerged as an organized body, with regular yearly meetings, all subscribing to the belief that peace and persuasion were better politics, and had more force, than war and the use of weapons. A peace document, originally worded by Fox, is still the basis of a leaflet used by Quakers when explaining their principles about warfare. 'We utterly deny all outward wars and strife, and fighting with outward weapons, for any end, or under any pretence whatever . . . the spirit of Christ, which leads us unto all Truth, will never move us to fight and war against any man . . .'

It was in America that the struggle for freedom of conscience, later to provide the roots for non-violent disobedience, took shape, chiefly in New England and Pennsylvania, where in the 17th century religious pacifists won the right to refuse to bear arms. Asserting that the state had no authority over matters of conscience, and taking literally the New Testament words "resist not evil", many of the peace Churches, the Mennonites, Brethren and Amish, withdrew to a large extent from the world, becoming known in the process as the "non- resistants".

The Quakers, refusing to see their meetings as little islands to be preserved from the wickedness of the world, took a different view and argued that, on the contrary, it would be their vision, one of goodness and peace, that would conquer. When the Society of Friends established the government of Pennsylvania, they planned that civil authority should flow from their own direct understanding of what was right, their "inner light". Nothing that could be construed as support for state violence in any of its forms was to be endorsed: the Friends would pay no war taxes, give no fees to others to take their place as soldiers, and they would serve the war machine in no alternative capacity. The Great Law, introduced by William Penn in 1682, at a moment when in Britain over a hundred crimes were still punishable by death, made murder and treason the only two capital offences. During both the Revolution and the Civil War, Quakers were repeatedly imprisoned, fined, and their property confiscated. They were little liked. In 1660 a report in Virginia had referred to them as an "unreasonable and turbulent sort of people"—not militant, but they could be fiercely and provocatively stubborn.

Right up until the 20th century, however, direct action of a pacifist nature was seen, not as something that might become an organized mass movement towards social change, but as an individual's testimony, a gesture of personal creed. Individuals, not groups, are remembered and honoured for their stands. John Woolman, one of the most significant figures in the early history of non-violence, castigated fellow Quakers who were also slave-holders in the South, and refused to pay his taxes in support of the war against the French or of that against the Indians. Henry David Thoreau, the philosopher-naturalist, is best loved of all American civil libertarians. For some years he had refused to pay his poll tax, though he paid other taxes, like the highway tax, insisting that the poll tax went directly to support a government which sanctioned slavery, of which he did not approve. In 1846, he was arrested as he was on his way to the shoemaker to collect a shoe that had just been mended. His friend Ralph Waldo Emerson is said to have visited him in his cell and asked: 'Henry, why are you here?' 'Why,' Thoreau replied, 'are you not here?'

The result of his one night in captivity is possibly the best known of all American pacifist texts and the most widely quoted, for in it Thoreau defines the exact nature of the division that every pacifist faces when he feels that he can no longer serve his government in war and violence. "The authority of government", writes Thoreau, " . . is still an impure one: to be strictly just, it must have the sanction and consent of the governed . . . There will never be a really free and enlightened State, until the State comes to recognize the individual as a higher and independent Power, from which all its own power and authority are derived, and treats him accordingly."

Throughout the 18th and 19th centuries, Europe produced a growing number of protesters against war. Philosophers and statesmen drew up visions of a united Europe, in which war would be seen as a crime against humanity, and wrote a series of carefully argued peace plans to give substance to their dreams. From 1815 on, peace societies sprang up in most states—some radical and socialist, seeing peace as part of a new order, others conservative, seeing it as a preserver of the old one. The Peace Society, founded in London in 1816, drew together pacifists from across the whole spectrum of religious and moral belief, rallying a call for peace to other reforms, such as the abolition of slavery and penal reform. In New York, the previous year, David Low Dodge, a merchant and keen peace pamphleteer, had founded a similar American society. Both were "principled against all wars, under any pretence." By 1825, however, when there were 25 pacifist societies in Britain alone and more than 30 in the United States, the realization had spread that something more was needed: that it was no longer enough to appeal simply to morality. A peace programme was drawn up by the British Peace Society, calling for the settlement of international disputes by arbitration, and expressing support for the "policeman but not the soldier."

From the early 1840s on, Europe saw many international peace congresses and late in the century a 'great peace crusade' was launched in Western Europe, which put forward a phased programme of disarmament and the building up of antimilitaristic international laws. Individual men and women continued to speak out against war: men like Jean de Triac, a Catholic writer, who described war as "meurtre en grand." By the end of the century, anti-militarism was written into the manifestos of the nascent socialist parties all the way from the Balkans to France.

It was also towards the end of the century that pacifism acquired one of its most eloquent spokesmen. In 1857 Tolstoy had watched a man being guillotined in Paris and had been revolted; once an enthusiastic soldier, his conversion to total pacifism took place in the late 1870s, when he began equating war and capital punishment with murder, and in A Confession he wrote of non-resistance to evil. Tolstoy's pacifism was based on the need for personal responsibility; he saw it as an ethical imperative, expressed most purely and most simply in the teaching of Christ. The state itself, he maintained, was the greatest obstacle to the law of love. 'Government is violence,' he wrote to a Hungarian admirer, 'Christianity is meekness, nonresistance, love. And therefore, government cannot be Christian, and a man who wishes to be a Christian must not serve government' nor swear official oaths, collaborate with the police, or perform military service. To resist war was to liberate mankind from its shadow. "Universal military service," declared Tolstoy in The Kingdom of God is Within You, 'is the last stage of violence that governments need for the maintenance of thewhole structure . . . and its removal would bring down the whole building." In this, he was anticipating the arguments of the most persuasive of the 20th century pacifists.

If Tolstoy's doctrine of social protest by withdrawal was hard to follow, his influence over later pacifists was immense, largely because of his realization that pacifism had to emerge from its Christian roots. It was, he believed universal to all mankind, precisely because its origins lay in an ethical principle "intelligible and common to all men, of whatever religion or nation, whether Catholic, Mohammedan, Buddhist, Confucian, whether Spanish or Japanese", and that the day had to be sought when—of wars and armies as there are now, there will remain only the recollection. Soon after it was published, Gandhi read *The Kingdom of God is Within You*. Russia gave me in Tolstoy, he was to write, many years later, a teacher who furnished a reasoned basis for my non-violence.

"Troublesome People: The Warriors of Pacifism"
Adler & Adler, 1987

Nonviolence and Moral Courage
by Aldous Huxley

Pacifists believe and their belief is based upon individual experience and a study of history, past and contemporary—that the most effective, the most equitable, the most economical way of meeting violence is to use non-violence.

If violence is answered by violence, the result is a physical struggle. Now, a physical struggle inevitably arouses hatred, fear, rage and resentment. In the heat of passion all scruples are thrown to the winds, all the habits of forbearance and humaneness acquired during years of civilized living are forgotten. Nothing matters any more except victory. And when at last victory comes to one or other of the parties, this final outcome of physical struggle bears no relation to the rights or wrongs of the case; nor, in most instances, does it provide any lasting settlement to the dispute at issue. The cases in which victory does provide some kind of lasting settlement may be classified as follows: (1) Victory is final where the vanquished are completely or very nearly exterminated. In the case of war between two populous countries extermination is unlikely: one war tends therefore to beget another. (2) Victory may lead to an unquestioned settlement where the fighting forces involved are so small that the mass of the population is left unaffected by the struggle. Today the entire population is liable to be affected by war. The relatively harmless wars conducted according to an elaborate code of rules by a small warrior-caste are things of the past. (3) Victory may lead to permanent peace where the victors settle down among the vanquished as a ruling minority and are, in due course, absorbed by them. This does not apply to contemporary wars. (4) Finally, victory may be followed by an act of reparation on the part of the victors to the vanquished. This will disarm resentment and lead to a genuine settlement. It was the policy pursued by the English after the Boer War. Such a policy is essentially an application of the principles of non-violence. The longer and the more savage the conflict, the more difficult is it to make an act of reparation after victory. It was relatively easy to be just after the Boer War; it was psychologically all but impossible to be just in 1918. That is why the pacifist insists that the principles of nonviolence should be applied, wherever possible, before physical conflict has actually broken out.

Nonviolence does not mean doing nothing. It means making the enormous effort required to overcome evil with good. Nonviolence does not rely on strong muscles and devilish armaments; it relies on moral courage, self-control and the knowledge, unswervingly acted upon, that there is in every human being, however brutal, however personally hostile, a fund of kindness, a love of justice, a respect for goodness and truth which can be reached by anyone who uses the right means. To use these means is often extraordinarily hard; but history shows that it can be done—and done not only by exceptional individuals, but by large groups of ordinary men and women and even by governments.

Pacifism is often opposed on the ground that "civilization is based on force," "there cannot be justice unless it is imposed by force," and so on. What exactly does this word "force" stand for? The answer is that, when used in reference to human relations, it has no single definite meaning. "Force" is used by parents, when, without resort to any kind of physical compulsion, they make their children obey them. "Force" is used by the attendants in an asylum, when they restrain a maniac from hurting himself or others. "Force" is used by the police when they control traffic and "force" of another kind and in greater quantity is used by them when they make a baton charge. Finally, there is the "force" that is used in war. This varies with the mentality of the combatants and the weapons and other technical devices at their disposal. Chivalry has disappeared and the "rules of war" are coming to be ignored; in any future war "force" will probably mean violence and fraud used to the extreme limit of the belligerents' capacity.

"Force" used by armies making use of modern weapons is morally unjustifiable and is not even likely to secure its object, for the simple reason that these weapons are so destructive that a war cannot now preserve any of a nation's vital interests; it can only bring ruin and death indiscriminately to all who come within its range, innocent and guilty, attacker and attacked, soldier and civilian alike. Merely in order to be effective, "force" must be used in moderation.

Experience shows that the forces which accomplish most are psychological forces--the force of persuasion, the force of loyalty, the force of social tradition, the force of good example and the like.

It is often objected that pacifism is morally unjustifiable. "Your position in society," the critic of pacifism argues, "is that of a parasite. You are profiting by what the armed forces of your country are doing to preserve you and your family from danger but you refuse to undertake defence work yourself and you try to persuade others to follow your example. You have no right to take from the society in which you live without giving anything in return." Several answers to these criticisms present themselves:

(1) In the contemporary world, the armed forces of a country do not provide its inhabitants with protection. On the contrary, their existence is one of the principal sources of national danger. There is no more effective way of provoking people to attack than to treaten them. At the present time Great Britain combines extreme vulnerability with formidable aggressive armament. Our policy of rearmament with weapons of aggression is one which positively invites attack. The pacifist is criticized as a shirker who seeks security behind a line of soldiers, sailors and airmen, whom he refuses to help. In reality, his dearest wish is to get rid of the soldiers, sailors and airmen, and all their machinery of destruction; for he knows that so long as they are there, security will be unattainable. Tanks, bombers and battleships do not give security; on the contrary, they are a constant source of danger.

(2) Those who accuse pacifists of being parasites upon the society in which they live should pause for a moment to consider a few facts and figures. Since the last war this country has spent sixteen hundred millions of pounds upon its armaments, and the rate of expenditure is now to be increased. The world as a whole spends nearly two thousand millions a year on its "defence forces." These "defence forces" live at the expense of the working community, performing no constructive work, absorbing an increasing amount of the world's energy and not only failing to provide the individual citizens of the various nations with adequate protection, but actually inviting attack from abroad. To the inhabitant of a bombarded London it will be no satisfaction to learn that the planes for which

he has been paying so heavily in taxation are bombarding some foreign capital.

(3) Refusal to obey the government of the society of which one is a member is a very serious matter. Still, most moralists and political philosophers have been of opinion that individuals are fully justified in disobeying the State if the State commands them to do something which they are convinced to be wrong. Social solidarity is not always desirable. There is such a thing as solidarity with evil as well as solidarity with good. A man who finds himself on a pirate ship is morally justified in refusing to co-operate with his shipmates in their nefarious activities. All reformers have been men who refused to co-operate, on some important issue, with the societies of which they were members. That is why so many of them have been persecuted by their contemporaries. The Christian religion takes its name from a persecuted reformer.

Criticisms and answers:

(1) The State provides free schools, libraries, pensions, etc. In return the individual should do what the State demands of him.

Answer: (a) The individual pays for State services in taxation.

(b) The State is not God and its demands are not categorical imperatives. The State was made for man, not man for the State. The State is a convenience, like drains or the telephone; its demand that it should be treated as an allwise divinity is inadmissible and leads, as the history of tyrannies and dictatorships shows, to every kind of crime and disaster.

(c) If the State may justifiably demand of an individual that he should commit murder for the sake of his country, then it is equally justified in demanding that he should commit lesser crimes. But we can imagine the outcry that would be raised by pious militarists if, for example, in an effort to raise the birthrate and improve the quality of the race, the State were to conscribe all women and compel them to have sexual intercourse with eugenically selected men.

(2) "The pacifist method of dealing with war is too slow and there will be another war before there are enough pacifists to stop it."

The pacifist method is certainly slow; but the militarist's method is far slower. Indeed, the militarist's method is foredoomed to make no advance whatever towards the goal of peace. War produces more

17

war. Only nonviolence can produce non-violence. Pacifism is admittedly slow and hard to practise; but the fact remains that it is the only method of getting universal peace which promises to be in the least effective.

(3) "There is something worse than war, and that is injustice." But war inevitably commits injustices far greater and more widespread than those it was called upon to redress.

(4) "Pacifism tends to increase the arrogance and power of dictators."

(a) None of the modern dictators has been faced with largescale pacifism. Where nonviolence has been used on a large scale even violent and ruthless rulers have been nonplussed.

(b) What increases the arrogance of dictators is not so much pacifism as the half-hearted use of their own violent methods. The violence of dictators must be opposed either by violence greater than theirs with the certainty of prolonging the war habit and the possibility of doing irreparable damage to civilization

or else by complete pacifism which, however slow and difficult, will ultimately lead to the establishment of peace .

from "An Encyclopedia of Pacifism"
1937. Reprinted in "The Handbook of
Nonviolence" by Robert Seeley, 1986.
Lawrence Hill & Company, 520 Riverside
Avenue, Westport CT 06880

Nonviolent Strategies
by Hildegaard Goss-Mayr

Now I should like to ask you not to take the expression nonviolence in a negative sense. It is a very negative expression for something which is highly active, aggressive and strong; which is a force. We regret that we have not found a better word to express this type of action. I hope we will not limit ourselves to discuss this term but try to get the sense, the real meaning for which it stands.

There are in man three possibilities to react against injustice:

1. Once you have become aware of an injustice you can remain passive. This is the first and I think the most common attitude. Probably each one of us has had this experience in his own life. We have accepted passively many injustices, many things that we considered wrong. This is the most negative attitude that man can take.

2. The second is the traditional way of reacting against injustice, the way that has been taken in history in general, that is, to react against injustice, aggression and other forms of evil with the same means. We could say to oppose the institutional forms of violence with counter-violence in the effort to overcome existing injustices. This means to resort to the same means with which the established forces are operating. By doing this, we remain, however, within the system, that is to say, we accept to remain within the vicious circle of violence and counter-violence which necessarily creates new forms of violence, even if we succeed to overcome certain injustices through the application of violence. It must be made very clear that the means are linked to the aim. That is to say, the use of violence in the effort to overcome injustice necessarily creates new forms of suppression and exploitation. Acting in this way one remains within the vicious circle of arms' trade, money speculation, verbal promises etc., and the mass of the people continue to suffer exploitation and injustice. There has been, perhaps more in our time than before, more serious research concerning a new way of fighting against injustice by using means that do

not include hatred, violence, etc.

3. Perhaps this third way of reacting against an injustice could be explained through a very simple example. I have two children. If, for instance, my boy, who is ten and by nature violent, has done something wrong and if I use the same aggressive means as he does, we shall just hurt each other. He does not improve and I must tell myself: "Well, you have not done anything to overcome the evil." On the contrary, if one really wanted to solve the problem, a teacher or parent would explain to the young person why his way of acting is wrong and help him to direct his forces toward positive tasks. That is to say, you dialogue, you begin to use methods and techniques in order to solve the conflict. In this process neither of us is diminished; on the contrary, he advances and I begin to understand him better and to learn about what he has to contribute. This force is the force of intelligence but also the force of truth, of love and justice that has been brought into play in this effort of solving a problem. This is the type of strength which is at the core of nonviolent action.

There are always two aspects in this form of action which are inseparable. If they are separated, we can no longer speak of an authentic nonviolent action. These two aspects are: (1) a specific view of man, a certain attitude toward men and society, and (2) certain techniques and methods that correspond to this attitude and that incarnate this force in a given conflict. This technique and this view go together and cannot be separated.

Now, which attitude toward life, toward man does it imply? First of all, an *absolute respect* of man, of his whole life, in body and spirit. Secondly, the conviction that man is man. We very often do not believe anymore that *man is man*, but we put a label, we say he is a communist, he is a conservative, he is black, he is white, and we do not see anymore the man behind the ideology, the religion or the race which he presents.

Those who work with this power of non-violence believe that *every man has a conscience*. This conscience may be uneducated, underdeveloped; it may, by tradition, be deformed; but it is there—and if work is done, this conscience can be awakened, it can be challenged, it can be reached. I think this is truly an aspect of hope; if we cannot believe anymore that man is man, in this

20

sense, in the final analysis, there is then no other way than to use the old traditional forms of violence in trying to solve our problems. This implies that *man must never be identified with evil.* As long as we identify him with evil we sacrifice him to an ideology. On the contrary the task of the nonviolent action is to *fight the injustice and to liberate men,* those who suffer the injustice as well as those who are responsible for it. This therefore is a very constructive, positive and active form of living.

I think it has already become clear that this kind of action has nothing to do with a sentimental form of love or of being nice. It is a strategy, it is a way to act, it is a struggle that has to be carried on to the last consequences. If it remains only a single, sporadic action it will not succeed. This implies that non-violent workers have to undergo training just as a soldier is trained for violent combat.

During recent years research on non-violent alternatives has been taken up on various scientific levels, as for instance political science, sociology, education, psychology, etc., in various Peace Research Institutes. Only very recently, however, non-violent action is being given more and serious attention and an effort is made to relate it to the various levels of human life. But we are still only at the very beginning and nobody can propose a complete and perfect strategy. There is no universal model of action. Nonviolent strategy has to be adapted to the need, to the particular situation and problem that is involved. Thus Gandhi's or Martin Luther King's methods cannot simply be transferred to the Latin American scene. From their strategies we can learn certain basic principles and develop and apply them in an adequate way to given conditions.

I should like to add that it is significant that these methods, so far, have mainly been used by the poor; I think nonviolence is essentially an arm of the poor, a force of liberation for them. Not only do they have no access to the arms of the rich, they often passively accept injustice because they are unaware of the power of resistance that lies within them because they are human beings. It is an essential task to make them aware of this force and train them to apply it. Most of the nonviolent actions that have been realized in Latin America so far have been carried out

21

by the very poor people, by industrial workers and campesinos, on the plantations or in the barrios of the cities.

1. Analysis. One has to be aware of the injustice in order to be able to fight it. You have to analyze very well the situation, not only its local aspect but the whole context in which it occurs; for instance, if you work for economic and social justice in Latin America, you must make the complete analysis and see how it is linked to the economic and military policy of the rich countries.

2. Form action groups and train leadership. If there is no local leadership, an action will not succeed; I think so far this has been one of the weak points in nonviolent action.

3. Then select a limited and well-defined first project. It must be at the level where the people with whom you work can understand it and where they are capable to solve it with their small forces. It is very important, in particular if you work with poor people for whom it may be the first time that they act, that this action makes them aware of their own strength. I remember working in Medellin, Colombia, with such a group in a barrio. There were about 5,000 people who had occupied land on a steep hill above the city. They had neither water nor electricity, canalization or schools. Many were unemployed. A priest who came to live with them developed leadership and tried to stimulate initiatives among the people to change their dismal conditions. With his help a seminar on nonviolent action was organized in which did participate not only representatives of the barrio but also students, teachers, social workers, intellectuals, priests, etc. It was for them, who knew poverty only from statistics, a challenging experience to live in the mud of the barrio. It helped to bridge the gap between the poor and the educated and to make them understand the necessity of working together for justice for all. The objective was, after having transmitted the basic facts about non-violence and its methods of action, and after having analyzed their situation, to make the poor people themselves decide upon their first project and to outline their plan of action. They decided that their most urgent problem was water: they learned how to negotiate, how to bring their problem before the mind of the responsible people—who live far from the reality of the poor—how to build up their forces with the help of conscious and educated people

and to win the support of a growing section of the population. They learned to use their imagination and to try out their human, moral and political power in this first project. They did win and helped themselves to build their water pipes. From there they went on to electricity, schooling, labor, etc. They experienced the power of man to work for change.

4. Expansion to the international level. The, once you act against one injustice, you see how it is linked to others, nationally and internationally. Therefore in the future the strategy must be to join actions in Africa, Asia or Latin America where people are working, for instance for land reform or where they are suffering particularly from the exploitation by certain international companies or from certain economic policies of the industrialized countries, with efforts in Europe and in the United States which are directed at changing these injustices. This means to put pressure on our political, economic and cultural groups, and upon our Churches in order to finally transform this system of exploitation. We are facing a task that concerns humanity. It is impossible for the developing countries to bring about the necessary changes unless in the rich countries as well the change of our economic, political and military system is obtained.

5. Progression of means. Direct action, strike, boycott, and immobilization are some of the heavier arms of non-violent action. Again, these actions must be adapted to the situation in which the struggle is taking place. However, after serious reflection and preparation much more is possible in the way of action than we imagine in general, even under most difficult circumstances. The most instructive example of recent times is that of the Czech people who did succeed in organizing the whole nation in a boycott against the invading Soviet troops. It showed what a whole nation is able to do if her people are very deeply concerned about certain injustices and are willing to accept the consequences of their collective action.

"Writings by Prophetic Voices in the World Religions"
Edited by Edward Guinan.
1973. Paulist Press, 1865 Broadway,
New York NY 10023

The Energy of Nonviolence
by Michael True

Violence is so much a part of American culture in the late twentieth century that one is likely to think of it as the dominant characteristic. People from abroad who know the United States only through its aggressive foreign policy and its popular culture—including gangster/counterinsurgency/war films—certainly perceive us as a violent people. D. H. Lawrence, writing in the 1920s, said that the "essential American soul is hard, isolate, stoic, and a killer." H. Rap Brown's argument, in the 1960s, that "violence is as American as apple pie" is supported by the actual and latent violence inherent in our trilliondollar military budget and our role as the major supplier of armaments to the world. At any moment, forty or so countries—adversaries and allies—are killing with or dying by weapons "Made in the U.S.A."

There is considerable evidence, nonetheless, that violence is abhorrent to the culture of the United States. A natural revulsion against war made it necessary for Woodrow Wilson, for example, to "win" a propaganda campaign at home in 1917, before waging war abroad. The president "saved the world for democracy" by sending seventy-five thousand proselytizers across the United States advocating armed intervention, then by imposing congressional statutes, imprisoning dissenters, suppressing publications, and harassing critics. And still workers and conscientious objectors resisted.

Numerous pamphlets, songs, and books from the seventeenth century to the present suggest that the impulse to resist injustice, to resolve conflict, and to bring about social change while rejecting violence is also "as American as apple pie." Or so a broad literary history indicates to anyone interested in recovering important elements of our buried or "disguised" past, in poetry, fiction, and nonfiction.

Although only occasionally recognized in standard histories of American culture, the literary record of nonviolence is extensive, dramatizing a persistent, occasionally disciplined countercultural search for alternatives to violence. A poem by John

Beecher (1904-1989), descendant of the great abolitionist family, is representative. A description of the San Francisco-to-Moscow peace walk as it crossed the Oklahoma prairie in the late winter of 1961, "Engagement at the Salt Fork" conveys a sense of the gentle, persistent strength of the American tradition of nonviolence:

> Like tumbleweeds before the wind we moved across the continent's huge heedless face. Blasts, born on Yukon tundras, knifed us through and buffeted our sign: Man Will End War or War Will End Man. Handful that we were, armed men patrolled us, secret agents sped ahead to warn the elevator towns .... As if we were the ghosts of banished Cherokees come back, the guilty strip shook in its cowboy boots.

"Handful" that they were—and are—nonviolent activists over three and one-half centuries have evoked a considerable literary response from their contemporaries. And as Beecher suggests, their enduring challenge to violence and injustice evokes memories of earlier Native American resistance to conquest.

The signs of the nonviolent tradition are everywhere in the literary history of the United States, including that most elemental and influential Leaves of Grass (1835). One of Whitman's hopes for that book—and the voice informing it—are relevant here: that "before me all the armies and soldiers of the earth shall yet bow—and all the weapons of war become impotent." With writings by Quaker mystics George Fox and John Woolman in his background, Whitman's poems and essays anticipate the work of later authors, from Jane Addams to Allen Ginsberg, who acknowledge their indebtedness.

Early European settlers, particularly those associated with William Penn's Holy Experiment, thought about and acted out various ways of living at peace with their neighbors. Even before coming to live in the colonies, they made important decisions about community that influenced the course of literary and social history and shaped the new nation. Often, as with Penn and John Woolman, the quest for peace brought nonviolent activists into close association with Native American cultures. These influences regarding community are evident in artifacts and social movements-including utopian communities related to but beyond the scope of this study-from the beginning.

Nonviolent activists offered alternatives—choices, one

might say—to accepted, more conventional ways of resisting injustice and resolving conflict. In their efforts to understand and to live these values, they challenged, if somewhat inadvertently, the so-called just-war theory (that is, justifications for making war) associated with Augustine and Thomas Aquinas that has dominated most ethical thinking about war and conflict in Western culture.

Poets, novelists, and social and literary critics of the nineteenth and twentieth centuries have been similarly preoccupied with the implications of nonviolence, in their writing about the struggles of individual abolitionists, feminists, Christian anarchists, conscientious objectors, nuclear resisters and the communities that sustained them. Exploring concepts associated with nonviolence—pacifism and civil disobedience, as well as love and power—this body of literature includes work by people both sympathetic and unsympathetic to the influence of nonviolence.

In some instances, writers associated with nonviolence are religious pacifists, people for whom nonresistance is a way of life; in other instances, they are nonpacifists, people committed to nonviolence as a tactic or interested in it merely as a focal point or theme in fiction and poetry. During the abolitionist and feminist movements of the 1840s and 1850s, for example, William Lloyd Garrison and Adin Ballou were visible, vocal advocates of nonviolent direct action. At the same time, Nathaniel Hawthome criticized, even satirized, social reformers—both violent and nonviolent—and their effect on (he would say their threat to) civil society. Politically conservative, Hawthorne nonetheless wrote insightful dramatizations, in fiction, of concepts associated with nonviolence, including the theoretical and practical implications of what is now called "conflict resolution."

The theme of nonviolence in American literature is obviously related to the theme of violence, as well as to other preoccupations that have characterized written discourse in the United States since the early European settlements. For this reason, it is important, in the midst of occasional confusion, to be as precise as possible about terminology, particularly violence and nonviolence. Among activists and strategists, the relationship between the two has been cause for considerable discussion, as the words take on new associations and implications. These statements, by Gandhi and Dorothy Day respectively, are representative: "Violence is any day preferable to impotence. There is hope for a violent man to become nonviolent. There is no such hope for the impotent." "Far better to revolt violently than to do nothing about the poor destitute."

The confusion surrounding the word violence is the result of considerable change in its denotation and connotation since 1800. As E. J. Hobsbawm said, "Of all the vague words of the late 1960s, violence is very nearly the trendiest and most meaningless." In the midst of what he calls "a general atmosphere of disorientation and hysteria," old confusions perpetuate themselves. When the same word, violence, is used to describe both the destruction of property, as in the Boston Tea Party, and the destruction of thousands (potentially millions) of people in a nuclear war, we become aware of the word's limitations in "naming" the concept. As late as 1968, violence did not even appear in the *International Encyclopedia of Social Science*. In the apocalyptic rush of contemporary events, we risk destroying ourselves before we have a word to describe what has happened to us, as Hannah Arendt once suggested.

The Latin root (violencia) signified vehemence, a passionate and uncontrolled force, the opposite of a calculated exercise of power. Traditionally, it meant "to pervert some object, natural or human, from its 'natural' course of development" and "to exceed some limit or norm." Political theorists of the eighteenth century—Locke, Rousseau, Montesquieu agreed, generally, that violence could not regenerate people or society and they, unlike later political philosophers, set limits to its "justifiable province."I In the American colonies, as well, people used the word without necessarily meaning violence in the modern sense, connoting limitless destruction. Colonists generally regarded violence as a last resort, and hoped initially to accomplish political reform by nonviolent means.

Since Marx and perhaps Edmund Burke violence has been extended to include ever widening, particularly calculated, means of destruction. This is quite understandable, given the proliferation of technological weapons over the last two centuries. The change has deprived us of an earlier tradition, nevertheless, which allowed for radical social change (revolution) without people resorting inevitably to war and killing.

Our understanding of nonviolence, a new word, is similarly frustrated by the word's failure to convey the concept's meaning and purpose. Still omitted from some dictionaries, nonviolence is burdened by a negative prefix that causes inevitable confusion for anyone unfamiliar with its history, much as non-European, non-white, and non-Catholic do in other contexts. New experience evokes, eventually, more precise "naming," as I. A. Richards indicated years ago; in the meantime, activists, strategists, and researchers attempt to clarify basic terms and issues already current. Gene Sharp, a major theorist and strategist, has said that the trouble with most discussions of nonviolence is that they say what you cannot do, rather than what you can do. In a poem about religious pacifists in India, William Meredith suggests that the inadequacy of the English word nonviolence relates to a deeper cultural problem. In "The Jain Bird Hospital in Delhi," he describes the Jains' "trust in faith, cognition and non-violence / to release them from rebirth." They "preached the doctrine of ahimsa, / which in our belligerent tongue becomes non-violence."

"Between wars," as Ammon Hennacy used to say, "everybody is for peace."

"Nonviolent movements," on the other hand, have been inherently "pro-active." They depend upon individual initiative, symbolized by the man who responded to the 1962 Cuban missile crisis by carrying a sign saying "NO!" into the town square. Nonviolent movements usually begin as responses to particular injustices. Like "violent" movements for social change, they introduce a new factor into the power equation, even when public opinion and policy are heavily weighted against them. The early abolitionists and the activists against the war in Vietnam in 1965, for example, faced overwhelming opposition. In the latter case, less than 25 percent of the voters opposed the war, and anyone who advocated ending the draft (central to national policy from about 1940 on) was regarded as a romantic or a fool. Then, unexpectedly, in 1973, inductions ended, as a result of nonviolent resistance at various levels. Similarly, "the Brotherhood Movement," initiated in the early 1940s, required disciplined resistance to the status quo, where thousands of people risked beatings, imprisonment, and death, before it achieved victory for Civil Rights in the 1960s.

Although they may employ conventional efforts for change, such as petitions and legislative lobbying, nonviolent activists assume direct responsibility for change. They challenge the legitimacy of those in authority and sometimes threaten their power base; their purpose, as Gandhi often said, is to provoke a response. The Wobblies, the Socialist Party, and the Non-Conscription League disobeyed the draft law, for example, after it was initiated in 1917, and suffered harassment, jail, and exile for doing so. During the Vietnam War, members of RESIST publicly advocated outright rejection of "illegitimate authority," as the government tried unsuccessfully, through various conspiracy trials, to discredit, then to crush, the antiwar movement.

Philosophically, nonviolence owes much more to the seventeenth than to the nineteenth century—to Hobbes, Milton, and Locke, rather than Rousseau, Shelley, or Marx. It is more closely associated with those crying "No taxation without representation" than with those calling for "Liberty, Equality, Fraternity." Although the terms may be general (and potentially misleading), nonviolence is primarily practical and strategic, rather than romantic or utopian. In attempting to make ends and means compatible with each other, as Mulford Sibley said of the pacifist, the nonviolent activist "is both a revolutionary and a political realist," while remaining skeptical about any revolution that advocates "killing the killers in order to stop the killing."

The Quaker and Mennonite responses to war and violence in the seventeenth century, though tentative and exploratory, were thoughtful, political (one might even say tactical) decisions, maintained in the face of opposition; they were not impulsive gestures to "bring on the revolution." Nonviolence in the seventeenth century, as with Hobbes's Leviathan image for the State, coincided with the effort to bring an end to religious strife, as Christians randomly killed one another in the name of Christ.

Nonviolence is obviously "a"—not "the"—tradition in American letters, one layer in a multilayered archeological dig, one voice in a chorus, one of several trails into the new world. Only periodically aware of itself, it is sometimes halting and contradictory in its development. Although the path is wiggly and overgrown, it is nonetheless significantly there, distinctive. Regarding it as such enables one to understand how, at various points in history, it veered, went astray, or practically disappeared, then reemerged and moved confidently in several directions.

from "An Energy Field More Intense Than War:
The Nonviolent Tradition and American Literature"
Syracuse University; 1600 Jamesville Ave, Syracuse NY 13244

Violence, Legal and Illegal
By Colman McCarthy

For cheekiness, here is a peak moment in Bill Clinton's presidency: On April 22,1999 he travels a few miles south of the White House to Alexandria, Va., to T.C. Williams High School to hail the virtues of nonviolent conflict resolution.

For nearly an hour, the war-making president who in the past 10 months has ordered his military to deliver death by bombs and missile warheads to people in Afghanistan, Sudan, Iraq and Yugoslavia, speaks earnestly to about 25 students in the school's peer mediation program. Television cameras are feeding the event to several thousand schools throughout the traumatized land, the citizenry shocked and benumbed by the massacre at Columbine High in Littleton, Colo. Clinton offered fatherly counsel: "Parents should take this moment to ask what else they can do to shield our children from violent images and experiences that warp young perceptions and obscure the consequences of violence—to show our children by the power of our own example how to resolve conflicts peacefully."

Two days before, while bloodied bodies still lay on the floor of the Colorado high school, Clinton had the same advice: "We must do more to reach out to our children and teach them to express their anger and to resolve their conflicts with words, not weapons."

These are statements of duplicity and hypocrisy. Clinton tells the nation to adopt the ways of peacemaking - the ways of Gandhi, Martin Luther King Jr., Dorothy Day, St. Francis, Jan Addams - while he pushes on with the killing of Serbs in Yugoslavia. Are Clinton and his warrior advisers so obtuse as to think that citizens in this country and abroad can't see that he talks peace while practicing killing? Or that his own example of trying to resolve conflicts in Iraq and Yugoslavia by bombing people is itself teaching that weapons are good. Weapons of the U.S. military, that is. And the weapons of the Columbine High killers? Those are evil.

Hours after the worst act of schoolhouse violence in the

31

nation's history, Belgrade suffered its most intense bombing since NATO and United States pilots were turned loose March 24. That same night, Virginia did some killing, too: the execution of still another death-row prisoner, this one a man known to be mentally ill, intellectually disabled and whose last words in the death chamber were: "Please forgive me for my sins." Virginia, backed by the Supreme Court, said no, you die.

As governor of Arkansas, Clinton oversaw four executions, the last one in February 1992 of a brain-damaged inmate who thought he would come back and eat part of his last meal after the execution. As president, Clinton is on to death-dealing on a wider global scale. But his lectures on nonviolence to students and his ordering up violence via bombing runs in the Balkans fits the pattern of double-standard ethics. Two types of violence exist: official and legalized, and unofficial and illegal.

The first kind has the blessing of political leaders, who, predictably, perfume the stench of state-sanctioned killing with high-toned phrases. When George Bush sent troops to Somalia in late 1992, he described the mission as "God's work." It was loftily labeled, "Operation Restore Hope." On Oct. 3, 1993, with 18 elite U.S. soldiers killed in an ambush and at least 500 Somalis dead, God's work became dirty work. Nearly seven years later, stability remains elusive in Somalia and famine has eased only slightly.

In the current Colorado-inspired national discussion about violence, the boundaries are rigidly set: Let's talk only about illegal violence by deranged criminals. Violence by the state—from U.S. responsibility for killing people in Grenada (1983), Libya (1986), Panama (1989), the Persian Gulf (1990, 1992, 1993, 1998, 1999), Sudan (1998), Afghanistan (1998), Yugoslavia (1999), for death-row executions, for police brutality—is conveniently omitted from the debate

Why? Some sociologists provide an answer. In "Violence: Perspectives of Murder and Aggression" (Jossey-Bass Publishers), Dane Archer and Rosemary Gartner wrote: "The most obvious explanation is that wars and other forms of official violence are unique in that they wear the mantle of governmental legitimacy. When aircraft bomb a village, when the CIA hires assassins to kill foreign leaders, when a policeman shoots a looter, when a prison firing squad kills a convicted murderer the killings that occur are the result of governmental orders. These orders originate in a hierarchical organization. They are issued by appointed or elected officials and carried out collectively by uniformed deputies who perform the actual killing. Official killings, therefore, differ from illegal violence in that they result from governmental orders, are usually performed by several agents acting collectively, and are justified as instruments to some higher purpose."Killing Serbs in Belgrade is moral. Classmates killing classmates in Colorado is evil. "Ethnic cleansing" by Slobodan Milosevic in Kosovo is wrong. Low-life cleansing of murderous thugs on U.S. death rows by state governments is right. Trigger-happy cops in New York City are defended by the mayor. The deaths of Iraqi citizens caused by the U.S.-U.N.-backed sanctions (as many as 200 people a day, according to UNESCO figures) is acceptable to Madeleine Albright.

Occasionally, a politician is able to see that violence is violence, and it is evil regardless of who does it. When Clinton went to Central America this year and heard from the victims of violence backed or condoned by one U.S. administration after another, he said: "Support for military forces and intelligence units which engaged in violence and widespread repression was wrong. And the United States must not make that mistake again."

Stirring but hollow words. As long as the United States retains its ranking as the world's largest seller of weapons, as long as U.S.made weapons are being used in well over half of the world's 35 wars or conflicts, most of them the poor killing the poor, as long as U.S. death rows are filled with the highest number of people in our history, Clinton's words of regret are meaningless. What Martin Luther King Jr. said on April 1, 1967, remains depressingly true: "The greatest purveyor of violence in the world today [is] my own government."

Clinton wants high school kids to disarm: Rely on words, not weapons. What about his own efforts? He remains steadfast in ordering up more and more bombing runs in Yugoslavia, regardless of the evidence that Milosevic is not changing his ways—it appears the opposite, that he is more entrenched—and regardless of the continued killing of Serb civilians. Their funerals are not shown on U.S. television screens the way the ones in Littleton,

Colo., are. Colin Powell and Al Gore do not beat their breasts in mourning for the dead of Belgrade as they did for the dead at Columbine High.

Curiously, it was Powell who said in 1991 when American warriors were sent to create peace through death in the Persian Gulf that he wanted them to "kill it." He meant the Iraqi army. The soldiers were an "it," not human beings, not a "them." And "it" doesn't bleed or moan when killed in what one U.S. pilot called a "turkey shoot" when defenseless Iraqi soldiers were fleeing in retreat. The one-time death ordering Powell has transformed himself into Mr. Humanitarian who preaches to kids on the joys of community service. But what about the tens of thousands of Iraqi children who have died, or will die, because of U.S. military violence in 1991 and the economic sanctions since?

This also was a time when the sensibilities of children became the concern of adults. The same day in late January 1991 that Colin Powell was telling his troops to "kill it," Barbara Bush told reporters: "Parents should monitor their children and just be sure that they're understanding what they're seeing so they're not getting terrible nightmares."

Indeed. Let's not upset the kiddies with the gore of war. Keep it sanitized. Show only U.S. warplanes taking off—a nightly staple on television these past 40 days, a staple in 1991—and never show the human beings who lay dead at the other end of the bombing runs.

The Baltimore Sun
May 2, 1999

2

To Reach Peace, Teach Peace

It is quite strange, in fact, that as yet there is no such thing as a science of peace, since the science of war appears to be highly advanced ....As a collective human phenomenon, however, even war involves a mystery, for all the people of the earth, who profess to be eager to banish war as the worst of scourges, are nonetheless the very ones who concur in the starting of wars and who willingly support armed combat.

Establishing lasting peace is the work of education; all politics can do is keep us out of war.

Maria Montesorri

The Rigor of Peace Studies
by Ian Harris

The word "education" comes from the Latin word educare, to draw or lead out. "Peace education" implies drawing out from people their instincts to live peacefully with others and emphasizes peaceful values upon which society should be based. Human beings will always have aggressive impulses. They project their feelings of anger out onto the world and categorize others as good or bad, friends or enemies. Human beings have within them destructive and aggressive forces that need to be controlled through a civilizing process. Peace education deals with both internal conflicts within the human psyche and violent situations in the world.

Traditionally, peace education has focused on the causes of war. More recently, with the inclusion of structural violence, peace education has expanded to include the study of all the causes of human conflict. A European peace educator has defined peace education as "the initiation of learning processes aiming at the actualization and rational resolution of conflicts regarding man as subject of action." According to this definition, peace education teaches the skills of peacemaking. A Japanese peace educator states that peace education is concerned with peaceless situations. These include struggles for power and resources, the nuclear race among superpowers, ethical conflicts in local communities, threats of violence, and wars. In this way peace education studies structures which support peacelessness as well as the values that give credibility to those structures. An American peace educator, Betty Reardon, defines peace education as "learning intended to prepare the learners to contribute toward the achievement of peace." She goes on to state that peace education "might be education for authentic security,"where a need for security motivates humans to form communities and nations. Because individuals disagree about how to achieve security, there are many different paths to peace. Peace education teaches about the various ways to provide security so that students can select which paths to follow. Peace education has a moral thrust where, through education, human beings work together to create a better social order. The attempt of teachers to use their professional skills to address the problems associated with a commitment to militarism responds to a moral imperative to work for the well-being of others.

Although most of the current effort to educate about peace comes as a response to the impending nuclear threat, peace education in both formal schools and informal community settings implies much more than awareness of nuclear weapons. It implies teaching people how to manage violence and conflict without physical force. The study of peace attempts to nourish those energies and impulses that make possible a meaningful and life enhancing existence:

The advantage of peace education and peace research is that it enables us to keep criticizing the structure and using brains and imaginations on alternatives, so that when the opportunities come—and they do come—we can use them.

Peace education addresses the violent nature of society, and asks: Must it be this way? Aren't there other ways human beings can solve their conflicts? How do we get to these other ways? Just as war has its adherents and its schools, peace needs to be taught and promoted so that it becomes active in the minds of citizens and world leaders.

Throughout history many educational efforts have supported and promoted war: It is obvious that a warfare curriculum for human beings has been developed and refined over the entire course of man's history. Its teachings have been part of man's education in almost all societies in each succeeding generation.

Traditional education glorifies established political power that uses brute force to oppress people and legitimize its authority. History books praise military heroes and ignore the contributions of peacemakers. Violence is carried on by governments oppressing weaker nations and exhibited in homes where physical assault is used in situations of conflict, disobedience, anger, and frustration. Structural violence condemns people to substandard levels of existence, while educational systems support those structures which contribute to the militarization of social life. Peace education questions the structures of violence that dominate everyday life and tries to create a peaceful disposition to counteract the omnipotent values of militarism.

Educational activity is purposeful. Teachers try, through instructional activities, to achieve certain goals that help structure and evaluate learning. As Douglas Sloan has pointed out, peace education has short and long-term goals. The short-term goals are to turn things around so that life will be more stable. At this level peace educators respond to immediate situations that threaten life on this planet. The longer term goals are to create in human consciousness concepts and beliefs that desire peaceful existence and hence transform human values to promote nonviolence.

A good illustration of the short-term goals of peace education has been provided by a Romanian peace educator, Adrian Nastase. Quoting the French philosopher Pascal, he observed that human beings are "running carelessly towards a precipice after having put something in front of us to hinder us from seeing it." Drawing from this analogy he suggests that the goals of peace education are to discover the "precipice" and to understand the irrational state of the present world, where the development of technology contains the tremendous contradictions of both improving the human condition and threatening its destruction. Peace education alerts people to the danger of their own destructive fantasies and demonstrates the obstacles that keep us from focusing on our suicidal behavior. Once this awareness has been achieved, peace education develops alternatives that could become the basis for gradually braking and finally stopping this mad rush towards the "precipice." Another way of stating the urgency of peace education is the famous statement by H.G. Wells that human beings are embarked upon "a race between education and catastrophe."

The field of peace studies varies from studying the causes of human violence to studying the causes of war. The study of human violence involves the human psyche and aspects of aggression, while the study of war focuses on the behavior of armies and nation-states. In between these two poles lies a vast academic domain that includes the study of conditions of survival, problems of communication, international relations, legal theory, and environmental awareness.

Whether working to achieve immediate or long-range objectives, peace education has ten main goals: (1) To appreciate the richness of the concept of peace; (2) to address fears; (3) to provide information about defense systems; (4) to understand war behavior; (5) to develop intercultural understanding; (6) to provide a future orientation; (7) to teach peace as a process; (8) to promote a concept of peace accompanied by social justice; (9) to stimulate a respect for life; and (10) to end violence. These ten goals describe the sorts of things taught in peace education classes. They are neither exhaustive nor exclusive. Peace education is a broad field that includes many different academic disciplines. These ten goals do not necessarily incorporate all the various academic topics of peace studies, but they do provide a framework for planning educational activities and constitute a set of learning objectives for peace classes. Optimally, peace education students will be exposed to the various concepts implied within all ten of these goals.

(1) Peace education provides in students' minds a dynamic vision of peace to counteract the violent images that dominate culture. Peace implies love and respect for all forms of life. Many examples of the richness of the concept "peace" come from arts and literature—the film Gandhi, the novels War and Peace and Fail Safe, and sections from the Bible. Throughout history peace has stimulated human imagination. Every major religion values peace. Peace education teaches about past, present and proposed future efforts to achieve justice.

(2) Peace educators address people's fears. Children are abused at home. Citizens fear being attacked on streets. Violence permeates schools. Increases in teenage suicide have been linked to despair about the future. Recent research indicates profound psychological effects of growing up in the nuclear age. People fear for their own security, as they realize that stockpiling nuclear weapons does not necessarily achieve world stability but rather threatens mass destruction. As Jonathan Schell has said:

The Hiroshima people's experience, accordingly, is of much more than historical interest. It is a picture of what our whole world is always poised to become -a backdrop of scarcely imaginable horror lying just behind the surface of our normal life, and capable of breaking through into that normal life at any second. Whether we choose to think about it or not, it is an omnipresent, inescapable truth about our lives today.

Studies indicate that the majority of children in the United

States fear for their future, and that children can be reassured when parents and adults face these fears by doing something to avert war.

People upset about violent situations often have strong emotions. Those who have been physically abused have deep-seated resentments and insecurities. Citizens grieve about violence and fear conflict. Because powerful emotions about violent experiences can interfere with pedagogical efforts, peace educators enter the affective domain to become aware of the tensions and problems created by living in a violent world. Understanding these problems can help address student concerns and make relevant the study of tensions that threaten human existence.

(3) Citizens of all countries need information about defense systems. The notion of collective security implies that nations build weapons and create armies, navies, and air forces because they provide protection from attack. Citizens need to know what goes into these systems, the implications of developing and depending upon them, and their cost. Because a citizenry ignorant of what these weapons represent cannot make informed decisions about them, peace educators need to teach about the causes, nature, and consequences of the arms race. At the same time that each nation develops a war apparatus, often referred to as "the national security state," to defend itself, many nations shroud their security operations in secrecy. Peace education demystifies the public structures created to provide national security, so citizens can make enlightened choices about the best security systems for their circumstances. Leaving these decisions in the hands of the military guarantees the perpetuation of militaristic policies. Peace educators discuss the modern ramifications of peace through strength and encourage students to draw their own conclusions about defense policies.

(4) Students in peace education classes study the major causes of injustice, violence, and war. In the 3000 years of recorded history there have been only 250 years wherein war or armed conflict did not occur. Human societies try to control destructive impulses. Is aggression a natural part of human nature or is it learned through socialization? Individuals such as Alexander the Great, Napoleon Bonaparte, and Adolf Hitler have played a strong role

in promoting wars, but we all have destructive fantasies. Because human groupings have different values and differing security needs, peace education includes the psychology, sociology and anthropology of human aggression. Peace educators provide their students with an understanding of how different individuals, cultures and political systems respond to conflict.

(5) Since wars occur as a result of conflicts between individuals, cultures, religions, and nations, peace education promotes respect for different cultures. Awareness of the role of the United Nations and other world systems is crucial to understanding what institutions human being can create to bridge different culturaes and guarantee survival on "spaceship earth." International studies, where students learn about different values of human communities, have always been a part of peace education. Peace studies focus on how human institutions manage large-scale conflicts on the international level, as well as learning about how those conflicts originated.

(6) Peace education, by providing students with a future orientation, strives to recreate society as it should be. Students and teachers in peace studies classes imagine what the future will be like and then discuss what can be done to achieve peace. Peace studies include courses about the future that stimulate students to think about less violent ways of managing human behavior.

(7) As important as it is to emphasize knowledge, peace education also teaches skills. To move the world away from violence will require change. How can we bring peace to the world if we can't even create it in our own personal lives? Peace education focuses on strategies to achieve both individual and societal change. Peacemaking is a process that must be taught if human beings are to alter their violent behavior. People wishing to achieve peace understand that peace is a process that transforms their own lives as they start personifying their visions of the future. In peace education classes students examine how their daily actions and beliefs contribute to the perpetration of injustice and the development of war. They learn strategies to deal with aggressive behaviors and concrete skills that will help them become effective peacemakers.

(8) Because the struggle for peace embraces justice, peace education students learn about the problems of human rights and

justice. Since the absence of war does not necessarily bring peace or harmony, peace studies programs do not focus only on national security issues but also include the study of social justice, human rights, development, feminism, racism, nonviolence, and strategies for social change.

To facilitate education for justice and peace, one must, above all, believe: believe that justice and peace are
possible, believe that each and every one of us can do something to bring justice and peace into being.

Peace educators teach about the problems brought about by injustice and use this knowledge to empower others.

(9) The achievement of peace represents a humanizing process whereby individuals overcome their violent tendencies. Peace education teaches a respect for life. Peace education students need to develop positive self images, a sense of responsibility for self and others, and a capacity to trust others. Peace education contributes to the social growth of all children if it helps them develop characteristics essential for the attainment of peace—a sense of dignity and self-worth, a confidence to question their values, communication skills, an ethical awareness, and an empathy for others:

To prevent future upheavals human beings must be lifted from their selfish natural state to the social and finally to the moral state. Education must help the people regain their sense of moral independence and inner security. This training should be extended to all children, and should be rooted in love.

Peace educators teach caring and a spirit of empathy, not just a rational understanding of the problems faced by others. This caring applies not just to other human beings but also to the planet with an appreciation of the ecological balances that support life. We have to hear within ourselves the sound of the earth crying, the pain of people who suffer in war, and the agony of people repressed by militarism. In this way peace education emphasizes the spiritual and moral development of human beings.

(10) The ultimate goal of peace education is to redress the problems created in a world consumed with violent behavior. Street crime, war, domestic quarrels, and poverty result in millions of people having to live in violent conditions where they

have little or no security and struggle to survive. Peace education can't directly halt violence, but it does teach about violent situations, the effects of violence, and alternatives to violent behavior. Peace education students learn how to resolve disputes nonviolently and how to make the world a more secure place. Until violence is curtailed, human beings will not be able to achieve their full potential.

To achieve these goals will not be easy. The task is heroic, energizing, and crucial. Violent crimes are increasing. Wars are occurring throughout the world. Weapons are growing more awesome, and a frightened populace seems compliant in the face of ever-increasing defense budgets. Most members of modern nation-states believe that military institutions are a necessary component of contemporary life. The repeated failure of arms negotiations and a continuing worldwide arms race paint a picture of civilization heading towards oblivion with little respect for the citizens of the earth or the fragile ecosystems that support life. Unless something is done to control the spread of violence, citizens of the world face at best terror, mass poverty and starvation; at worst nuclear annihilation.

Educators help ward off such disasters by teaching about the nature of violence and developing in their classes strong visions of peace that provide alternatives to violent behavior. In order to create a less violent world, human beings must delegitimize the basic premises underlying the current global order and reassess fundamental assumptions regarding human motivations, essential values, and ultimate goals. Educators, need to ask their students what kind of world they really want, and help them achieve a vision that will motivate a fundamental change in the way humans conduct their affairs.

from "Peace Education" by Ian Harris.
McFarland Publishers
Ian Harris is a peace educator at the University of Wisconsin, Milwaukee.

Peace Education Beyond the Classroom
by Linda Lantieri

When I was a child and walked the six blocks to my elementary school by myself each day, I was hardly alone. I was greeted by neighbors who knew me by my first name and watched out for me until I reached the next adult sitting on another porch.

Today some children open the doors of their homes and witness drug deals in the hallway on the way to the elevator. Going to school they pass people on the street who frighten them. One of our mediators in New York City describes it this way: "It's real bad. Sometimes when I come outside, I'm scared because there are crack people in my building, on the same floor where I live. They sell their drugs right in front of me. And sometimes I'm scared that they'll hurt me."

One of my fondest memories is the way my family celebrated birthdays when I was a child. In the morning, we chose exactly what we wanted for dinner and put on a special outfit to wear to school that day. I would come home to the love and warmth of my family, a stack of gifts, and my favorite meal on the table.

Today we live in a world that robs some children of even these happy and safe moments. Interviewed for the video documentary The Last Hit, Micah, who lives in a Detroit housing project, spoke about his ninth birthday:

On the night of my birthday, December 32, New Year's Eve, we were coming up from the basement to eat some ice cream and cake. So what happened was my mother was about to put out the ice cream and I was behind her talking to my friends, and I heard about five shots-pow, pow, pow. As soon as I got shot I saw our cabinet door open, and the other last thing I saw was the clock, and I looked dead at it and I looked everywhere, but I didn't see anybody. I saw my mother in the dining room and she said, "What's the matter? What's the matter?" I went into the bathroom—there was light there. So I said, "I'm shot, I'm shot. Help me." My auntie came and wiped my hand and said, "You'll be all right." My father didn't know I said I was shot. He said, "You're not shot, you're not shot." But about the time we got to the hospital, that's when he finally figured out that I was shot .

Every child in this country has a right to safety, especially in their own home. Not one single child growing up in America should be robbed of his or her childhood because we as adults cannot protect them.

Clearly we have made the case for the important role of schools in addressing the issues of our wider society. And yet schools working alone cannot make a big enough dent in the crisis we face. Even if we could put into place a comprehensive, multi-year commitment to the teaching of emotional and social competency and conflict resolution skills in every school in America—rural, suburban, or inner-city—we would still be unable to turn the tide. As we wage peace in our schools, children are getting strong, frequent, and extreme messages from the society at large and from their own communities. They have ready access to real and simulated violence. Some live in homes and neighborhoods where violence is often the accepted norm. An eight-year old boy from Hartford, Connecticut, said, "I like school, but I have to worry about getting home alive."

There is no single, simple remedy to this problem. Our response to these complicated issues has to be a wide-ranging and public one. When we think about solutions, our focus needs to be not on any one program or project, but beyond that—to joining a local and national movement that involves the private sector, national and local governments, neighborhood organizations, religious communities, law enforcement, researchers, businesses. We must all mobilize. .

We are finally realizing that something must drastically change. As our collective psychic numbness fades away we start to feel the effects of our indifference and not one of us is left untouched. Several years ago I had the opportunity to work in Mother Teresa's Home for the Dying, in Calcutta. I learned an important lesson that gives me hope. A visitor can't miss the purpose of this place: "Home for the Dying" is written in large letters above the building in both Hindi and English. Yet a strange phenomenon consistently occurs—fifty percent of the people who are brought to this place get well and are able to leave. I'm convinced that when the severity of a problem is acknowledged, we have the best chance of healing to occur. It seems that this is where many of us are now in our society—beginning to acknowledge that the home for the dying is right here on the streets of our country and that our concerted effort can heal the situation. As Monica, a mediator in a South Bronx high school, put it, "I'm not going to be a statistic. I'm going to walk out of here alive!"

Several years ago, I experienced a remarkable example of community in Southern India, where I was helping in a health clinic. One day, after a long and difficult delivery, a very young mother gave birth to a child without arms. Just moments after the birth, several village women arrived. Helping the mother come to terms with what she was seeing, the women eased into picking the little girl up, figuring out how best to hold her. During the first week of this child's life, a different woman from the village would visit the family each day with yet another beautiful piece of clothing she had sewn in a way that adapted to the child's disability. By the end of the week, young Satinder had an entire wardrobe of clothing that demonstrated the collective, loving acceptance of her as the newest member of the village.

The way most of us live today seems to create more and more distance between ourselves and our neighbors, and so many of us yearn for that sense of community. We need the kind of heart-to-heart resuscitation that will transform neighborhoods into functional villages again.

There is a two-way street here that gives us hope: while the education of the heart requires changes in society in order for its most revolutionary ideals to be realized, emotionally literate people are exactly the kind of people most likely to bring about that change.

Although the curriculum we advocate is skill-based, the development and promotion of social responsibility is an expected outcome. In our work, we are hoping to inspire everyone to play an activist role in shaping our society's future. We want both young people and adults to feel as though they can change the world by their individual actions. The peaceable classrooms and schools we work to create are more than refuges from harm, they are interdependent and interconnected models for the larger community.

Since young people from peaceable schools and classrooms have experienced the power of constructive action, they are usually more hopeful about tackling problems and effecting social change. Instead of feeling they can do very little to change the world, they are armed with the experience of having done so. The skills that we teach and the values and attitudes we nurture help young people see themselves as active citizens participating in a democratic process.

In peaceable schools, young people experience a community where empathy, equality, and respect are the norm. They have a taste of what their larger world could be like. To give young people a greater opportunity to integrate these skills and attitudes, we encourage an active engagement with the wider community while they are still in school.

For schools and communities to reach out to one another, a porous boundary needs to be created between the two. Teachers, administrators, and kids need to become part of community life and schools need to let communities in.

I was walking down a street in my New York City neighborhood one day and came upon three girls, all about ten or eleven years old. One of the girls had her arm around another's shoulder, comforting her as she cried uncontrollably. The third girl seemed quite troubled, possibly guilty for having caused the situation. I decided to intervene. "I'm wondering if you need any help. I'm a teacher," I said, hoping that telling them I was a teacher would elicit their trust in a stranger's help. They began to share. The one girl had in fact said something derogatory to the girl who was upset, something unthinking about her parents not caring because she was adopted. It turns out this girl was adopted and the comments hit a sensitive nerve. I engaged them in a discussion that ended with tears of forgiveness and hugs among all three girls. As I started to say good-bye and compliment them for working it out so beautifully, one of the girls looked back at me and said, "I just have to say one thing to you. I don't think you're really a teacher because a teacher wouldn't have taken all this time with us when we're not even in school." I didn't quite know what to say. I was reminded that this is how some kids view adults in their lives—in separate corners, with clear and low expectations about who we will help and when.

Practical Ways Schools and Communities Can Work Together

There are numerous ways schools and communities create these "porous boundaries" we speak of. Here are a few ideas for what schools can do:

Get students and teachers actively involved in neighborhood efforts, from cleanup campaigns to adults volunteering for community patrol.

Lobby for students to serve on community planning committees, so the voices of youth can help shape the community's future.

Support local mediation centers as a way of dealing with neighborhood disputes, with peer mediators and school mediation coaches volunteering their expertise.

Cooperate with local TV, radio, and print media by helping them to report on positive events happening in schools and co-producing public service announcements with nonviolent messages.

Support community efforts in the martial arts and other self-defense skills by introducing young people to them during school hours.

Invite local policy makers, police, and judges to participate in school celebrations as well as in conflict resolution trainings.

Consider using the school's facilities as a community center, collaborating with nonprofit organizations to provide safe and stimulating opportunities for youth after school.

Support the idea of school-based health clinics, which can help reinforce violence prevention programming.

Work along with community artists to create murals and billboards in the community with positive-pro-social peace messages.

Co-sponsor forums where all sectors of the community-staff, parents, students, law enforcement officials, etc.-can share ideas, expertise and points of view.

Support mentoring efforts linking up adults in the community with youth who would benefit from ongoing one-to-one contact with a caring person.

Sponsor discussion groups that invite neighbors in the community, using such materials as the Study Circles Resource

Center's guide *Confronting Violence in Our Communities: A Guide for Involving Citizens in Public Dialogue and Problem Solving.* Youth can be included in the study circle as well.

Our challenge in this next decade, in a country that now spends more on prisons than on education, is to let our next act today bring this reality closer for a child we know and love so that his or her tomorrow will be better. We believe many of us across the country are already living our lives this way. Each day people perform isolated, unseen, loving conscious acts of peace in our homes, schools, and neighborhoods. In the words of Robert Kennedy,

Each time one stands up for an ideal, or acts to improve the lot of the rest, or strikes out against injustice, one sends forth a ripple of hope, and crossing each other from a million different centers of energy and daring, those ripples build a current that can sweep down the mightiest walls of oppression and resistance. Moral courage is a rarer commodity than bravery in battle or great intelligence. Yet it is one essential, vital quality for those who seek to change a world that yields most painfully to change.

We envision the younger generation, the ones who will build the future, telling their kids how they learned to de-escalate violence and turn conflict into opportunity, how they learned to value each unique individual, and how they were part of building a future full of hope and gentleness. This vision continues to unfold in thousands of schools across the country, and we are grateful to be playing our part.

from "Waging Peace in Our Schools"
by Linda Lantieri and Janet Patti
Beacon Press 1996

Linda Lantieri is the co-founder and national director of the Resolving Conflict Creatively Program, a school-base conflict resolution program in New York City.

49

Creating a Peace Studies Class: Think It's Easy?
by Colman McCarthy

At Walter Johnson High School in Bethesda, nearly 40 students are taking an academically accredited course called Peace Studies. A year ago the course wasn't offered. How this change came about is a story of practical idealism and gritty persistence as practiced by a member of last spring's graduating class, Jeremy Fischer.

Creating a foothold for peace education—whether in elementary, middle or high schools, or colleges and universities—almost always is traceable to one singularly resolute person who says, "This will happen and I'll make it happen." The peace movement is more than marching in antiwar rallies or denouncing militarism. It also includes the lone lover of long shots—sometimes a student, teacher, principal, school superintendent, or parent—who sees the value of studying nonviolence as the sane, moral and effective alternative to violence in all its forms, from governmental wars among nations to living room wars among spouses and families.

Somewhere along the educational way, Jeremy Fischer came across the writings of Peter Kropotkin—the early 20th-century Russian pacifist, communitarian and author of *Mutual Aid* who advised students: "Think about the kind of world you want to live and work in. What do you need to build that world? Demand that your teachers teach you that."

So Jeremy Fischer became a demander—as a sophomore, three years ago—when he embraced the idea and ideal that the kind of world he wanted was peace-based, not violence-based. He didn't see that as overbearingly too much to ask of his teachers, considering that all human hearts yearn for peace and all governments keep claiming they seek only peace.

Jeremy didn't realize it then but he was about to learn the oldest lesson of social reform: The trouble with a good idea is that it soon degenerates into hard work. His degeneracy began quickly.

"Save for a few idealists," he wrote in an essay about waking up and shaking up his school, "most people took the idea of a peace studies case to be fine in principle but unworkable and unimaginable for our school. Many students were apathetic. Counselors and administrators seemed busy enough without another goal to pursue. The faculty told me that if this course was to be created, I would have to organize support for it."

That he did. Jeremy wrote articles for the school newspaper. He wrote letters and made phone calls to school officials. He endured brushoffs, runarounds, frowns, yawns and countless can't you-see-I'm-busy looks from big desk rajahs. But he didn't go away. He had learned to hang on, hang in, hang out—everything but hang it up. The peace education he wasn't getting in the classroom was acquired by his own reading of such books as Gandhi's autobiography and "Nonviolence in America," edited by Staughton and Alice Lynd. He embraced the philosophy of pacifism, quickly understanding that pacifism is not passivity or appeasement but is taking direct nonviolent action to prevent or stop violence.

"Violence is not only physically attacking others," he has written, "but is also leaving the poor unassisted, allowing racism to flourish, and imprisoning those who are most in need of assistance. Pacifism does not seek merely to end all violent international conflicts. It seeks to transform our everyday world into a compassionate family, void of racism, hatred, violence and misunderstanding. I know I can't do it alone, but this means I must keep trying to persuade others to help."

A payoff came: In the spring semester of his senior year at Walter Johnson—his 9th inning—Jeremy found Ty Healey, a sympathetic faculty member ready to teach the course. About 30 students enrolled, far more than scoffers had predicted.

As happens, education reform came from below, not above. It took one student's energy at one school to get one course in place. For all the opposition, it was as if his proposal was for a course in bookmaking, not peacemaking.

Healey, 26, is in his second year at Walter Johnson, after earning a master's degree in education at George Washington University. He isn't surprised by the high enrollment numbers: "Feedback from last year's students has been very positive. They saw the benefits, both in their personal lives and in having the rare opportunity to discuss contemporary issues involving peace and justice."

In all his 18 years of education, Healey had never taken a class similar to the one he now teaches. "This course," he says, "has been a worthwfle experience for me, to begin learning about something truly important."

When the course ended last spring, the students collectively wtote a letter to their schoolmates, hailing peace studies as "one of the most beneficial experiences of our high school careers." They said peace studies is "one tangible solution to the problem of violence in our community and schools."

In nearly 20 years of working in the field of peace education—including classroom teaching of more than 5,000 students, running a nonprofit, conducting teacher training workshops in conflict resolution, lecturing at schools and colleges—I've seen more than a few reformers laboring the way Jeremy Fischer did.

Customarily, they come up against two brick walls thickly laid by conventional educators. The instinctual reaction of a school administrator when someone proposes that a course be offered in peace studies is, "What's the cost?" and not, "What's the benefit?" Money decides. When school shootings occur, and the inevitable call goes out "to do something," dollars are spent on metal detectors, hallway police or ID badges for the kids—not textbooks on nonviolence or salaries for potential peace studies teachers. An unimaginative school administrator is like a prison warden: Why improve the place, a steady population is guaranteed.

The second objection to broadening curricula to include courses in nonviolence is the alleged onesidedness of peace education: Students need exposure to both sides. I have heard this argument from many of my own students after they have been assigned to read essays by Gandhi, Martin Luther King Jr., Dorothy Day, Jane Addams, Tolstoy, Gene Sharp or Joan Baez. "Why doesn't this course give us the other side?" they ask.

The answer? This course is the other side. Most history texts—with such exceptions as Howard Zinn's *A People's History of the United States*—showcase the events and makers of war, not of peace.

Through their actions and speeches, political leaders are teachers—routinely instructing the young that governmental violence is necessary and good, from the waging of wars to death row executions. Children from dysfunctional families have been ably taught by example the ways of violence.

Still another non-classroom teacher is the television. With more than 90 percent of Saturday morning TV cartoons having violent themes—former senator Paul Simon of Illinois has reported this--children are educated early by media violence. Got a problem? Belt somebody.

From these multiple sources, students in the nation's 78,000 elementary schools, 32,000 high schools and 3,000 colleges are steeped in violence education. They deserve an intellectual rest in a class on peace education.. Even then, it's usually minimal: one course, at most, in 12 years of primary and secondary education, and perhaps another in college.

Some school officials are grandiose in their claims to be peace educators. A principal who invited me to speak on nonviolence at a student assembly said afterward that his commitment was strong: Every year he organizes "peace day." Impressive, I said. But a question: Do you have math day once a year? Literature day? Science day?

To have any chance at all for a long-term decrease in violence—in whatever form—academic, for-credit courses in peace studies, mediation and nonviolent conflict resolution need to be offered every year of schooling.. Every gunman killing people in schools or workplaces, every spouse abuser, every street thug: They were all in first grade somewhere at sometime, then second grade and on up. Had they been exposed to the literature, methods, history, theories and practitioners of nonviolence, perhaps they would have had second thoughts—rejecting thoughts—about violence.

Every semester, I call on my students to go beyond . merely asking questions. Do something bolder and braver. Instead of asking questions, question the answers—those given by anyone who says the answer is violence. That requires courage, because it means taking on nearly an entire culture whose leaders justify war making, gun-owning, arms-selling and other forms of legal institutionalized violence that exploits whole social classes.

It also can mean, as it did for Jeremy Fischer, taking, on a school. I met him three years ago when I had been invited to speak at Walter Johnson. Jeremy hung around after the talk. He wanted a reading list for books on nonviolence. He wanted to know about groups I had praised in my speech--the War Resisters League, the Fellowship of Reconciliation, the Peace Education Foundation. He asked about courses he might take. I invited him to enroll in one of my summer courses, which he did—consecutive summers, and bringing along his father both times. I gave Jeremy full support as he labored to bring peace education to his school.

Jeremy Fischer--every high school in America has a few students of firm resolve like him-is attending Guilford College this fall on a full, four-year scholarship. Guilford, a peaceable school well known for campus activism, had a slot for a student with proven talents to agitate, not merely cogitate. It found one.

from The Washington Post
September 28, 1999

3

Peace Follows Service

This is the true joy in life, being used for a purpose recognized by yourself as a mighty one; being a force of nature instead of a feverish selfish little clod of ailments and grievances complaining that the world will not devote itself to making you happy.

I am of the opinion that my life belongs to the whole community, and as long as I live, it is my privilege to do for it whatever I can.

I want to be thoroughly used up when I die, for the harder I work the more I live. I rejoice in life for its own sake. Life is no brief candle to me. It is a sort of splendid torch which I have

got hold of for the moment, and I want to make it burn as brightly as possible before handing it on to future generations.

George Bernard Shaw, Man and Superman

The Cure Is Care
by Sargent Shriver

The Peace Corps gave me the most memorable, continuing, morally unblemished, and uncompromised chance ever given any American to serve his country, his countrymen, and his fellow human beings worldwide, simultaneously, and at the grassroots level with the poor everywhere.

Never in war, and I have served in war; never in peace, and I have served in many places in peace, has anyone ever received, from a secular state, a greater opportunity for pure service.

I was privileged to be part of a great band of people. From among the Volunteers who served overseas when I was director have come senators, congressmen, directors of overseas programs both public and private, foreign service officers, bankers, congressional staff members, state government officials, city mayors, and on and on. The Peace Corps proved to be the best talent agency for public servants in this century of American history.

Despite this, can there be optimism now for the future of the Peace Corps?

The Peace Corps budget is only 3/100,000 of the Defense Department's. Its numbers are only 3/1,000 of the Armed Forces. One thousand men and women are enrolled to serve our needs in war for every three—repeat three—in the Peace Corps. Talk about David and Goliath! By any quantitative measure known to the Rand Corporation, the American Enterprise Institute, or Office of Management and Budget, the Peace Corps is almost inconsequential, irrelevant perhaps, a cipher in the great game of world politics and power.

Then why are we here—two thousand of us attending this anniversary celebration?

Are we grown men and women but still talking about juvenile things? Are we just on a nostalgia kick? Are we puerile romantics, idealists, flower children, merely tolerated by mature, realistic, worldly wise leaders? Are we just accepted because all human societies have their soft-headed dreamers, their physically crippled and mentally retarded, their psychologically immature? Aren't the draft and military service the best way to deal with

Peace Corps Volunteer types, past, present, and future? Wouldn't the draft teach Peace Corps people to shape up, learn about the real world, guarantee their passage from illusion to realism? Can we as a nation, in difficult economic times, spend taxpayers' dollars on such a whimsical, peripheral activity as a corps dedicated to peace?

Many experts today say no. They say we should not dissipate our national resources and strength. Government was not established, they say, to create, finance, or direct such activities. The "private sector" is the proper place for idealistic experiments. The Peace Corps has little or nothing to do, they say, with our Constitutional purposes to create a more perfect union, establish justice, provide for the common defense, promote the general welfare, and secure the blessings of liberty for ourselves and our posterity. The Peace Corps, it is alleged, does not contribute to the defense of the United States. It does not protect the people from dangers abroad or at home. It's a misplaced, vestigial remainder of a messianic culture of the past. Good, perhaps, for Mormons, Mennonites, Quakers, left-wing Catholics, Pacifists, Evangelicals — but only a sideshow in an era controlled by the hard sciences, technology, finance, economics, and military matters. The threat is from without, not from within; from the U.S.S.R., not from ourselves. We're all right; they're all wrong; and we will prove it by our strength. The Peace Corps has little or no role in dealing with the real threat to America.

Thoughts like these may predominate in many places today, but the Peace Corps is always full of surprises, and happiness, and truth.

I experienced that joy and that truth all over again when I met again Beulah Bartlett and Blythe Monroe, two of our first PCVs to Ethiopia. Those two women were 68 and 66 when they volunteered for the Peace Corps, and yesterday they both received tumultuous applause for their work and their spirit. They inspired us all just by their presence on the platform.

After they left the stage, Beulah looked up at me and said, "You saved my life."

What a lovely thing for her to say, I thought. It was beautiful ...but, of course, it wasn't true!

I never saved Beulah's life. Beulah saved her own life by giving it away. She offered it to service. Her gift of herself to the poor and uneducated in Ethiopia gave her a new lease on a new life ...a life of service and peace.

The Peace Corps is thousands of human beings at peace—with themselves, with their fellow man, with the world. Why? Because they have saved their own lives. How? By giving themselves away!

We never own anything till we give it away. That's the heart of peace; that's the heart of the Peace Corps.

When will we learn that truth, here in our beloved U.S.A., the land of conspicuous consumption and wealth?

We must learn it ...without tragedy or suffering to teach it to us, if possible, because it has the power to save our lives just as it saved Beulah's.

I used the word power just then. I used it on purpose. I used it to emphasize the power of peace. It is peace that gives strength. It is peace that provides "the force"—an unconquerable, unsurpassable force—not arms, not bombs, not fear or threat of destruction. Those things just arouse resistance and resentment. They produce the opposite of what they intend. The alleged "power of arms" is a sham. The man with the pistol in his hand blazing away is the pitiful, fearful weakling afraid of another person, killing and marauding like a frustrated child because he's angry and hurt and alone and desperate, looking for love and finding only hatred and opposition. No, I never saved Beulah's life or Blythe's life. They saved themselves ...because they learned to give themselves away ...as the Declaration of Independence says in its last and most important words: "We pledge our lives, our fortunes, and our sacred honor." Risking their lives, giving their fortunes, and themselves, the original American Revolutionaries found peace.

That's why I am less confused and more knowledgeable and realistic about peace than in 1960 when we began the Peace Corps. In the 1960s we thought it would be easy. We thought Congress would always increase our size and our budget, if we produced results.

We thought we could defeat poverty, enlighten the ignorant, eradicate disease, win over our enemies, given enough time, given enough Volunteers. Now I know different, not better, but deeper. I know we still need money and Volunteers. I know the U.S.A. and the world needs the Peace Corps. But now I think we can achieve peace without eradicating poverty or ignorance or disease. The "power of peace" does not lie in the vain hope that we can change the human condition everywhere and for everyone. Our American faith in a technological fix for every problem is naive and irrelevant. Millions of people don't want our technology, our culture, our values. They've heard promises about a materialistic heaven on earth from communists and capitalists. Great improvements in the materialistic conditions of life are promised by both. But neither system has ever produced anything but an imposed peace—which is peace only for the mighty, and not even pure peace for them. Look how rich men and Politburo members employ guards and guard dogs, TV monitors, and elaborate alarm systems to protect themselves and their possessions and positions. The leader of the free world, ironically, needs more protection than anyone, except the leader of the communist world.

Those men are not creating or enjoying peace; they are creating and enjoying power. Augustus Caesar, the greatest of Roman Emperors, built a Temple of Peace—but only after he had gained absolute power. He encouraged people to worship him, the state he had created, the armies that sustained them. Deus, Imperator, Rex-God, Emperor, Leader. Augustus had it all! But was it peace?

Jesus Christ said no. And the Christians had to go underground because they worshiped a different God. They threatened the stability of the kingdom of Augustus by declaring that another kingdom exists ...a kingdom where peace comes from below, from the ground up, not from the top down, from inside the hearts of human beings, not from the barrel of a gun no matter who's holding it.

Many Peace Corps Volunteers have possessed this kind of power. They were at peace with themselves and with their work. That's why the Peace Corps nurses in the Dominican Republic were asked to stay when the revolutionary slogans all said "Yankees Go Home." That's why no Peace Corps Volunteers were attacked or injured in the Panamanian uprisings against the U.S.A.

in 1964 or during the 1981 violence in El Salvador. That's why "terrorists" have not assaulted Peace Corps Volunteers even in remote locations in the underdeveloped world.

Certainly there have been accidents. Surely there will be deaths. PCVs could get killed just as the nuns were killed in El Salvador, just as priests, missionaries and others sometimes get killed—overseas or here at home. But the peace of the Peace Corps Volunteers is not something that can be taken from them, even by death. It's a peace they can give endlessly because giving it away does not diminish the supply.

Expressed differently, it's the quality of caring—caring for others, willingness, even eagerness, to teach the ignorant or bathe the dirty, nurse the leper, or serve as a farmer, lawyer, doctor, technician, nurses' aide in places where thousands, even millions, need what you have, in skills, yes, but most of all in human warmth.

No free market can ever replace free human services rendered by one free human being to another human being. A "good society" is the result of billions of such good acts. Government is good, not overreaching or intrusive, when government encourages, supports, and facilitates good, moral activity by the citizens. We are being swamped, night and day, with propaganda for selfishness, for excessive consumption, for killing, for domination of peoples, of nature, of history.

Is it too much to ask ourselves, we who believe in the Peace Corps, is it too much to ask ourselves?
Shouldn't we swing back into action? Shouldn't we volunteer again?

How should we begin? Exactly the way human beings always begin by organizing ourselves. Into what? Into "communities of caring."

In Latin America, basic caring communities have been started right in the villages. Those are caring communities—people caring for one another. That's what Peace Corps administrators meant in 1960 when we talked about community development—developing a sense of community spirit, community action at the grassroots or the rice roots. That's why Americans with only a bachelor's degree were sought after and sent abroad. We were looking for caring people, not just curing people, those able to cure a disease or a problem. Sure we wanted curing people, but only if they were caring people, too.

In a phrase, (the cure is care) Caring for others is the practice of peace. Caring becomes as important as curing. Caring produces the cure, not the reverse. Caring about nuclear war and its victims is the beginning of a cure for our obsession with war. Peace does not come through strength. Quite the opposite. Strength comes through peace. The practices of peace strengthen us for every vicissitude.

The task is immense!

Twenty years ago we called it "the towering task." Well, my friends, in 1981, "the towering task" still towers before us; but, thank God, we still have the Corps of Peace—that body of human beings who know, and have known, that America's destiny is not to be policeman of the world, monarch of the world, Caesar, Imperator, Rex, or Deus. But servant—servant of people, servant of peace, saviors of humanity.

It's a big task. But it's fun; it's joy; it's the true pursuit of happiness! May you all grow young in the achievement of it. Volunteer!!

from remarks at Howard University in 1981 at the 2nd National Conference of Former Peace Corps Volunteers

To Be of Use
by Marge Piercy

The people I love the best jump into work head first without dallying in the shallows and swim off with sure strokes almost
out of sight. They seem to become natives of that element, the
black sleek heads of seals bounding like half-submerged balls.

I love people who harness themselves, an ox to a heavy
cart, who pull like water buffalo, with massive patience, who strain
in the mud and the muck to move things forward, who do what
has to be done, again and again.

I want to be with people who submerge in the task, who
go into the fields to harvest and work in a row and pass the bags
along, who are not parlor generals and field deserters but move in
a common rhythm when the food must come in or the fire be put
out.

The work of the world is common as mud. Botched, it
smears the hands, crumbles to dust. But the thing worth doing
well done has a shape that satisfies, clean and evident. Greek am-
phoras for wine or oil, hopi vases that held corn, are put in museums. But you know they were made to be used. The pitcher cries
for water to carry and a person for work that is real.

Reverence for Life
by Albert Schweitzer

No human being is ever totally and permanently a stranger to another human being. Man belongs to man. Man is entitled to man. Large and small circumstances break in to dispel the estrangement we impose upon ourselves in daily living, and to bring us close to one another, man to man. We obey a law of proper reserve; but that law is bound to give way at times to the rule of cordiality.

There is much coldness among men because we do not dare to be as cordial as we truly are.

Just as the wave cannot exist for itself but must always participate in the swell of the ocean, so we can never experience our lives by ourselves but must always share the experiencing of life that takes place all around us.

The ethics of reverence for life requires that all of us somehow and in something shall act as men toward other men. Those who in their occupations have nothing to give as men to other men, and who possess nothing else they can give away, must sacrifice some of their time and leisure, no matter now sparse it may be. Choose an avocation, the ethics of reverence for life commands-an inconspicuous, perhaps a secret avocation. Open your eyes and seek another human being in need of a little time, a little friendliness, a little company, a little work. It may be a lonely, an embittered, a sick, or an awkward person for whom you can do something, to whom you can mean something. Perhaps it will be an old person or a child. Or else a good cause needs volunteer workers, people who can give up a free evening or run errands. Who can list all the uses to which that precious working capital called man can be put? Do not lose heart, even if you must wait a bit before finding the right thing, even if you must make several attempts.

Be prepared for disappointments also! But do not abandon your quest for the avocation, for that sideline in which you can act as a man for other men. There is one waiting for you, if only you really want it.

This is the message of true ethics to those who have

only a little time and a little humanity to give. Fortunate are those who listen. Their own humanity will be enriched, whereas in moral isolation from their fellow men, their store of humanity would dwindle.

Each of us, no matter what our position and occupation, must try to act in such a way as to further true humanity.

Those who have to opportunity to serve others freely and personally should see this good fortune as grounds for humility. The practice of humility will strengthen their will to be of service.

No one has the right to take for granted his own advantages over others in health, in talents, in ability, in success, in a happy childhood or congenial home conditions. One must pay a price for all these boons. What one owes in return is a special responsibility for other lives.

All through the world, there is a special league of those who have known anxiety and physical suffering. A mysterious bond connects those marked by pain. They know the terrible things man can undergo; they know the longing to be free of pain. Those who have been liberated from pain must not think they are now completely free again and can calmly return to life as it was before. With their experience of pain and anxiety, they must help alleviate the pain and anxiety of others, insofar as that lies within human powers. They must bring release to others as they received release.

He who has experienced good in his life must feel the obligation to dedicate some of his own life in order to alleviate suffering.

Technical progress, extension of knowledge, do indeed represent progress, but not in fundamentals. The essential thing is that we become more finely and deeply human.

Doing and suffering, we have the chance to prove our mettle as people who have painfully fought our way to the peace that can never be attained by reason alone.

We are headed right when we trust subjective thinking and look to it to yield the insights and truths we need for living.

Just as white light consists of colored rays, so reverence for life contains all the components of ethics; love, kindliness, sympathy, empathy, peacefulness, power to forgive.

We must all bid ourselves to be natural and to express our unexpressed gratitude. That will mean more sunlight in the world, and more strength for the good. Let us be careful not to incorporate bitter phrases about the world's ingratitude into our philosophy of life. There is much water flowing underground which does not well up from springs. We can take comfort from that. But we ourselves should try to be water that finds its way to a spring, where people can gratefully quench their thirst.

Thoughtlessness is to blame for the paucity of gratitude in our lives. Resist this thoughtlessness. Tell yourself to feel and express gratitude in a natural way. It will make you happy, and you will make others happy

The man who has the courage to examine and to judge himself makes progress in kindness.

It is a hard fight for all of us to become truly peaceable.

Right thinking leaves room for the heart to add its word.

Constant kindness can accomplish much. As the sun makes ice melt, kindness causes misunderstandings, mistrust, and hostility to evaporate.

The kindness a man pours out into the world affects the hearts and the minds of men.

Where there is energy, it will have effects. No ray of sunlight is lost; but the green growth that sunlight awakens need time to sprout, and the sower is not always destined to witness the harvest. All worthwhile accomplishment is acting on faith.

The one thing that truly matters is that we struggle for light to be within us. Each feels the others' struggle, and when a man has light within him it shines out upon others.

The great secret is to go through life as an unspoiledhuman being. This can be done by one who does not cavil at men and facts, but who in all experiences is thrown back upon himself and looks within himself for the explanation of whatever happens to him.

None of us knows what he accomplishes and what he gives to humanity. That is hidden from us, and should remain so. Sometimes we are allowed to see just a little of it, so we will not be discouraged. The effects of energy are mysterious in all realms.

The epithet "mature," when applied to people, has always struck me as somewhat uncomplimentary. It carries overtones of spiritual impoverishment, stunting, blunting of sensibilities. What we usually call maturity in a person is a form of resigned reasonableness. A man acquires it by modeling himself on others and bit by bit abandoning the ideas and convictions that were precious to him in his youth. He once believed in the victory of truth; now he no longer does. He believed in humanity; that is over. He believed in the Good; that is over. He eagerly sought justice; that is over. He trusted in the power of kindness and peaceableness; that is over. He could become enthusiastic; that is over. In order to steer more safely through the perils and storms of life, he has lightened his boat. He has thrown overboard goods that he considered dispensable. But the ballast he dumped was actually his food and drink. Now he skims more lightly over the waves, but he is hungry and parched.

Adults are only too partial to the sorry task of warning youth that some day they will view most of the things that now inspire their hearts and minds as mere illusions. But those who have a deeper experience of life take another tone. They exhort youth to try to preserve throughout their lives the ideas that inspire them. In youthful idealism man perceives the truth. In youthful idealism he possesses riches that should not be bartered for anything on earth.

Those who vow to do good should not expect people to clear the stones from their path on this account. They must expect the contrary: that others will roll great boulders down upon them. Such obstacles can be overcome only by the kind of strength gained in the very struggle. Those who merely resent obstacles will waste whatever force they have.

Reverence for Life
Albert Schweitzer

The Call to Service
by Robert Coles

As a child I often heard my mother use the word "charity" in referring to her constant involvement in the Red Cross, the League of Women Voters, a Catholic Worker soup kitchen, and in numerous hospital fund drives, as well as in her reading to sick children and helping people in the hospital as a volunteer. Still, my so-called research, which would become a lifetime of observation, of conversations and more conversations and efforts to understand what I'd heard, all began in the South, with the children and young volunteers I got to know there. I have chronicled that research many times, but as I have already indicated in connection with young Tessie, I wasn't always prepared to think of my work as a study of service. Nor were many of the boys and girls and older people who got involved in those momentous confrontations inclined to think of themselves as Tessie did, as people trying to offer what they could to others.

As Stan, a civil rights activist who would later become a VISTA volunteer, declared to me one day, "You keep asking me why, why I'm here. I'm here because I believe in something. I believe in racial equality—'black and white together,' and I'm willing to stand up for it, for what I believe. That's what I'm doing here. You could even call it selfish—it's important to me, and I feel I'm lucky to be here with others, doing this. Do I think of them, the segregationists? [I had asked.] No, I really don't. I mean, I do, of course—the sheriffs, the mobs. But a lot of the time I close my eyes to all of that, to them. I say to myself, Hey, you're here, and you're ready to keep putting yourself on the line, and that's as far as I let my mind go—one day at a time, one step at a time."

He had carried to the South the values he had learned in a white, fairly well-to-do, secular home up North. Or, it might be said, those values had carried him to Dixie, and though he might not have dwelt on them explicitly, they were a part of his life, as he acknowledged, and they help us understand what he was doing, what others like him were doing and continue to do. There he was in Canton, Mississippi, in 1964, amid the frantic activity and constant anxiety of the SNCC Summer Project, stopping for a while to think about his parents and what they taught him, and how that helped to characterize what he was doing with his life.

"I was brought up on the idea that you have to think of others, the poor, not just yourself. My dad is a lawyer, and he makes a good living; but he always contributes some of his time to causes - to people who need his help and can't afford it, or to politics. He joined the NAACP when he was a young man, when that was itself a real political statement, at least in the neighborhood where he and my mother lived.

"Neither of my parents are religious; my mom never goes to church, and my dad says his parents were agnostics, though they went to a Congregationalist church at Christmas and Easter. But both my parents had strong political ideals: they wanted the New Deal to last forever, and to expand, and make the country more egalitarian. They weren't socialists or communists. They were old fashioned liberals or progressives, but they really believed in political commitments—and those commitments were sort of their meal, the bread and potatoes of their life. I think it was always like that for me too—it really mattered who was president, which party ran Congress, what laws were being passed, how the Supreme Court voted. The ways some kids are all tied up with church calendars or Hebrew school, I was tied up with this law (will it get through the Senate?) or that idea (will the president really push it?), and it's still like that for me.

"I guess you'd say that I'm here because this is a big moment in American history, and it really matters that Negroes get the vote and that the segregationists lose this political struggle, and it matters not only to me as a voter, an American, but to me and my family, [because] that's the kind of people we are, and this is what we believe in doing: to stand up for your ideas, your beliefs, and, like we say in SNCC, to put your body on the line, and if it's dangerous, then you don't walk away then, not if you want to hold on to your self-respect."

He didn't mention the real help, the genuine and important service he was offering every day as a teacher, as an advocate. In the above-quoted remarks and in hours of other comments, his emphasis was always on his politics, his activist purposes, his willingness (indeed, eagerness) to join with others, to link arms in a movement dedicated to those purposes—all on behalf of his principles, which he eagerly discussed at great length. For him, tutoring children in Mississippi, providing health information to families, and teaching a civics class to men and women in hopes that they would take the considerable risk of walking to the county courthouse and attempting to register as voters—all these activities were part of a social and political struggle that he used as his defining compass. He pursued those directions that served "the movement's ends," a phrase that appeared repeatedly in his sometimes urgently impatient statements.

"I have so damn much to do," he would say over and over, as if uttering mere words—which he liked to do and could do very well—was an indulgence. When I told him how impressive his work with schoolchildren was, he brushed aside the compliment and made a point of indicating the relationship between his teaching and his social activism: "We need to earn the confidence of the people here. We can't just come in and ask them to put their lives on the line—and that's what they feel they're doing when they go into that courthouse, and who can blame them!" He had little apparent interest in acknowledging the worth of the tutoring per se. And given the risks he was taking—his life on the line!—I felt I could not press the matter.

from "The Call To Service"
Houghton Mifflin, Boston

Answering the Call
by Colman McCarthy

On the eve of the national summit on volunteerism in Philadelphia, A. Franklin Burgess Jr., a District of Columbia Superior Court judge traveled to Frederick, Md., with Anthony Taylor, a sixth grader at Garrison Elementary School in the Shaw neighborhood of Washington. Burgess has been mentoring the youngster for the past three years. On this spring evening, the judge and the student took in the Class-A Carolina League contest between the Frederick Keys and the Wilmington Blue Rocks. That was the first treat for Taylor. The second came after the game when he and Burgess went to a restaurant for dinner with a friend who brought along some players from the Keys and Blue Rocks.

What Bill Clinton, Colin Powell, George Bush and assorted other exhorters to goodness were preaching in Philadelphia, Judge Burgess was practicing. And it should be noted that writing of his involvement in the life of Anthony Taylor is more than another exercise in journalism for me. The program in which they participate is Elementary Baseball, a non-profit venture that my son John McCarthy started four years ago after a stint in the minor leagues.

In 1993, John, who attended public schools from first grade through college, gave a motivational talk at Garrison Elementary. He told stories about Satchel Paige and Hank Aaron—both went to the same grade school in Mobile—and encouraged the Garrison kids to be the best baseball players they could be.

Baseball? they asked. What's that?

Few had ever played. For poor inner city kids, baseball is unaffordable: Families have little money for gloves, balls, bats. Then too, what families? Baseball is a game passed from fathers to children. More than 90 percent of Garrison's students live in fatherless homes. Many are raised by grandmothers.

John was invited by the Garrison principal to organize a baseball program. In a year, the school was the only one in the District with its own team. At the first practice, kids had to be told to run the bases counter-clockwise. They called runs "points."

If baseball was foreign to many, so also was literacy and the habit of reading. Few had an adult who pushed them educationally outside the classroom. Most males in the lives of these children were failures: relatives in prison, drug abusers, layabouts.

After teaching the Garrison children that first base was to the right, not left, John expanded Elementary Baseball into a literacy program. To be on the baseball team—Garrison now has six—the kids also had to attend an afterschool reading program where they were matched with a mentor and a tutor. To find the mentors, John turned to Chief Judge Eugene Hamilton of the Superior Court. John offered a simple, but persuasive case for why members of the court bench should come to the bench at the ballfield: Get into the lives of at-risk kids now in a positive way as mentors, he argued, or you may be in their lives in 10 or 15 years in a negative way as you're dispatching them off to jail.

At Hamilton's urging, judges and other members of the court heeded the call. By the time of the Philadelphia summit, Elementary Baseball—supported by foundation and federal funds— was matching more than 60 adults from the court with Garrison children.

Frank Burgess, Princeton '65 and Harvard Law '71, with two years of the Peace Corps in between, has been mentoring Anthony Taylor for three years. There have been lunch dates in the judge's chambers, at least two outings a month, and regular attendance at Anthony's baseball games.

Burgess, who is the presiding judge in the court's criminal division and who oversees cases in which up to 90 percent of the defendants are young black males from the kind of neighborhood where Garrison Elementary is located, says he has seen improvement in Anthony's self-control: fewer tantrums during games, fewer outbursts at umpires. Though not immediately measurable, apart from the rise in his scores on national reading exams, Anthony appears to be benefiting from his involvement in the program. I know him to be more sociable, less withdrawn. Still, there are no guarantees. "In volunteer work," Burgess says, "we're not dealing in solutions to large-scale problems. It's on an individual basis, one on one. We have to believe we're fulfilling our responsibilities if we help one or two people along the way. Within any culture, it's difficult to know who's going to achieve and avoid crime and who won't. Kids can come from the most poverty-stricken background and [not] have mentors like me and still rise above it and not commit crimes."

In addition to Garrison's mentor program, during the last school year over 70 literacy tutors—primarily college and high school students—were working individually with Garrison children. In late March, the President and Hillary Clinton spent a morning at the school, advancing what is part of the administration's proposed $2.7 billion 'America Reads Challenge.' The goal is to recruit more than one million literacy volunteers for elementary school students to ensure that every child learns to read.

Will it happen? After four years of observing Elementary Baseball close—up and recruiting tutors from my peace studies classes at Bethesda-Chevy Chase High School, the University of Maryland, and Georgetown University Law Center, I can report this about mentoring and literacy volunteerism: We can be more certain about the benefits it gives to the service providers than those it brings to the service receivers.

One of the main reasons that I've been pushing my students to get out of the classrooms and into the lives of people in pain is to lessen the intellectual damage that we teachers do to our students. We are so intent on cramming theories and abstractions into their heads that they leave us idea-rich but experience-poor. Be smart, be brainy, we tell them: Make A's in school and you are predestined to make A's in life. We lie to the students.

To correct the problem of experience-poverty, I've been sending students to Garrison and Elementary Baseball for the past four years. What they learn through service is a way of tying ideas in the head to actions of the heart.

The benefits are as obvious as they are unsentimental, even if the way my students express themselves is still tentative. Sarah Heard, one of my Bethesda-Chevy Chase seniors now doing well at Amherst, wrote last year of working with a child at Garrison: "I definitely gained a great amount from this experience. It was sad to have it end. It has given me an inspiration to follow up on tutoring activities after high school. I gained an enormous amount from the teachers at Garrison as well. Those who stayed after school to tutor genuinely cared for their students. The experience opened up a whole new area for me, and perhaps I will go into teaching in the future."

Dilshad Husain was in my University of Maryland honors class in the fall semester of 1996. One of eight students who became involved with Elementary Baseball, Dilshad was paired for 14 weeks with a boy named Anthony Brown. She described him as "dynamic, smart and smart-mouthed, fun-loving and handsome:" "I *may* be helping him," Dilshad wrote at the end of the semester. "I may be helping him to improve his reading skills. I may be teaching him a modicum of patience. I may be showing him that higher education is a thing to strive for. I may be teaching him that mental solutions are better than physical ones. I may be changing some stereotypes for him—that Spanish people aren't the only ones to play soccer! I may be teaching him how the world is enlarged through books. I may be doing a lot of things for him, intentionally and unintentionally. I am aware of this, and I know he is happy to see me every week because of these things and more."

"But I don't think he realized his gift to me. I don't think he knows how much he is helping me. It's a `may' when it comes to my helping him. I won't know if I have done any long-term good for a while. But it is an `is' when it comes to him helping me. I can see and feel everyday how I have been changed by him—the way he reacts to things and the way he sees things. He may not know yet that this tutoring is a two-way street, but I aim to correct that. Anthony Brown needs to know that he has a gift, and I am glad and grateful that he is giving it to me."

The after-school reading tutor for Anthony Taylor last fall was Eric Speigel from my Maryland class. His experience was much less smooth than that of his schoolmates. Anthony often came late to tutoring, let himself be distracted, and preferred to talk about sports. Sometimes, Eric Speigel wrote:

"I left Garrison feeling that I was wasting my resources. There were so many other kids that I had gotten to know and like. Why wasn't I with one of them? But on this roller coaster ride, next week could be a great one. Dedication entails commitment through the good and bad . ...At times, I've wished I could be with one of those cute little kids that shower their tutors with affection and excitement every time they see them. I could take pictures, show them to my friends at school and say 'Here's my little buddy.' I'm sure there are many advantages to an experience like that. There have been times when I've wondered if I could have made a bigger difference if paired with someone who accepted and appreciated my efforts. Still, I wanted and received a realistic experience. These kids need someone who will be there for them week in and week out. Whether they show their appreciation is irrelevant. After all, we are here to fill one of the many voids in their lives and satisfy their needs, not worry about own needs. In filling some of the potholes and pitfalls in their own road to the future, we can only hope that it will one day be as smooth a ride as our own."

The current debate about teaching values in school might be resolved if more schools demanded community service and service learning programs. Only one state—Maryland—does. Students given chances to care for the victims of economic and social injustice will likely develop a value system that questions the people in power who let that injustice persist. That's risky. It's how revolutionaries get started, it's how a few teachers begin to wake up and realize the truth of Martin Luther King Jr.'s call: "We must encourage creative dissenters. .. We must demonstrate, teach, and preach, until the very foundations of our nation are shaken.'

Ironically, the gang of exhorters on the platform at the Philadelphia volunteerism summit—Clinton, Powell, Bush, Ford— are among those of one generation who helped create the mess and despair that the creative dissenters of the next generation are now called on, as altruists and idealists, to ease. Colin Powell was a ranking part of the Pentagon establishment that saw the United Sates bankrupt itself through military spending. The $700 million a day that Congress gives the Pentagon is three times what the Peace Corps spends in a year. The current military budget is 17 times greater than the combined spending of the six nations— North Korea, Iran, Iraq, Syria, Libya, and Cuba—we are instructed to worry about.

Is there no linkage between the money wasted on militarism and the money now wanted for social uplift? I don't recall

Powell decrying this squandering of the nation's wealth, neither while wearing his uniform nor in his autobiography detailing the glories of his career. Now he preens about as the savior of Generation X: "Let's volunteer together to take care of our youth and help shape America's future:"

No. Reshape it. What's getting underway now in the literacy programs is catch-up work that wouldn't have been necessary if the country hadn't been impoverished by the military spending binge. Jimmy Carter administered a trillion dollar military budget, yet now he troops around the globe as Mr. Peacemaker. Powell gets away with his Mr. Volunteerism number, thanks to a fawning media.

Before enticing high school and college kids to cure the ills of society, those doing the enticing could use some instruction on accountability. That, too, would be one of the benefits of volunteerism, available to both servers and served.

from The Washington Monthly
June 1997

4

How Does Goodness Happen?

Anyway

People are unreasonable, illogical, and self-centered.
Love them anyway.
If you do good, people may accuse you of selfish motives.
Do good anyway.
If you are successful, you may win false friends and true enemies.
Succeed anyway.
The good you do today may be forgotten tomorrow.
Do good anyway.
Honesty and transparency make you vulnerable.
Be honest and transparent anyway.
What you spend years building may be destroyed overnight.
Build anyway.
People who really want help may attack you if you help them.
Help them anyway.
Give the world the best you have and you may get hurt.
Give the world your best anyway.

Meditations From A Simple Path
by Mother Teresa

The Moral Imagination
by Edward Tivnan

Following a tour of the burned-out neighborhoods of South Central Los Angeles after the riots in the spring of 1992, President George Bush admitted, "I can hardly imagine—I try, but I can hardly imagine—the fear and the anger that people must feel to terrorize one another and burn each other's property." It is not surprising that a sixty-eight-year-old Connecticut-born son of a U.S. senator and an alumnus of Andover, Yale, the US. Congress, and the Central Intelligence Agency cannot put himself into the sneakers of a looter in South Central L.A. Yet any leader who claims, as ours so often do, to be committed to wiping out moral ugliness had better try, for while it might not be right to terrorize one another or burn one another's property, it is crucial—especially for presidents—to understand the urge.

I wondered if the President had read the op-ed essay in the *New York Times* the previous day in which the author noted, "White people sometimes think that if blacks could just act like whites, everything would be all right." The author, of course, is black, which gives some authority to his comments about blacks. But what does he know about how whites think? Plenty, it turns out. His father, you see, is white. The author is also an eighth grader in a Chicago school. He is able to see the problem in a way that most of us cannot imagine. But that doesn't mean that, with the help of such reports from the much too distant world of black life, we cannot at least try to imagine the differences.

The facts are unavoidable: one in five American children lives in poverty, banks and other money lenders still discriminate against blacks applying for mortgages, white males are more likely to work at the best jobs for the highest salaries. In 1989, President Bush vetoed a bill that over three years would have raised the minimum wage to $4.55 an hour. In 1991 that same president (who had once called for a "kinder and gentler nation") vetoed a civil rights act passed by Congress to set aside Supreme Court rulings that make it more difficult for women and minorities to win employment and discrimination suits.

Some things in any society are not worth "conserving."

Surely, even conservatives do not oppose moral progress. I hear no one lamenting the passing of slavery, male suffrage, child labor, and indiscriminate pollution of the air and rivers. Yet these were all values that American society once lived with. It was the Civil War—not morality—that ended slavery. But today we recognize all of them as clear examples of moral ugliness and, in the case of slavery and child labor, cruelty. That we want to stamp out cruelty and the morally ugly is, I believe, a common trait of Americans, on the Right and the Left. Recognizing what is morally ugly is another matter. Our standards are typically different. Poverty may be an injustice for me and the breaks of the game for you. What does it take for people to recognize moral ugliness or cruelty?

God will not help us here; nor will some overarching sense of "community." Being a decent, compassionate, good person in a diverse community requires considerable imagination—moral imagination.

We all have our ghettos to escape. It takes no less a leap of the imagination for a privileged white president to see his way into the ghetto than for a poor black to see his way out.

That our values are so different and incompatible is a fact of life in a pluralistic democracy, as I demonstrated in the previous chapter. But how such people who see the world in such different ways can live together peacefully in a society is one of philosophy's most vexing problems. I want to argue that the only peace available in American democracy is an unstable one. And to keep the peace, we must learn to live with our lack of moral knowledge and the inevitable clash of values around us. We must try to become the historians of our own society, the novelists of our own lives, the screenwriters of the suffering and humiliation on the streets, in hospitals, in abortion clinics, even on death row. We must try to feel the frustration and bitterness, the hatred and fear of the poor, the black, the female, the pregnant, the dying, and the condemned.

If that sounds too politically correct, let me add quickly that from the Left we must also try to feel the frustration and bitterness, the hatred and fear of hardworking, God-fearing, loyal, tax-paying Americans who, with good reason, question the crime, disorder, and social chaos in their midst. As I argued in the last chapter, neither liberals nor conservatives have a lock on The Truth. Liberals who press political correctness on their neighbors are no better than conservatives who want to impose their values on the rest of us. Both are strategies for religious and cultural warfare. Oppression is no less so when it comes from the Left.

Of course, there are those who do not want to listen, who have no interest in what the other side believes. They prefer shouting to civil conversation. But I am not talking about the extremists and fanatics. I am addressing the moral conversation that might take place between people with divergent attitudes who proudly call themselves liberal and conservative but also view themselves as people of good will who share at least the common goal of a decent society. To them, I suggest that the moral conversation is more likely to continue if we can imagine the world from the other side of the barricade. Standing among "the enemy" for a moment, we might be able to see similarities between them and us, not some common "human nature" or some ineffable "essence" shared by all men, but the fact that we are all bundles of opinions and beliefs, of theories and prejudices about how we and our world are or ought to be. To be able to make this imaginary leap is to have a well-developed moral imagination.

A few of us seem to be born with this kind of moral creativity—people with such natural compassion that they strike us as saintly (Mother Teresa comes to mind first, but pick your favorite "living saint"). But the rest of us can become more morally imaginative about what we might value and what others value. This should not be beyond our powers. Our moral adversaries are not ancient Greeks, medieval knights, warring Zulus, evil Russians, or any of the other people that historians and anthropologists claim to understand. These are our fellow Americans, indeed they are likely to be our neighbors, our relatives, even our very selves.

I hear the objections: If burning down another's place of business is wrong, what good does it do me to imagine the anger of a black looter? What's wrong is wrong. If I believe abortion is murder, then sympathizing with a murderer seems to be stretching it.

Yes, but what about the possibility that the L.A. arsonist

might be justified in his anger (if not his actions)? What if abortion is not murder—and capital punishment is? To explore these possibilities, you have to understand more about the intellectual source of your moral conflict, listen a little harder to the other side of the story. By trying to understand a black person's rage, or why a husband feels morally obliged to kill his wife suffering from the pain of terminal cancer, you might see the possibility of sometimes being wrong. You don't have to change your mind about one issue or another. You don't have to believe that anything goes. (Who does?) But by developing your moral imagination, you will be less likely to burn your adversary at the stake for fear that no matter how strongly you feel that the death penalty is right, say, or that affirmative action is unjust, you may actually be wrong.

To create a decent society from millions of people who disagree with one another on matters of life and death requires getting comfortable with "screwed-up" people and their ideas.

This same gift to penetrate the minds and beliefs of others is also what makes for a great novelist, the kind of writer who can help us understand the deepest thoughts, motives, and complexities of men and women. It is a prerequisite for art.

Such imaginative sympathy is also, I believe, a prerequisite for democratic pluralists to meet Dewey's task of philosophy—to clarify men's ideas as to the social and moral strifes of their own day. What I have in mind is the kind of imaginative leap it takes to understand what it is like to be poor, black, female, and pregnant without the option of abortion; it requires the kind of insight into the shame and defeat or numbing depression someone might feel when he decides he has no reason to continue living; it requires understanding what it is like to be terminally ill and kept alive by machines; it requires understanding what makes a person angry enough to burn down and loot his neighborhood in East Los Angeles. And it is also the same kind of imaginative leap required to understand why some Americans are appalled by feminists, abortion, euthanasia, and black people unable to find a job or so angry that they burn their neighbors' property.

Supreme Court Justice Thurgood Marshall once asked the deputy solicitor general arguing for the constitutionality of a regulation prohibiting people from sleeping in public parks whether he had ever been homeless. Marshall knew that sometimes even the imaginations of the most well-intentioned people, stunted by ignorance or inexperience, could use some prodding.

For centuries white Americans have found it difficult to understand the frustration, anger, indeed the hatred of some black Americans. Slavery, after all, once was legal in the United States and rationalized by the best political, philosophical, and religious minds of the day. Neither morality nor piety ended slavery; a murderous civil war did. And even after the Constitution was amended to grant black Americans their equal citizenship before the laws, state legislatures treated them as second-class citizens for the next century, until the civil rights battles of the 1960s helped expand our moral imaginations.

As I was writing this chapter, the newspapers reported the death of Thurgood Marshall, the first black Supreme Court justice who as the chief attorney of the NAACP had pursued the school discrimination cases that resulted in Brown v. Board of Education, the landmark reversal in 1954 of the "separate but equal" doctrine. The *New York Times* obituary quoted from a tribute to Marshall written by a former law clerk:

He grew up in a ruthlessly discriminatory world—a world in which segregation of the races was pervasive and taken for granted, where lynching was common, where the black man's inherent inferiority was proclaimed widely and wantonly. Thurgood Marshall had the capacity to imagine a radically different world, the imaginative capacity to believe that such a world was possible, the strength to sustain that image in the mind's eye and the heart's longing, and the courage and ability to make that imagined world real.

Apparently, Marshall's own imaginative powers were contagious. The obituary reminded me of another newspaper story about Marshall I had clipped months before: "LIBERAL GIANTS INSPIRE THREE CENTRIST JUSTICES" was the headline of a story about the personal reminiscences of Justices Anthony Kennedy, Sandra Day O'Connor, and David Souter—all Republican appointees to the Court and moderate conservatives—about their recently retired colleagues Justices Marshall and William Brennan. O'Connor had written that she was surprised by the extent to which Marshall "would profoundly influence me" during the ten years they had served together on the Court. Discussing cases during conference, Marshall liked to tell personal stories that spoke to a particular issue before the Court. O'Connor recalled one example of racial prejudice and the miscarriage of justice in a death penalty case Marshall had handled as a trial lawyer. "His story made clear what legal briefs often obscure: the impact of legal rules on human lives," wrote justice O'Connor, who described Marshall's stories as "a source of amazement and inspiration."

This is what makes great moral leaders: they amaze and inspire us and help us reimagine the world we think we know so well, until we realize that something is so wrong with it that we have to create a new world.

from "The Moral Imagination"
Simon & Shuster 1995

Peace of Mind, the Mind of Peace
by the Dalai Lama

Do you think humans are inherently good, and succumb to evil, or that we are balanced between good and evil equally?

I believe the answer is more neutral. I'm always telling people, basic human nature is gentleness, human affection. So if human affection is actually the foundation or the basis of human existence right at the beginning of our life until our death, the rule of human affection is very, very powerful—the more compassionate, more affectionate person is naturally healthier: physically healthier, mentally healthier, and happier.

Your comment about balance is also very true. Now, if we ask, "is this person good or bad?" the answer, I think, is the person can be good, can be bad, or can be indifferent. From that angle, basic human nature, the basic human being, is something good, but can either be good or bad. What is the main factor of good and bad? It's not your face, not money, but rather, a part of mind, a part of thought. We make a distinction, good or bad. In terms of thought, there are negative thoughts such as hatred, jealousy, fear; they are called negative because these thoughts bring us disaster, destroy our happiness, destroy our future, destroy our family, and eventually destroy our world. With nuclear weapons, we have the potential to destroy the whole world. Nobody is utilizing nuclear weapons with a happy mood. There is a lot of frustration, hatred.

Human affection gives us peace of mind; this is positive because this makes us not only happy, but also brings happier days in our family, in our society. Therefore, we call this positive.

In each individual human being, there are both qualities: Negative and positive. But human intelligence, if we are thinking properly, thinking fully, allows us the capacity to realize that these negative thoughts are negative and also realize the positive things.

Human beings have the ability to increase positive thought and reduce negative thought. Therefore, the conclusion is that the human being, basically, is positive, because of human intelligence and human compassion.

Combine these two things, and in spite of the negative

things which are also part of human life, they are more dominant. From that viewpoint, the human being is positive.

from Spin Magazine
April 1994

Provide Love

by Bobby Muller

I'm just going to share a little bit of a personal thing that happened. I really considered myself a very righteous guy, a very good guy, and when I went into the Marine Corps, you know, I was really sensitive to kids. And I went through the whole training thing, went to Vietnam, and—

Vietnam was a very confusing war. You didn't have a front-line, and you didn't have a clear identification of who your enemy was. And I had a lot of situations—I was a platoon commander—where I had my guys out doing operations. And as they would often do, you know, they would have the kids come in and we'd give them C-rations, we'd give them stuff. And a couple of times actually, you know, that night we would get hit, we would get attacked. And our command position and our critical positions were obviously known to the attacking force, the Vietcong, and it turned out that it was the kids that we had befriended and given the C-rats to, et cetera, that had gotten their brothers to come in and attack us that night.

I won't get carried away with it, but a lot of things happened in my interactions with the Vietnamese that I remember. At one point, you know, we used to have these heating tabs that we would light up, and they'd burn with an invisible flame to cook up the C-rats. And we were on a truck convoy going down the highway, and my guys were lighting up these heating tabs and throwing them off the truck. And they were a valued little commodity, so, you know, kids would be coming out of the villages, and they would pick up these heating tabs, and being that they had an invisible flame, the kids couldn't tell that it had been lit up, and it would stick to their hand, their fingers, and burn them.

And I remember laughing at that.

When I got shot, I was medevacked to a hospital ship and they had me in intensive care for several days, and they had a psychiatrist come and talk to me. He said, "Is there anything you want to talk about?" He was presumably inquiring about the fact that I was going to be a paraplegic. But my question to him was, two days before, I had sat down, chowed down, and had a big lunch amongst a whole bunch of dead bodies. And it meant nothing to me. And I said, "Is there something wrong with me?" And he said, "No, there's nothing wrong with you. You've been in an extraordinary circumstance, and your mind has its automatic defense mechanisms that come into play to allow you to get through these extraordinary circumstances." He said, "You go back to New York City, and next year, you see somebody get hit by a cab, and you're going to be as affected as anybody else."

Which is exactly what happened. What I'm saying to you is that I think people are inherently good. I think the power of love and the power of good is a very, very strong force, but we can be affected by the negative. We can be affected by the forces of, for lack of a better term, darkness. And in being on the ground, and getting involved in a situation of killing people and having my guys killed, I sometimes say that I think I took a little bit of a walk down that path of darkness, and I personally realized how a good guy could wind up doing unconscionable things, have a value structure so fundamentally altered.

And remember My Lai, okay? In My Lai, it was "the good guys," it was an American infantry unit that went in and murdered 505 Vietnamese women and children and old people without one single shot being fired in return. That was the good guys, okay?

So, what I'm saying may not be clear but, you know, when you get exposed to evil and when you get into darkness, and the circumstances around you are of that nature, they can have an affect on all of us. Those of you that may say that could never happen to me, let me tell you something: you're kidding yourself. I didn't think it could happen to me. I was shocked when I realized it did happen.

But the positive part of this story, to wrap it up, is that by coming back, getting love, getting nurturing, getting out of where the forces of darkness and the negative energy of, basically, evil can work on you, [it] allows you the opportunity to rehabilitate, to rejuvenate. And I've seen it with literally hundreds of veterans that were exposed to the most horrific combat. I've seen it in kids. I've seen it with a lot of people in war zones that I've gone to.

So we have a rejuvenative capability. You know, stop feeding the negative. Take them out of those situations. Provide love, and get a decent environment, and even with those that have been crushed, you can so oftentimes bring them back to wholeness and good health.

Remarks on Nov. 5, 1998 at the University of Virginia.

Do Small Things In a Great Way
by Colman McCarthy

To the question, can people be made to be good, Gandhi of India replied: No, all that's possible is to create conditions in which it will be easier to choose the good. How are those conditions created? After some 30 years as a journalist interviewing specialists in the good life - a life of seeking the good - I'm leaning toward a conclusion: The good life is a peacemaking life. Every government claims it seeks peace. Every human heart yearns for it. No calling is higher or more noble than that of peacemaker, no matter the form it may take. Peace is the result of love. But if love were easy, we'd all be good at it.

It isn't so easy, because creating the conditions for both a heart at peace and a peaceable society demands commitments to three forces - one spiritual, one social and one intellectual. The forces are prayer, service and nonviolence.

By prayer, I don't mean the vulgarized, trivialized or Pat Robertsonized prayer of asking God for self-serving benefits or boons: a successful bypass operation, a better job, electing a politician who votes my way. True prayer - the prayer of Amos and Isaiah, of such Christian saints as Teresa of Avila and Clare of Assisi, of the Moslem, Hindu, Buddhist, Jain and B'hai saints, and Chief Little Priest of the Native American Church - reverses it. Nothing is asked from God. Instead, God is asked, what do you want from me?

That's risky. The answer might demand new ways of thinking or acting. If religion has no risks, it's mere religiosity: surface piety, not inner morals. Ties to organized religion are not needed for prayerfulness, as can be observed by the deep spirituality practiced by many atheists and agnostics. Albert Camus, the French novelist, professed atheism, yet he was invited by the Dominicans to speak at their retreats. Prayer is no more than asking "How should I be using my gifts?" and then acting on the answer. One of those answers, surely, is to help others discover their gifts. What is parenthood about, if not that? Or teaching? What teachers do we remember except those who nudged or pushed us to discover our gifts?

The second essential commitment is service. My wife and I have three sons - one of them Notre Dame class of '90 and all of them thrivingly on their own. When they were younger, we would have friends over for dinner. We discussed the issues. In Washington, D.C., we are required to have issues dinners. You can't just sit and enjoy a meal together like normal people! Campaign financing, our China policy, Whitewater: half an hour on each one. Then it was into the living room, where someone would notice the kids and, eager to relate, ask the inevitable question: What do you want to be when you grow up?

The question always unsettled me. Don't ask them that, I would say to myself. It's inane and irrelevant. Instead, ask young people the question that truly matters: How do you want to serve society when you are ready? Get it into their minds, hearts, spirits and souls at an early age that we expect service from them, that that's where they'll find their joy and their life's meaning.

In the high school, college and law school classes I've been teaching for the past 15 years, my students have one handicap: Their minds are crammed with so many academic theories and book-learned thoughts that they leave school idea rich but experience poor. They're unbalanced. I worry about them, especially those who make too many A's. As Walker Percy wrote, you can make all A's and go out and flunk life. As a way to involve all my brainy students in experiential knowledge, I offer them a service alternative: Go into an elementary school or a high school and teach conflict resolution skills, or tutor in a literacy program.

Ten years ago, I had an English major in my class at the University of Maryland. She had made all A's and could quote Shakespeare and Milton by the linear yard. I suggested she learn about English from the other end, by teaching an illiterate how to read. She went to a local literacy program and was matched with a truck driver. They spent a semester together. Both were liberated. The truck driver learned how to read and my English major learned how to live. Near the end, she came to me and said how much the experience had changed her life. But why, she wondered, hadn't I asked her to do that sooner? Well, I replied, we professors are busy making you smart, so you get rich and get ahead.

We lie to the students, rarely issuing a challenge by leading them into the life of service. In many schools and among many teachers, including me, that's changing. More than a fourth of my University of Maryland students last year were literacy tutors to third- and fourth-graders at a District of Columbia elementary school where more than 90 percent of the children come from fatherless families and where a majority have relatives or close neighbors in prison. Some of the gains are measurable - the reading scores of the tutored kids went up - and some are not: the stirrings of conscience among my college folk, the new awareness of their gifts, a shift in thinking so that now the good life means a giving life.

What these students learned outside the classroom twins with some of the teachings of the peacemakers we study inside. There is Albert Schweitzer, the German theologian and medical missionary in Gabon, West Africa, who wrote in Reverence for Life "No one has the right to take for granted his own advantages over others in health, in talent, in ability, in success, in a happy childhood or congenial home conditions. One must pay a price for al l these boons. What one owes in return is a special responsibility for other lives .... He who has experienced good in his life must feel the obligation to dedicate some of his own life in order to alleviate suffering."

The third commitment is to nonviolent conflict resolution. As a lifelong pacifist, I wanted to find out whether peacemaking can be taught. In 1982, I went to an inner-city high school near my office at the Washington Post and asked the principal if I could teach a course called "Solutions to Violence." Give it a try, she said. I've been teaching it ever since. It isn't a difficult course. We read some Gandhi, King, Merton, Day, Muste, Jesus, Francis, Amos, Isaiah, Tolstoy, Einstein, Buddha, Adin Ballou, Sojourner Truth, Jeannette Rankin, Jane Addams, George Fox, John Woolman, Scott Nearing, Eugene Debs, David Dellinger, Dan and Philip Berrigan, Albert Schweitzer, Thich Nhat Hanh, William Lloyd Garrison, Michael True, Vincent Harding, Mulford Sibley and Howard Zinn. For starters.

When I rattle off those names on the first day of class, someone inevitably raises a hand to ask, "How'd you hear of all

those people?" Then I'm asked, "Why haven't we heard of them"""
To the second question: You haven't heard of them because you go
to American schools. In our 3,000 colleges, 28,000 high schools
and 78,000 elementary schools, students are graduated as peace
illiterates.

Imagine the clamor for reform if we were suddenly to realize that we are a nation of math illiterates. Imagine that you knew
of a faraway country where the citizens insisted that $2+2=93$ or
that $3x3=85$. This was a nation of otherwise intelligent people,
with great achievements of intellect in the arts and sciences.

When you inquired about their obvious deficiencies in
math, you were told the schools didn't teach it. A few citizens
sought to change that but were dismissed as cranks. So no politicians dared run for office with a proposal that math be taught in
the schools. Teachers who told students that $2+2=4$, not 93. were
reported to the school boards as radicals not to be entrusted with
impressionable young minds. Newspaper editorials were forever
deploring the ignorance and calling for commissions to study the
problem, but none argued that schools hire math teachers.

That's about where we are regarding peace education. Few
know how to teach it because few were taught. Few can imagine
that other answers besides fists, guns, armies, bombs and nukes
should be considered as solutions to conflicts, whether the conflicts are within families or workplaces or among governments.
The consequence of our peace illiteracy is that the good life is all
but impossible. Instead, the wounded life, the destroyed life the
oppressed life is tolerated.

How? The forms vary. Some 22,000 murders are committed annually in the United States. The leading cause of injury
among American women is being beaten at home by a man. Abortions have averaged 1.5 million annually. The United States is the
world's major arms dealer, with more than 75 percent of the combatants in the planet's 35 wars or conflicts using American-made
weapons. Congress gives the Pentagon $700 million a day, a sum
three times the Peace Corps budget for a year. In 1995, the Center
for Defense Information reported that the proposed $258 billion
military budget is 17 times as large as the combined military spending of the six nations identified by the Pentagon as our most likely

adversaries (North Korea, Iraq, Iran, Syria, Libya and Cuba). What Martin Luther King Jr. said on April 4, 1967, in Riverside Church in New York remains true: "The greatest purveyor of violence in the world today [is] my own government."

The good life is incompatible with the violent life. Who does not feel overwhelmed by the enormity of the problem or feel nearly helpless by the smallness of one's personal response? Those realities ought to be irrelevant: We aren't called on to do great things, we are asked to do small things in a great way. Prayer, service and nonviolence are the small things. If done in a great way, what else follows but the good life?

from Notre Dame Magazine, Summer 1997

5

Is Gandhi Right?

It is the law of love that rules mankind. Had violence, i.e., hate ruled us, we should have become extinct long ago. And yet the tragedy of it is that the so-called civilized men and nations conduct themselves as if the basis of society was violence.

Gandhi

Gandhi on Nonviolence

Non-resistance is restraint voluntarily undertaken for the good of society. It is, therefore, an intensely active, purifying, inward force .... It presupposes ability to offer physical resistance.

Non-violence is the greatest and most active force in the world. One cannot be passively non-violent .... One person who can express ahimsa in life exercises a force superior to all the forces of brutality.

Non-violence cannot be preached. It has to be practiced.

[Human society is naturally non-violent.] All society is held together by non-violence, even as the earth is held in her position by gravitation. But when the law of gravitation was discovered the discovery yielded results of which our ancestors had no knowledge. Even so when society is deliberately constructed in accordance with the law of non-violence, its structure will be different in material particulars from what is today .... What is happening today is disregard of the law of non-violence and enthronement of violence as if it were an eternal law.

I know that the progress of non-violence is seemingly a terribly slow progress. But experience has taught me it is the surest way to the common goal.

My faith in the saying that what is gained by the sword will also be lost by the sword is imperishable.

Non-violence is impossible without self-purification.

My greatest weapon is mute prayer.

In the composition of the truly brave there should be no malice, no anger, no distrust, no fear of death or physical hurt. Non-violence is certainly not for those who lack these essential qualities.

Mental violence has no potency and injures only the person whose thoughts are violent. It is otherwise with mental non-violence. It has potency which the world does not yet know. And what I want is non-violence of thought and deed.

Self-respect and honor cannot be protected by others. They are for each individual himself or herself to guard.

If we remain non-violent, hatred will die as everything does, from disuse.

It is the law of love that rules mankind. Had violence, i.e., hate ruled us, we should have become extinct long ago. And yet the tragedy of it is that the so-called civilized men and nations conduct themselves as if the basis of society was violence.

Democracy can only be saved through non-violence, because democracy, so long as it is sustained by violence, cannot provide for or protect the weak. My notion of democracy is that under it the weakest should have the same opportunity as the strongest. This can never happen except through non-violence .... Western democracy, as it functions today, is diluted Nazism or fascism.

Non-violent defense presupposes recklessness about one's life and property.

The immovable force of satyagraha—suffering without retaliation.

Those who die unresistingly are likely to still the fury of violence by their wholly innocent sacrifice.

He who meets death without striking a blow fulfills his duty 100 percent. The result is in God's hands.

If intellect plays a large part in the field of violence, I hold that it plays a larger part in the field of non-violence.

As non-violence admits of no grossness, no fraud, no malice, it must raise the moral tone of the defenders. Hence there will be a corresponding rise in the moral tone of the "weak majority" to be defended.

Moral support cannot really be given in the sense of giving. It automatically comes to him who is qualified to take it. And such a one can take it in abundance.

A satyagrahi is dead to his body even before his enemy attempts to kill him, i.e., he is free from attachment to his body and only lives in the victory of his soul. Therefore when he is already thus dead, why should he yearn to kill anyone? To die in the act of killing is in essence to die defeated.

The general of a non-violent army has got to have greater presence of mind than that of a violent army, and God would bless him with the necessary resourcefulness to meet new situations as they arise.

A non-violent army need not have the resourcefulness or understanding of its general, but they will have a perfect sense of discipline to carry out faithfully his orders.

In this age of democracy it is essential that desired results are achieved by the collective effort of the people. It will no doubt be good to achieve an objective through the effort of an supremely powerful individual, but it can never make the community conscious of its corporate strength.

If freedom has got to come, it must be obtained by our own internal strength, by our closing our ranks, by unity between all sections of the community.

A weak man is just by accident. A strong but non-violent man is unjust by accident.

If liberty and democracy are to be truly saved, they will only be by non-violent resistance no less brave, no less glorious, than violent resistance. And it will be infinitely braver and more glorious because it will give life without taking any.

When in the face of an upheaval such as we are witnessing these are only a few individuals of immovable faith, they have to live up to their faith even though they may produce no visible effect on the course of events. They should believe that their action will produce tangible results in due course.

Such non-violent resisters will calmly die wherever they are but will not bend the knee before the aggressor. They will not be deceived by promises. They do not seek deliverance from the British yoke through the help of a third party [the Japanese]. They believe implicitly in their own way of fighting and no other. Their fight is on behalf of the dumb millions who do not perhaps know that there is such a thing a deliverance. They have neither hatred for the British nor love for the Japanese. They wish well to both as to all others. They would like both to do what is right. They believe that non-violence alone will lead men to do right under all circumstances.

The task before the votaries of non-violence is very difficult, but no difficulty can baffle men who have faith in their mission.

The best preparation for and even the expression of

non-violence lies in the determined pursuit of the constructive program .... He who has no belief in the constructive program has, in my opinion, no concrete feeling for the starved millions. He who is devoid of that feeling cannot fight non-violently. In actual practice the expansion of my non-violence has kept exact pace with that of my identification with starved humanity.

Non-violence knows no defeat. It must, however, be true non-violence, not a make-believe.

A satyagrahi must always be ready to die with a smile on his face, without retaliation and without rancor in his heart. Some people have come to have a wrong notion that satyagraha means only jail-going, perhaps facing blows, and nothing more. Such satyagraha cannot bring independence. To win independence you have to learn the art of dying without killing.

Must I do all the evil I can before I learn to shun it? Is it not enough to know the evil to shun it? If not, we should be sincere enough to admit that we love evil too well to give it up.

A satyagrahi cannot wait or delay action till perfect conditions are forthcoming. He will act with whatever material is at hand, purge it of dross and convert it into pure gold.

Truth and non-violence are not possible without a living belief in God, meaning a self-existent, all-knowing, living Force which inheres in every other force known to the world and which depends on none, and which will live when all other forces may conceivably perish or cease to act. I am unable to account for my life without belief in this all-embracing living Light.

Crime is a disease like any other malady and is a product of the prevalent social system. Therefore [in a non-violent India] all crime including murder will be treated as a disease.

Murder can never be avenged by either murder or taking compensation. The only way to avenge murder is to offer oneself as a willing sacrifice, with no desire for retaliation.

In this age of the atom bomb unadulterated non-violence is the only force that can confound all the tricks of violence put together.

The lawlessness, if it can be so described, that I have advocated is like prescribing wholesome and necessary food for the body. Behind my "lawlessness" there is discipline, construction and well-being of society. It is an effective protest against an unjust and injurious law or act. It can never take the form of selfish evasion of duty.

Gandhi and His Myths
by Mark Shepard

There are many myths about Gandhi. I'd like to point out a few of them and hopefully get rid of them for you.

First, a quick one: Gandhi was not a scrawny little man. Yes, his legs were scrawny-and bowed—but be had a barrel chest, and a deep, booming voice to match it . In pictures, you just don't notice his chest, because be usually had a cloth draped around it.

That was an easy one. Let's try another.

One of the most common and most dangerous myths about Gandhi is that be was a saint The name, or rather, the title Mahatma itself means "Great Soul." That's somewhere between a saint and a Messiah. Gandhi tried to avoid the title, but the people of India ignored his protests. Now I see that even the Library of Congress has begun to classify him under "Gandhi, Mahatma," so I guess he's lost that battle.

I've heard it argued that Gandhi indeed was a saint, since he was a master of meditation. Well, I must tell you that in all my readings of and about Gandhi, I've never come across anything to say that Gandhi was a master of meditation, or that he meditated at all—aside from observing a minute of silence at the beginning of his prayer meetings, a practice he said he borrowed from the Quakers.

Gandhi objected when people called him "a saint trying to be a politician." He said he was instead "a politician trying to be a saint" Personally, I go along with Gandhi's judgment on this

Not that Gandhi's spiritual efforts and achievements shouldn't be honored. They've certainly inspired me. But, if we label Gandhi a perfected being, we lose our chance to view his life and career critically and to learn from his mistakes.

Besides, if people see Gandhi as a saint, they'll think he's "too good for the world," and they won't take his example seriously as a model for concrete social change. I'm constantly annoyed at finding books on Gandhi in bookstore sections marked "Religious," or even "Occult." If his books are stashed away like that, how will the hard-boiled political scientists ever run across him?

Another myth about Gandhi is the idea that India's political leaders, beginning with Nehru, are the inheritors of his tradition and have carried it on.

I wish they had. But, really, India's leaders have rejected much more of Gandhi than they've adopted.

They abandoned nonviolent action as soon as they attained power. India now sports the world's fourth largest armed force, and the leaders haven't seemed at all reluctant to use it to settle conflicts, either inside or outside the country. No thought is given to possible Gandhi-style alternatives.

Maybe even worse, India's leaders have done their best to imitate Western countries by building an economy based on large-scale industry and large-scale agriculture.

Gandhi fought this kind of development. He warned that it would economically ruin India's villages, where 80% of India's people lived and still live. And Gandhi has proved correct

Yes, India is now overall a much richer country but it has more desperately poor people than ever. As many as half of its people can't afford enough food to sustain health. India prides itself now on growing enough grain so it doesn't need to import anyóbut the surplus rots in storage while people starve who can't afford to buy it.

Gandhi promoted a different kind of development. He stressed efforts based right in the villages, building on the villagers' own strengths and resources. Not many people here realize it, but Gandhi may be this century's greatest advocate of decentralism or basing economic and political power at the local level.

You may remember in the movie *Gandhi* seeing Gandhi spin cotton yarn on a compact spinning wheel. Gandhi and his colleagues were the ones who developed this wheel and introduced it into the villages. It's the first case of what's now called "appropriate technology" or "intermediate technology." Of course, E. F. Schumacher, the author of Small is Beautiful, later introduced the terms themselves. Schumacher was strongly influenced by Gandhi, calling him "the most important economic teacher today."

Gandhi set up a number of organizations to help carry out village development. He sent many workers to live in and among the villages.

Since his death, thousands have carried on this work. Now, though, the workers often combine development with campaigns against local injustice. Probably the closest thing in the United States to what they are doing is what we call "community organizing."

The people carrying on this work in India are among the true successors of Gandhi. Other modern-day Gandhians are in programs like the Chipko—Hug the Trees—Movement which blocks irresponsible logging in the Himalayas; a Shanti Sena, the "Peace Army," which intervenes nonviolently in urban riots. My book *Gandhi Today* describes a number of the Gandhians' programs.

I suspect, though, that most of the myths and misconceptions surrounding Gandhi have to do with nonviolence. For instance, it's surprising how many people still have the idea that nonviolent action is passive.

It's impotent for us to be clear about this: There is nothing passive about Gandhian nonviolent action.

I'm afraid Gandhi himself helped create this confusion by referring to his method at first as "passive resistance," because it was in some ways like techniques bearing that label. But he soon changed his mind and rejected the term.

Gandhi's nonviolent action was not an evasive strategy nor a defensive one. Gandhi was always on the offensive. He believed in confronting his opponents aggressively, in such a way that they could not avoid dealing with him.

But wasn't Gandhi's nonviolent action designed to avoid violence? Yes and no. Gandhi steadfastly avoided violence toward his opponents. He did not avoid violence toward himself or his followers.

Gandhi said that the nonviolent activist, like any soldier, had to be ready to die for the cause. And, in fact, during India's struggle for independence, hundreds of Indians were killed by the British.

The difference was that the nonviolent activist, while willing to die, was never willing to kill.

Gandhi pointed out three possible responses to oppression and injustice. One he described as the coward's way: to accept the wrong or run away from it. The second option was to stand and fight by force of arms, Gandhi said this was better than acceptance or running away.

But the third way, he said, was best of all, and required the most courage: to stand and fight solely by nonviolent means.

Another of the biggest myths about nonviolent action is the idea that Gandhi invented it.

Gandhi is often called "the father of nonviolence" Well, he did raise nonviolent action to a level never before achieved. Still, it wasn't at all his invention.

Gene Sharp of Harvard University, in his book Gandhi as a Political Strategist, shows that Gandhi and his Indian colleagues in South Africa were well aware of other nonviolent struggles before they adopted such methods themselves. That was in 1906. In the couple of years before that, they'd been impressed by mass nonviolent actions in India, China, Russia, and among blacks in South Africa itself.

In another of his books, The Politics of Nonviolent Action, Gene Sharp cites over 200 cases of mass nonviolent struggle throughout history. And he assures us that many more will be found if historians take the trouble to look.

Curiously, some of the best earlier examples come from right here in the United States, in the years leading up to the American Revolution. To oppose British rule, the colonists used many tactics amazingly like Gandhi's and, according to Sharp, they used these techniques with more skill and sophistication than anyone else before the time of Gandhi.

For instance, to resist the British Stamp Act, the colonists widely refused to pay for the official stamp required to appear on publications and legal documents: a case of civil disobedience and tax refusal, both used later by Gandhi. Boycotts of British imports were organized to protest the Stamp Act, the Townshend Acts, and the so-called Intolerable Acts. The campaign against the latter was organized by the First Continental Congress, which was really a nonviolent action organization.

Almost two centuries later, a boycott of British imports played a pivotal role in Gandhi's own struggle against colonial rule.

The colonists used another strategy later adopted by Gandhi, setting up parallel institutions to take over functions of government and had far greater success with it than Gandhi ever did. In fact, according to Sharp, colonial organizations had largely taken over control from the British in most of the colonies before a shot was fired.

Why aren't we more aware of such cases, including those in our own history? 1 think it's because of something we could call "filtering."

Probably most of you who've worked with cameras know about the kind of filter I mean. The filter fits over the camera lens and blocks out potions of the light-usually certain colors and lets the remainder pass through to the lens. In effect, the filter selects the portion of light that the camera will "see."

Each of us, too, sees the world through our own "filter"— a filter made up of our assumptions, our motivations, and the categories we use to sort out and organize our experience. This filter determines how we see the world.

When we come across something that doesn't match our assumptions, motivations, and categories, our filter blocks it out. It's not that we choose to reject it. Consciously, we don't even perceive it. Or else we perceive it in a partial, distorted form.

It seems that nonviolence has a particularly hard time passing through many people's filters.

To know about current and past events, we depend a great deal on journalists and historians.

Now, one thing that journalists and historians understand is military power. They know what comes from many people being shot or imprisoned. It's obvious when such power is being used, and a journalist or historian can feel professionally safe in describing and analyzing it.

But most of them do not deal so well with subtle, nonviolent forms of power. They don't understand how such power operates; or even how it could operate; or even that such a form of power could exist.

So, as often as not, they don't notice it at all. Or, if they do notice it, they don't grasp what they've seen. Or they don't connect it with its effects.

For example, say that a Third World country undergoes a spontaneous country-wide, mass noncooperation campaign and say the things Gandhi said and really mean them? Well, surely these critics couldn't!

Other, "kinder" critics have felt Gandhi was simply an idealistic fool, with no conception of how power works in the real world. Translated, this means that these critics can't understand how Gandhi's methods worked.

Let's look at these methods of Gandhi's and see if we can spot where their power might come from. And maybe we can clear up some other myths along the way

Gandhi called his overall method of nonviolent action Satyagraha. This translates roughly as "Truth-force." A fuller rendering, though, would be "the force that is generated through adherence to Truth."

Nowadays, it's usually called nonviolence. But, for Gandhi, nonviolence was the word for a different, broader concept: namely, "a way of life based on love and compassion." In Gandhi's terminology, Satyagraha—Truthforce—was an outgrowth of nonviolence.

It may also help to keep to mind that the terms Satyagraha and nonviolent action, though often used one for the other. don't actually refer to the exact same thing. Satyagraha is really one special form of nonviolent action: Gandhi's own version of it. Much of what's called nonviolent action wouldn't qualify as Satyagraha. But we'll come back to that, later.

Gandhi practiced two types of Satyagraha in his mass campaigns. The first was civil disobedience, which entailed breaking a law and courting arrest. When we today hear this term, our minds tend to stress the "disobedience" part of it. But, for Gandhi, "civil" was just as important. He used "civil" here not just in its meaning of "relating to citizenship and government" but also in its meaning of "civilized" or "polite." And that's exactly what Gandhi strove for.

We also tend to lay stress differently than Gandhi on the phase of civil disobedience. We tend to think breaking the law is the core of it. But, to Gandhi, the core of it was going to prison. Breaking the law was mostly just a way to get there.

Now, why was that? Was Gandhi trying to fill the jails? Overwhelm and embarrass his captors? Make them "give in" through force of numbers?

Not at all. He just wanted to make a statement. He wanted to say. "I care so deeply about this matter that I'm willing to take on the legal penalties, to sit in this prison cell, to sacrifice my freedom, in order to show you how deeply I care. Because, when you see the depth of my concern, and how 'civil' 1 am in going about this, you're bound to change your mind about me, to abandon your rigid, unjust position, and to let me help you see the truth of my cause."

In other words, Gandhi's method aimed to win not by overwhelming but by converting his opponent: or, as the Gandhians say, by bringing about a "change of heart."

Now, to many people, that sounds pretty naive. Well, I'll let you in on a secret. It was naive. The belief that civil disobedience succeeded by converting the opponent happened to be a myth held by Gandhi himself. And it's shared try most of his admirers, who take his word for it without bothering to check it out.

Of course, noncooperation and civil disobedience overlapped. Noncooperation too was to be carried out in a "civil" manner. Here, too, Gandhi's followers had to cheerfully face beating, imprisonment, confiscation of their property—and it was hoped that this willing suffering would cause a "change of heart."

But noncooperation also had a dynamic of its own, a dynamic that didn't at all depend on converting the opponent or even molding public opinion. It was a dynamic based not on appeals but on the power of the people themselves.

Gandhi saw that the power of any tyrant depends entirely on people being willing to obey. The tyrant may get people to obey by threatening to throw them in prison, or by holding guns to their heads. But the power still resides in the obedience, not in the prison or the guns.

Now, what happens if those people begin to say, 'We're not afraid of prison. We're even willing to die. But we're not willing to obey you any longer.'?

It's very simple. The tyrant has no power. He may rant and scream and hurt and destroy, but, if the people hold to it, he's finished.

Gandhi said, "1 believe that no government can exist for a single moment without the cooperation of the people, willing or forced, and, if people suddenly withdraw their cooperation in every detail, the government will come to a standstill." That was Gandhi's concept of power: the one he's accused of not having. It's a hard one to grasp, for those used to seeing power in the barrel of a gun. Their filters do not pass it. And so they call Gandhi idealistic, impractical.

Then there are the critics who say nonviolent action worked fine in India, but they don't think it would make sense to use it elsewhere. These critics believe that Indians are particularly suited to nonviolent action, because of the ethic of nonviolence built into their religion.

This is a very interesting myth, and those who believe in it certainly possess a very selective filter. Personally, I don't think you can follow the news from India for long and still believe Indians are less violent than other people.

Besides, Gandhi's philosophy of nonviolence seems to have been consciously inspired first by the New Testament: the Sermon on the Mount. Only later it seems, did he find similar ideas in Hindu scriptures.

It's surprising how easy it is to forget that we too have an ethic of nonviolence built into our society's chief religion. We just don't happen to follow it. Just as the Indians don't normally follow theirs.

But, really, the easiest way to see that nonviolent action is suitable outside India is simply to look at all the cases of nonviolent action outside India. Unless your filter is pretty murky, you can hardly miss them. It certainly can't be easy to ignore the example of Martin Luther King Jr., or to forget the Solidarity movement in Poland, or to overlook the overthrow of Ferdinand Marcos in the Philippines.

Then there is the cousin of the "only-in-India" argument. This one says that nonviolent action can work only against "easy" enemies like the British, and not against, say, the Soviets, or Central American dictators, or those villains of last resort, the Nazis.

First of all, a violent struggle will tend to bring about much more destruction of life, property, and environment.

Of course, there can be destruction in nonviolent struggles, too. Just because you're nonviolent doesn't mean your opponent will be. As I said before, Gandhi's campaigns in India saw hundreds of Indians killed by the British. Still, this doesn't compare with the tens or hundreds of thousands, or even millions, killed in some violent revolutions.

The difference, by the way, doesn't arise because nonviolent struggles are aimed at "nice" enemies. After all, the British aren't so much nicer than the French, who killed 800,000 Algerians—that's one out of every thirteen during Algeria's war of independence.

No, the difference arises because, in a violent struggle, the violence of each side goads the other to greater violence. Also, each side uses the violence of the other side to justify its own violence. A nonviolent struggle, on the other hand, doesn't so much encourage the violence of the opponent.

Other negative side-effects of violence come into view once the struggle comes to an end. For instance, violence generally leaves the two sides as long-standing enemies.

Maybe the most amazing thing about Gandhi's nonviolent revolution is, not that the British left, but that they left as friends, and that Britain and India became partners in the British Commonwealth.

"Gandhi and His Myths"
by Mark Shepard

Ahimsa
by Eknath Easwaran

Ahimsa, nonviolence, was the noblest expression of Truth for Gandhi—or, properly speaking, the way to truth.

Ahimsa and Truth are so intertwined that it is practically impossible to disentangle and separate them. They are like the two sides of a coin, or rather a smooth unstamped metallic disc. Who can say which is the obverse and which the reverse? Nevertheless, ahimsa is the means; Truth is the end.

Ahimsa is the bedrock of satyagraha, the "irreducible minimum" to which satyagraha adheres and the final measure of its value.

In the traditional lore of India there is a story about an old sannyasi, a Hindu monk, who was sitting on the bank of a river silently repeating his mantram. Nearby a scorpion fell from a tree into the river, and the sannyasi, seeing it struggling in the water, bent over and pulled it out. He placed the scorpion back in the tree, but as he did so, the creature bit him on the hand. He paid no heed to the bite, but went on repeating his mantram. A little while later, the scorpion again fell into the water. As before, the monk pulled him out and set him back in the tree and again was bitten. This little drama was repeated several times, and each time the sannyasi rescued the scorpion, he received a bite.

It happened that a villager, ignorant of the ways of holy men, had come to the river for water and had seen the whole affair. Unable to contain himself any longer, the villager told the sannyasi with some vexation:
"Swamiji, I have seen you save that foolish scorpion several times now and each time he has bitten you. Why not let the rascal go?"

"Brother," replied the sannyasi, "the fellow cannot help himself. It is his nature to bite. "Agreed," answered the villager. "But knowing this, why don't you avoid him?"

"Ah, brother," replied the monk, "you see, I cannot help myself either. I am a human being; it is my nature to save."

Ahimsa is usually translated as "nonviolence," but as we have seen, its meaning goes much beyond that. Ahimsa is derived from the Sanskrit verb hims, which means to kill. The form hims means "desirous to kill"; the prefix a- is a negation. So a-himsa means literally "lacking any desire to kill," which is perhaps the central theme upon which Hindu, Jain, and Buddhist morality is built. In the Manu Smriti, the great lawbook of Hinduism, it is written, "Ahimsa paramo dharma": ahimsa is the highest law. It is, as Gandhi puts it, the very essence of human nature.

"Nonviolence is the law of our species as violence is the law of the brute. The spirit lies dormant in the brute and he knows no law but that of physical might. The dignity of man requires obedience to a higher law—to the strength of the spirit . . . ."

The word nonviolence connotes a negative, almost passive condition, whereas the Sanskrit term ahimsa suggests a dynamic state of mind in which power is released. "Strength," Gandhi said, "does not come from physical capacity. It comes from an indomitable will." Therein he found his own strength, and there he exhorted others to look for theirs. Latent in the depths of human consciousness, this inner strength can be cultivated by the observance of complete ahimsa. Whereas violence checks this energy within, and is ultimately disruptive in its consequences, ahimsa, properly understood, is invincible. "With satya combined with ahimsa," Gandhi writes, "you can bring the world to your feet."

When Gandhi speaks of ahimsa as a law, we should take him at his word. Indeed, it was a law for him like gravity, and could be demonstrated in the midst of human affairs. Gandhi even characterized his practice of ahimsa as a science, and said once, "I have been practicing with scientific precision nonviolence and its possibilities for an unbroken period of over fifty years." He was a precise man, meticulous and exacting, fond of quoting a Marathi hymn that goes, "Give me love, give me peace, O Lord, but don't deny me common sense." He valued experience as the test of truth, and the nonviolence he pursued and called "true nonviolence" had to conform to experience in all levels of human affairs. "1 have applied it," he declares, "in every walk of life: domestic, institutional, economic, political. And I know of no single case in which it has failed." Anything short of this total application did not interest Gandhi, because ahimsa sprang from and worked in the same continuum as his religion, politics, and personal life. Only practice could determine its value, "when it acts in the midst of and in spite of opposition," and he advised critics to observe the results of his experiments rather than dissect his theories.

" . . . nonviolence is not a cloistered virtue to be practiced by the individual for his peace and final salvation, but it is a rule of conduct for society .... To practice nonviolence in mundane matters is to know its true value. It is to bring heaven upon earth .... ! hold it therefore to be wrong to limit the use of nonviolence to cave dwellers [hermits] and for acquiring merit for a favoured position in the other world. All virtue ceases to have use if it serves no purpose in every walk of life."

Gandhi's adherence to nonviolence grew from his experience that it was the only way to resolve the problem of conflict permanently. Violence, he felt, only made the pretense of a solution, and sowed seeds of bitterness and enmity that would ultimately disrupt the situation.

One needs to practice ahimsa to understand it. To profess nonviolence with sincerity or even to write a book about it was, for Gandhi, not adequate. "If one does not practice nonviolence in one's personal relationships with others one is vastly mistaken. Nonviolence, like charity, must begin at home." The practice of nonviolence is by no means a simple matter, and Gandhi never intimated that it was. As a discipline, a "code of conduct," true nonviolence demands endless vigilance over one's entire way of life, because it includes words and thought as well as actions.

Ahimsa is not the crude thing it has been made to appear. Not to hurt any living thing is no doubt a part of ahimsa. But it is its least expression. The principle of ahimsa is hurt by every evil thought, by undue haste, by lying, by hatred, by wishing ill to anybody. It is also violated by our holding on to what the world needs.

"Gandhi the Man"
by Eknath Gaswaran

Gandhi Goes To England
by Mildred Fahrni

I was doing voluntary social work in Kingsley Hall, the community center that Muriel Lester had established to offer recreation and education to the impoverished residents of Bow in London's East End. Muriel had met Gandhi when traveling in India as IFOR secretary. He came to stay at Kingsley Hall on his arrival in England in 1931. Gandhi had come to London for the Round Table Conference set up by the government to discuss Indian independence. He was welcomed by the curious but warm-hearted Cockneys and responded with humor when children called out, "Hi, Gandy, 'ows the old goat?" He preferred Kingsley Hall's simple cell-like rooms to the apartment that had been reserved for his party in Knightsbridge.

With little baggage, Gandhi's group moved in. Bapu, as we soon learned to call him, rejected the small cot and chair. "Take all this furniture out," he said, and put down his mat to sit and sleep on. The rest of the group—his son Devidas, two secretaries, Madelaine Slade and C.F. Andrews—succumbed to the "luxury" and settled in for four months, sharing in the life of our small community, with our vegetarian meals and fellowship. We in turn were able to share in their morning meditations ...when we could get up at 4:00 am. Seated cross-legged on the floor of a chilly, dimly lit room, we could participate in the devotion even though we did not understand the words of the chanted prayers.

Others came to join us at 5:30 as we bundled up in woolen scarves and garments (though Gandhi wore only his dhoti and shawl, with sandals on his otherwise bare feet). We were a strange procession as we set out for an hour's walk in the chill dawn, but this was our best time for a person-to-person talk as we took turns walking beside him and asking him political, economic, and religious questions. Each one was answered sincerely, sometimes with humor, always with concern for the questioner. It was at these times that I felt the magnetism of this man who had committed himself to seeking Truth, or God, so completely that he let nothing deter him from his search. He said, "To know God one must have the patience of a man who, standing by the sea, would seek to empty it drop by drop." He told us that every glimpse of truth is worth a lifetime of search, and that if one follows the light as he sees it, more glimpses will be given.

Gandhi was humble but confident. He knew the long years of struggle and self-training that brought the maturity that could say, "God is the whole of life. One must submerge oneself in the whole. Life can only be found in self-effacement. As the drop of water soon dies alone but lives forever in the ocean, so the individual can only live in the life of the whole. Then antagonisms and resistance are impossible." He had found the way through love and nonviolence.

When the time came to leave London, one of his group said, "Don't you think it has been a waste of time to come here? The British don't understand us any better than when we came." His reply was, "Oh no, I know it is right that India should have her freedom. It is right for England as well as India, for no country can hold herself free while she holds another in slavery. And because it is right, I work for it. It may not come this year or next year or for one hundred years, but it will come. I am not responsible for consequences." And so they gathered up their bundles, including the broken toys the poor children of Bow wanted "Uncle Gandhi" to take to the poor children of India, and departed.

On arrival in India, Gandhi was immediately put in jail, but when I visited him eight years later he was living in Sevagram, one of the poorest villages in India. There he had organized the All India Village Development program to provide housing and education, agriculture and crafts to make the village self-sufficient. Living in a simple mud hut, eating only the food necessary to nourish his body, which he called "the temple of God," he truly became the Mahatma, the father of his people. Many came to consult with him from all over the world, and wherever he went crowds gathered, each person hoping to receive darshan or blessing by being in his presence. Many did not understand the basis of his nonviolence, but they loved and trusted him and followed him.

Other leaders and holy men have received great acclaim, but none so great as Bapu. The reason for this, I feel, is that he portrayed in his own life the principles he propounded. He lived his message. He was the most transparent person I have ever met. There was no guile in him, no attempt to conceal, cover up, or withhold. He was open to one and all and willing and anxious to share his insights with the humblest as well as the most prestigious.

Today when the world is torn with violence, Gandhi's message has again arrested attention, and to many it becomes evident that there is only one way that will save us, the way of love and nonviolence. To this we must be committed, even unto the cross and unto death. There is no other way.

Mildred Fahrni (1900-1992), from Vancouver, British Columbia, was long a lender of the FOR in Canada.
As a reporter she covered the founding of the UN in
1945. She marched with King in Montgomery in
1956 and was in Saigon and Hanoi in 1960.
Throughout her life she stood with the poor and oppressed.

The Great Trial, 23 March, 1922

Throughout his life, Gandhi wrote an average of 500 words a day. In early 1922, he was prosecuted for three articles in "Young India". The charge: "attempting to excite dissaffection towards His Majaesty's Government established by law in British India." Gandhi, a lawyer who believed in reconciliation law, not adversarial law, pled guilty.

Before reading his written statement to the court, Mr. Gandhi spoke a few words as introductory remarks.

I have no desire whatsoever to conceal from this Court the fact that to preach disaffection towards the existing system of Government has become almost a passion with me, and the learned Advocate-General is also entirely in the right when he says that my preaching of disaffection did not commence with my connexion with Young India, but that it commenced much earlier; and in the statement that I am about to read, it will be my painful duty to admit before this Court that it commenced much earlier than the period stated by the Advocate-General. It is the most painful duty with me, but I have to discharge that duty knowing the responsibility that rests upon my shoulders, and I wish to endorse all the blame that the learned Advocate-General has thrown on my shoulders.

I want to avoid violence. Non-violence is the first article of my faith. It is also the last article of my creed. But I had to make my choice. I had either to submit to a system which I considered had done an irreparable harm to my country, or incur the risk of the mad fury of my people bursting forth when they understood the truth from my lips. I know that my people have sometimes gone mad. I am deeply sorry for it and I am therefore hereto submit not to a light penalty but to the highest penalty. I do not ask for mercy. I do not plead any extenuating act. 1 am here, therefore, to invite and cheerfully submit to the highest penalty that can be inflicted upon me for what in law is a deliberate crime and what appears to me to be the highest duty of a citizen. The only course open to you, the judge, is, as I am just going to say in my statement, either to resign your post, or inflict on me the severest penalty, if you believe that the system and law you are assisting to administer are good for the people. I do not expect that kind of conversion, but by the time 1 have finished with my statement, you will perhaps have a glimpse of what is raging within my breast to run this maddest risk which a sane man can run.

The Statement was then read.

I owe it perhaps to the Indian public and to the public in England to placate which this prosecution is mainly taken up that I should explain why from a staunch loyalist and cooperator I have become an uncompromising disaffectionist and Non-cooperator.

My public life began in 1893 in South Africa in troubled weather. My first contact with British authority in that country was not of a happy character. I discovered that as a man and an Indian I had no rights. More correctly, I discovered that I had no rights as a man, because I was an Indian.

But 1 was not baffled. I thought that this treatment of Indians was an excrescence upon a system that was intrinsically and mainly good. I gave the Government my voluntary and hearty cooperation, criticizing it freely where I felt it was faulty but never wishing its destruction.

Consequently when the existence of the Empire was threatened in 1899 by the Boer challenge, I offered my services to it, raised a volunteer ambulance corps and served at several actions that took place for the relief of Ladysmith. Similarly in 1906 at the time of the Zulu revolt, I raised a stretcher-bearer party and served till the end of the 'rebellion'. On both these occasions I received medals and was even mentioned in Dispatches. For my work in South Africa I was given by Lord Hardinge a Kaiser-i-Hind Gold Medal. When the war broke out in 1914 between England and Germany, I raised a volunteer ambulance corps in London consisting of the then resident Indians in London, chiefly students. Its work was acknowledged by the authorities to be valuable. Lastly, in India, when a special appeal was made at the War Conference in Delhi in 1918 by Lord Chelmsford for recruits, I struggled at the cost of my health to raise a corps in Kheda and the response was being made when the hostilities ceased and orders were received that no more recruits were wanted. In all these efforts at service I was actuated by the belief that it was possible by such services to gain a status of full equality in the Empire for my countrymen.

But all that hope was shattered. The Khilafat promise was not to be redeemed. The Punjab crime was white-washed and most culprits went not only unpunished but remained in service and some continued to draw pensions from the Indian revenue, and in some cases were even rewarded. I saw too that not only did the reforms not mark a change of heart, but they were only a method of further draining India of her wealth and of prolonging her servitude.

I came reluctantly to the conclusion that the British connexion had made India more helpless than she ever was before, politically and economically. A disarmed India has no power of resistance against any aggressor if she wanted to engage in an armed conflict with him. So much is this the case that some of our best men consider that India must take generations before she can achieve the Dominion status. She has become so poor that she has little power of resisting famines. Before the British advent, India spun and wove in her millions of cottages just the supplement she needed for adding to her meagre agricultural resources. This cottage industry, so vital for India's existence, has been ruined by incredibly heartless and inhuman processes as described by English witnesses. Little do town-dwellers know how the semi-starved masses of India are slowly sinking to lifelessness. Little do they know that their miserable comfort represents the brokerage they get for the work they do for the foreign exploiter, that the profits and the brokerage are sucked from the masses. Little do they realize that the Government established-by law in British India is carried on for this exploitation of the masses. No sophistry, no jugglery in figures can explain away the evidence that the skeletons in many villages present to the naked eye. I have no doubt whatsoever that both England and the town dwellers of India will have to answer, if there is a God above, for this crime against humanity which is perhaps unequalled in history. The law itself in this country has been used to serve the foreign exploiter. My unbiased examination of the Punjab Martial Law cases has led me to believe that at least ninety-five per cent of convictions were wholly bad. My experience of political cases in India leads me to the conclusion that in nine out of every ten the condemned men were totally innocent. Their crime consisted in the love of their country. In ninety-nine cases out of a hundred justice has been denied to Indians against Europeans in courts in India. This is not an exaggerated picture. It is the experience of almost every Indian who has had anything to do with such cases. In my opinion, the administration of the law is thus prostituted consciously or unconsciously for the benefit of the exploiter.

The greatest misfortune is that Englishmen and their Indian associates in the country do not know that they are engaged in the crime I have attempted to describe. I am satisfied that many Englishmen and Indian officials honestly believe that they are administering one of the best systems devised in the world and that India is making steady though slow progress. They do not know that a subtle but effective system of terrorism and an organised display of force on the one hand, and the deprivation of all powers of retaliation or self-defence on the other, have emasculated the people and induced in them the habit of simulation. This awful habit has added to the ignorance and self-deception of the administrators. Section 124-A under which I am happily charged is perhaps the prince among the political sections of the Indian Penal Code designed to suppress the liberty of the citizen. Affection cannot be manufactured or regulated by law. If one has no affection for a person or system, one should be free to give the fullest expression to his disaffection, so long as he does not contemplate, promote or incite to violence. But the section under which Mr. Banker and I are charged is one under which mere promotion of disaffection is a crime. I have studied some of the cases tried under it, and I know that some of the most loved of Indian patriots have been convicted under it. I consider it a privilege, therefore, to be charged under that section. I have endeavoured to give in their briefest outline the reasons for my disaffection. I have no personal ill-will against a single administration, much less can I have any disaffection towards the King's person. But I hold it to be a virtue to be disaffected towards a Government which in its totality has done more harm to India than any previous system. India is less manly under the British rule than she ever was before. Holding such a belief, I consider it to be a sin to have affection for the system.

And it has been a precious privilege for me to be able to write what I have in the various articles, tendered in evidence against me.

In fact, I believe that I have rendered a service to India and England by showing in Non-cooperation the way out of the unnatural state in which both are living. In my humble opinion, Non-cooperation with evil is as much a duty as is cooperation with good. But in the past, Noncooperation has been deliberately expressed in violence to the evil doer. I am endeavouring to show to my countrymen that violent Noncooperation only multiplies evil and that as evil can only be sustained by violence, withdrawal of support of evil requires complete abstention from violence. Non-violence implies voluntary submission to the penalty for Non-cooperation with evil. I am here, therefore, to invite and submit cheerfully to the highest penalty that can be inflicted upon men for what in law is a deliberate crime and what appears to me to be the highest duty of a citizen. The only course open to you, the judge, is either to resign your post and thus dissociate yourself from evil, if you feel that the law you are called upon to administer is an evil and that in reality I am innocent or to inflict on me the severest penalty if you believe that the system and the law you are assisting to administer are good for the people of this country and that my activity is therefore injurious to the public weal.

The Judgment

Mr. Gandhi, you have made my task easy in one way by pleading guilty to the charge. Nevertheless, what remains, namely, the determination of a just sentence, is perhaps as difficult a proposition as a judge in this country could have to face. The law is no respecter of persons. Nevertheless, it will be impossible to ignore the fact that you are in a different category from any person I have ever tried or am likely to have to try. It would be impossible to ignore the fact that in the eyes of millions of your countrymen, you are a great patriot and a great leader. Even those who differ from you in politics look upon you as a man of high ideals and of noble and of even saintly lift. I have to deal with you in one character only. It is not my duty and I do not presume to judge or criticize you in any other character. It is my duty to judge you as a man subject to the law, who by his own admission has broken the law and committed what to an ordinary man must appear to be a grave offence against the State. I do not forget that you have consistently preached against violence and that you have on many occasions, as I am willing to believe, done much to prevent violence. But having regard to the nature of your political teaching and the nature of many of those to whom it was addressed, how you could have continued to believe that violence would not be the inevitable consequence, it passes my capacity to understand.

There are probably few people in India, who do not sincerely regret that you should have made it impossible for any government to leave you at liberty. But it is so. I am trying to balance what is due to you against what appears to me to be necessary in the interest of the public, and I propose in passing sentence to follow the precedent of a case in many respects similar to this case that was deeded some twelve years ago, I mean the case against Bal Gangadhar Tilak under the same secion. The sentence that was passed upon him as it finally stood was a sentence of simple imprisonment for six years. You will not consider it unreasonable, I think, that you should be classed with Mr. Tilak, i.e., a sentence of two years simple imprisonment on each count of the charge; six years in all, which I feel it my duty to pass upon you, and I should like to say in doing so that, if the course of events in India should make it possible for the Government to reduce the period and release you, no one will be better pleased than I.

Gandhi on the Judgment

"I would say one word. Since you have done me the honour of recalling the trial of the late Lokamany a Bal Gangadhar Tilak, I just want to say that I consider it to be the proudest privilege and honour to be associated with his name. So far as the sentence itself is concerned, I certainly consider that it is as light as any judge would inflict on me, and so far as the whole proceedings are concerned, I must say that I could not have expected greater courtesy."

Then the friends of Gandhi crowded round him, as the Judge left the court, and fell at his feet. There was much sobbing on the part of both men and women. But all the while, Gandhi was smiling and cool and giving encouragement to everybody who came to him. After all his friends had taken leave of him, Gandhi was taken out of the court to the Sabarmati jail.

And thus the great trial finished.

Gandhi's Journey
by Colman McCarthy

Gandhian scholars and others in the know have told me that regardless of the number of biographies I may have read on the Mahatma, the breadth and luminousness of his life (1869-1948) assure that new information will keep turning up.

So it is in *Gandhi: A Life*, by Yogesh Chadha, a New Delhi writer, who uncovers what Louis Fischer and Judith M. Brown—to take two of the major Western biographers—missed in their seemingly thorough works: that in the spring of 1895, Gandhi, then practicing law in South Africa, made a day trip to a Trappist monastery near Durban.

Gandhi saw a brand of Christianity at the Mariann Hill community of 160 priests and brothers, and a separate enclosure of 60 nuns, that is rarely seen in Western religion. "They rose at two o'clock in the morning, devoting four hours to prayer and contemplation," Chadha writes. "They breakfasted at six on bread and coffee, and the midday meal consisted of soup, bread and fruits. Supper was at six in the evening, and by eight o'clock they were in bed. None of the brothers ate fish, fowl or meat, nor did they partake of eggs . . . No one drank alcohol, no one kept money for private use, no one left the confines of the community except on approved business, and there were no newspapers available. And yet everyone appeared happy, and visitors were received with humble bows."

The Trappists' personal self-discipline and collective simple living—both linked to daily prayer and manual labor—awed Gandhi. Of his day among these Christians, he wrote in the Vegetarian, a British magazine: "You see religion everywhere. I know from personal experience that a visit to the [Trappist] farm is worth a voyage from London to Natal."

Chadha has other offerings not found in conventional biographies. Where Judith Brown—whose 1989 *Gandhi: Prisoner of Hope* is both literate and analytical—describes Gandhi's relationship in the early 1930s with Lord Irwin, Britain's viceroy in India, Chadha does that and includes the full text of a long letter from the Indian to the Englishman. It endures as one of the 20th century's purest statements of protest against abusive authority. "Nothing but organized nonviolence can check the organized violence of the British government," Gandhi wrote to the lord whose regime was lording it over destitute India.

Ten days later Gandhi and 78 followers of strong will and stronger legs left their ashram near the city of Ahmedabad in a protest walk of 240 miles and 24 days to the sea at Dandi. This was the Salt March, taken to publicize the British government's ruthless tax and monopoly on salt. The march became a movement, with several thousand joining in from the stopover villages along the way. A nationwide defiance of the salt tax followed.

Gandhi was 61. He was known through his writing—500 words a day during his adulthood—and his political successes in South Africa, where he changed discrimination laws, and in India, where he opposed the salt tax. His political goal was Britain's expulsion from India.

Seventeen years would pass before the British were forced to vacate India. Historians disagree on the breadth of Gandhi's role in Indian independence. Chadha argues that Gandhi "cannot be acclaimed as the author of India's freedom." He came aboard a reform movement that dated back to his days in South Africa. Nor did he ever posture as the leader of independence. What is well beyond historical dispute is that, as Chadha writes, "the extraordinary manner in which [India's freedom] was achieved can be pointedly ascribed to him."

The manner was nonviolence. Gandhi disliked the word, arguing that it was a negative, with nonviolence saying only what it wasn't. He invented his own word, satyagraha, the force of truth and love. It was twinned with ahimsa, the Jain commandment to live harmlessly. After a few jailings—Gandhi spent 2,089 days in Indian prisons and 249 in South Africa's—he began avoiding the phrase "passive resistance," with its errant suggestion that pacifism equals passivity. It is, instead, violence-free direct action organized to convert abusive power. For satyagraha "to be a creed," Gandhi believed, it "has to be all pervasive. I cannot be nonviolent about one activity of mine and violent about others. That would be a policy, not a life force."

As with most Gandhi biographers, Chadha records that the Mahatma walked the earth with feet emphatically made of clay. He was an overly harsh disciplinarian with his four sons, temporarily disowning one for wanting to marry at age 18. (Gandhi himself had married at 13.) He quarreled with his brother Laxmidas over money. He refused to let his wife wear a necklace she received as a gift. At 37, he embraced celibacy and denied sexual relations with his wife for the rest of her life. When she became ill while jailed for civil disobedience (not against her husband, unfortunately), Gandhi wrote to say he was too busy saving the world to come to her. For all of these offenses, Gandhi would sink into deep remorse. He had the saving grace of self-awareness, the gift of seeing his own flaws and the energy to overcome them, however fallibly.

Attention will be turning soon to naming the "person of the century." Who else but Gandhi? In one of history's bloodiest centuries, only the advocates of nonviolence ought to be considered. Among them—Jane Addams, Martin Luther King Jr., Dorothy Day, Adolpho Perez Esquivel, Oscar Romero, Scott Nearing, Erwin Knoll—none is the match of Gandhi. He wrote of it, taught it, lived it and was persecuted for it.

By all of that, he also gave work to biographers, starting with France's Romain Rolland in 1923 and extending to Yogesh Chadha today. Until another Gandhi scholar comes along who digs deeper and can write more movingly Gandhi scholarship will be well served by Chadha's effort.

The Washington Post
June 4, 1998

6

Okay, But What About Hitler?

Denmark had not won the war but neither had it been defeated or destroyed. Most Danes had not been brutalized, by the Germans or each other. Nonviolent resistance saved the country and contributed more to the Allied victory than Danish arms ever could have done.

from the film "A Force More Powerful,"
a PBS documentary produced by Steve York,
Nov. 2000

The Reich Defied
by David McReynolds

At some point all pacifists face this classic question, stated in many different ways. "Yes, but what about Hitler" can also be "Yes, but what about Arafat . . . Netanyahu . . . Criminals . . . Fascists . . . Racists . . . Serbs . . . Croatians . . . Muslims".

At first glance nothing is stranger than the notion that a people without weapons could defeat an occupying force (India), or an oppressive and unjust racial structure (the U.S.). But then some dismiss these triumphs by saying the same tactics wouldn't work against Hitler - that "nonviolence really needs a humane, Christian, decent, democratic opponent . . . such as the white Southerner or the British . . . or it won't work."

Part of the problem here is myth. There was very little "nice" about the British. I will come back to that in a moment. But first there is a "terrible truth" we all have to face, whether we are pacifists or the most dedicated of violent terrorists—not all battles can be won. There are times when nothing will work. This does not mean we shouldn't try—we never know when the tide of history is about to change. Racism was not less evil in Montgomery, Alabama, in 1955 when the Montgomery Bus Boycott began than in 1915. Nor was this the first resistance. Blacks had risked their lives and lost their lives during their entire "American experience".

Sometimes Nothing Will Succeed
In South Africa, decades ago there had been nonviolent campaigns led by Gandhi's son, Manilil. They failed. So far—let's be blunt—we have failed in this country at the task of "turning America around." In some ways our job is harder than Gandhi's— the Indians knew they were militarily weak compared to the British and were willing to examine alternatives, while Americans think they are strong because of the weapons they possess and are reluctant to consider alternatives.

But back to the British and those "nice Christian Southerners." The British were imperial rulers, repressive, violent when necessary, and if there were paradoxes to their rule in India, they were less from some decency inherent in British Imperialism than from self-interest. The tropical climate of India did not attract large numbers of English. To rule the vastness of India, the colonizers relied on "natives" trained to manage the courts, police, transportation, postal services, etc. From a Marxist point of view there were contradictions built in. The British trained the Indians in the skills of running India. But the result was to create precisely that educated elite which led the independence movement.

Gandhi studied for the law in London, went on to South Africa, one of the many lawyers, and civil servants the British had trained to run their Empire. There was nothing about the English that was uniquely nicer than the Germans. Germany was the most civilized nation in Europe in the 1930's. Hitler was a monster, yes, but not an alien. Second, because the Holocaust was documented, and happened in the midst of Europe and because "our side" won we know a great deal about it—and may think it was unique. Unhappily it was not. Records of the slave trade suggest far higher numbers of Africans died during that trade, and the evidence of Belgian rule in the Congo is shocking—in a short period after the Belgians took over in the last century, they killed several million more Africans than the Germans did the Jews. Evil in human affairs is universal, the Nazis had no monopoly on it.

Evil in Human Affairs

Americans need to pay attention to our own history. I am not trying to downgrade the Holocaust. No pacifist should be in the business of arguing "my pain is greater than your pain." But we are charged to be honest about what we ourselves, or our nation, has been complicit in. The pain of 400 years of slavery is of the same level of evil as the Holocaust. In reading a *New York Times Magazine* piece about the Vietnam War (8.10.97), the figure accepted for Vietnamese deaths was 3.6 million. Their sole crime was defending their nation against a foreign invader - us. As the Times noted, that many dead is equivalent, on the basis of the relative populations, to 27 million Americans . When someone says "pacifism is fine but it wouldn't have worked against Hitler" they should consider that to the Vietnamese, Lyndon Johnson was Hitler, and to Black America Jim Crow was Hitler.

We will never know if nonviolence would have worked

against Hitler or if it might have worked against the Americans in Vietnam if the Vietnamese had chosen that method . The history of the Holocaust shows little resistance of any kind to Hitler from the Jews. This is not surprising—they could not believe anything as terrible as the "final solution" was contemplated. Historically the Jews survived anti-Semitism by keeping a low profile . Some have said "The Jews were pacifists and look what it got them!" Sorry, they were passive - there is a world of difference. There is no way of knowing if active pacifism would have had any chance of working. We only know it was not tried. I remember the chilling deduction of Hannah Arendt in her book on Eichmann, in which she concluded it was the passive cooperation of the Jews of Europe with the Nazis which helped make the Holocaust possible. If you think about this for a moment it is, unhappily, true. To track down, arrest, transport and kill six million people who are resisting— even by not showing up when ordered, would, at the very least, have caused massive public disorder. Nothing is easier than saying "I would have resisted"—a cheap sentiment expressed by people who weren't there. Documents show some resistance, such as the Warsaw Ghetto Uprising. Violent or nonviolent, radicals honor resistance.

Some Isolated Victories Against Hitler

But within Occupied Europe there were well documented victories for nonviolence. In Norway there was a successful teachers' strike against being forced to teach Nazi ideology. In Denmark the opposition to the Nazis was led by the King, who said that if the Jews had to put on the "Yellow Star of David", then he, the King, would be the first man in Denmark to put one on. When the Nazis moved to arrest the Danish Jews, members of the Gestapo leaked this news to the Danish authorities and in 48 hours virtually all the Jews in Denmark were gotten to safety in Sweden. In Bulgaria, which had no history of anti-Semitism, spontaneous civil resistance including crowds sitting on train tracks prevented the Nazis from shipping any Jews out of the country.

"Those Nice Christian Southerners"

Of all the places Americans thought resistance to Jim Crow would begin, Montgomery, Alabama, heart of the Confederacy was the last. I remember a bus ride through the Deep South in 1951, coming back from my first trip to Europe (a pacifist youth conference in Denmark). Inspired by Bayard Rustin and the Journey of Reconciliation I took the Greyhound bus's Southern route back from New York to Los Angeles. My challenges to Jim Crow were timid—I was alone and not very brave even in a crowd. But I had a good chance to see and feel what it was like to move through the Deep South in the early 1950's. So much time has now passed nearly a half century—that Alabama is as far removed from us as Nazi Germany. But the incredible mass opposition to racism began there, in the Deep South, where the greatest danger a civil rights worker faced was not from the Klan but from the Sheriff, where there was no appeal to law, where Blacks could not vote, where night was a time of terror, not rest. Don't tell older Black Southerners about how safe nonviolence was then!

Nonviolence cannot win every struggle—there are defeats. This is no more reason to abandon nonviolence than the military would give up its weapons if it lost a battle. Philosophic note: in every military struggle there is a winner and a loser, so half the time violence fails, and half the time it wins. But in nonviolent struggle the objective is not to have a victor but to change the situation itself—a radically different concept.

Having admitted our approach cannot win all battles, why does it work at all? Why did it work against the Nazis in Norway and Denmark, or against the power structure in the American South? Or against the British in India?

Let us concede that all human events have "plural explanations." It takes nothing from the Vietnam Peace movement in our country to see that while our nonviolence was effective, so, too, was the pain of the body bags coming home as a result of the military struggle the Vietnamese waged against our troops. Let us concede that while the British in India weren't terribly nice, Britain had a democratic society which permitted an anti-colonial politics to develop. Let us admit that the violence of Southern racists was limited by fear of federal intervention, due to strong Northern support for Martin Luther King Jr.

Looking farther back in history, to times before any "civil society", there are two examples of movements which spread in the face of great oppression. Buddhism is a totally non- violent philosophy which, despite hardship and persecution, spread throughout Asia, finally subduing the Mongols, who had so savaged Europe and China. Christianity, which did not make an alliance with the State until three hundred years after the death of Jesus, became the dominant religious force in the West, triumphing over the total power of Roman Emperors.

Neither Christianity nor Buddhism was a philosophy of social change—that awaited the teachings of Gandhi in this century.

But the fact remains like a stubborn rock - both Western and Eastern civilization are founded on the basis of ideologies that were nonviolent, and which for some time in their early period faced extreme persecution. Thus, when Gandhi began "to experiment with truth" in this century, and see if nonviolence could be used to challenge social injustice, he was working on a foundation that was not entirely new. Nonviolence is older than the Christian era.

David McReynolds is the president of The War Resisters League. He has been the Socialist candidate for president twice, most recently in the 2000 election.

Not a Just War, Just a War
by Erwin Knoll

I was born in Austria, and at the age of six I watched jackbooted Nazi troops march into Vienna. Millions of Austrians cheered. I was fortunate enough to escape with my life, but many members of my family weren't that lucky; they died in the camps. The Holocaust is, I suppose, the formative experience of my life.

As a teenager, even as a young adult, I loved to go to old World War II films so that I could watch the Germans die. It gave me special pleasure to see the violent end inevitably allotted to officers of the Waffen SS who invariably wore monocles, permanent sneers, and black uniforms adorned with swastikas and death's-head insignia. I assumed, somehow, that all the German soldiers who froze to death in the siege of Stalingrad and all the German civilians cremated in the firestorm bombing of Dresden were officers of the Waffen SS who wore monocles, black uniforms, and permanent sneers. It took me an embarrassingly long time to figure out that wasn't the case. Apparently, some people still haven't figured it out.

But wasn't it necessary, after all, to stop Hitler? Sure it was; it was necessary, in fact, not to let him get started. But of all the ways to stop Hitler or to keep him from getting started, war was the worst—the way that inflicted the most pain, the most suffering, the most damage on everyone—especially Hitler's victims. A few months ago, when I read and reviewed Howard Zinn's latest book, *Declarations of Independence*, I was deeply moved by the account of his moral and intellectual journey from World War II bombardier to pacifist. Zinn offers persuasive evidence that the war magnified rather than diminished Nazi atrocities. And he writes, "History is full of instances of successful resistance (although we are not informed very much about this) without violence and against tyranny, by people using strikes, boycotts, propaganda, and a dozen ingenious forms of struggle."

I believe in ingenious, nonviolent struggle for justice and against oppression. So I won't support our troops—not in the Persian Gulf or anywhere else. And I won't support anyone else's troops when they go about their murderous business. And I'll say, regretfully, to the fallen black soldiers of the 4th Massachusetts, and the guys dead on the beaches of Normandy, and the young people who threw stones at Brezhnev's tanks in the streets of Czechoslovakia, that they died in vain perpetuating a cycle of human violence that must be stopped, because there is no such thing as a just war. Never was. Never will be.

The Progressive, June 1991
Erwin Knoll was Editor of The Progressive, 1973-1994.

A War to Save the Jews ?
by Howard Zinn

Did the United States enter the war because of its indignation at Hitler's treatment of the Jews? Hitler had been in power a year, and his campaign against the Jews had already begun when, in January 1934, a resolution was introduced into the Senate expressing "surprise and pain" at what the Germans were doing and asking for a restoration of Jewish rights. The State Department used its influence to get the resolution buried in committee.

Even after we were in the war against Germany (it should be noted that after Pearl Harbor Germany declared war on the United States, not vice versa) and reports began to arrive that Hitler was planning the annihilation of the Jews, Roosevelt's administration failed to take steps that might have saved thousands of lives.

Goebbels, minister of propaganda for Hitler's Germany, wrote in his diary on December 13, 1942: "At bottom, however, I believe both the English and the Americans are happy we are exterminating the Jewish riffraff." Goebbels was undoubtedly engaging in wishful thinking, but in fact, the English and American governments had not shown by their actions that they were terribly concerned about the Jews. As for Roosevelt, he shunted the problem to the State Department, where it did not become a matter of high priority.

As an example of this failure to treat the situation as an emergency, Raul Hilberg, a leading scholar of the Holocaust, points to an event that took place in 1942. Early in August of that year, with 1,500,000 Jews already dead, the Jewish leader Stephen Wise was informed indirectly through a German industrialist that there was a plan in Hitler's headquarters for the extermination of all Jews; Wise brought the information to Under Secretary of State Sumner Welles. Welles asked him not to release the story until it was investigated for confirmation. Three months were spent checking the report. During that time a million Jews were killed in Europe.

It is doubtful that all those Jews could have been saved.

But thousands could have been rescued. All the entrenched governments and organizations were negligent.

The British were slow and cautious. In March 1943, in the presence of Franklin D. Roosevelt, Secretary of State Hull pressed British Foreign Minister Anthony Eden on plans to rescue the 60,000 Jews in Bulgaria threatened with death. According to a memo by Roosevelt aide Harry Hopkins who was at that meeting, Eden worried that Polish and German Jews might then also ask to be rescued. "Hitler might well take us up on any such offer and there simply are not enough ships and means of transportation in the world to handle them." When there was a possibility of bombing the railroad lines leading into the murder chambers of Auschwitz, to stop further transportation of Jews there, the opportunity was ignored.

It should be noted that the Jewish organizations themselves behaved shamefully. In 1984, the American Jewish Commission on the Holocaust reviewed the historical record. It found that the American Jewish Joint Distribution Committee, a relief agency set up during World War II by the various Jewish groups, "was dominated by the wealthier and more 'American' elements of U.S. Jewry.... Thus, its policy was to do nothing in wartime that the U.S. government would not officially contenance."

Raul Hilberg points out that the Hungarian Jews might have been saved by a bargain: the Allies would not make air raids on Hungary if the Jews would be kept in the cities and not sent away. But "the Jews could not think in terms of interfering with the war effort, and the Allies on their part could not conceive of such a promise .... The Allied bombers roared over Hungary at will, killing Hungarians and Jews alike."

As I read this I recalled that one of the bombing raids I had done was on a town in Hungary.

Not only did waging war against Hitler fail to save the Jews, it may be that the war itself brought on the Final Solution of genocide. This is not to remove the responsibility from Hitler and the Nazis, but there is much evidence that Germany's anti-Semitic actions, cruel as they were, would not have turned to mass murder were it not for the psychic distortions of war, acting on already distorted minds. Hitler's early aim was forced emigration, not extermination, but the frenzy of it created an atmosphere in which the policy turned to genocide. This is the view of Princteton historian Arno Mayer, in his book *Why Did the Heavens Not Darken*, and it is supported by the chronology that not until Germany was at war was the Final Solution adopted.

Hilberg, in his classic work on the Holocaust, says, "From 1938 to 1940, Hitler made extraordinary and unusual attempts to bring about a vast emigration scheme .... The Jews were not killed before the emigration policy was literally exhausted." The Nazis found that the Western powers were not anxious to cooperate in emigration and that no one wanted the Jews.

Declarations of Independence
HarperCollins 1990

The Danish Resistance
by Thomas Merton

One of the rare glimmers of humanity and reason in the detailed history of Eichmann's patient labors to exterminate the Jews, as recorded by Hannah Arendt's recent series of articles in The New Yorker, was the nonviolent resistance offered by the entire nation of Denmark against Nazi power mobilized for genocide.

Denmark was not the only European nation that disagreed with Hitler on this point. But it was one of the only nations which offered explicit, formal and successful nonviolent resistance to Nazi power. The adjectives are important. The resistance was successful because it was explicit and formal, and because it was practically speaking unanimous. The entire Danish nation simply refused to cooperate with the Nazis, and resisted every move of the Nazis against the Jews with nonviolent protest of the highest and most effective caliber, yet without any need for organization, training; or specialized activism: simply by unanimously and effectively expressing in word and action the force of their deeply held moral convictions. These moral convictions were nothing heroic or sublime. They were merely ordinary.

There had of course been subtle and covert refusals on the part of other nations. Italians in particular, while outwardly complying with Hitler's policy, often arranged to help the Jews evade capture or escape from unlocked freight cars. The Danish nation, from the King on down, formally and publically rejected the policy and opposed it with an open, calm, convinced resistance which shook the morale of the German troops and SS men occupying the country and changed their whole outlook on the Jewish question.

When the Germans first approached the Danes about the segregation of Jews, proposing the introduction of the yellow badge, the government officials replied that the King of Denmark would be the first to wear the badge, and that the introduction of any anti-Jewish measures would lead immediately to their own resignation.

At the same time, the Danes refused to make any distinction between Danish and non-Danish Jews. That is to say, they took the German Jewish refugees under their protection and refused to deport them back to Germany-an act which considerably disrupted the efficiency of Eichmann's organization and delayed anti-Jewish operations in Denmark until 1943 when Hitler personally ordered that the "final solution" go into effect without further postponement.

The Danes replied by strikes, by refusals to repair German ships in their shipyards, and by demonstrations of protest. The Germans then imposed martial law. But now it was realized that the German officials in Denmark were changed men. They could "no longer be trusted." They refused to cooperate in the liquidation of the Jews, not of course by open protest, but by delays, evasions, covert refusals and the raising of bureaucratic obstacles. Hence Eichmann was forced to send a "specialist" to Denmark, at the same time making a concession of monumental proportions: all the Jews from Denmark would go only to Theresienstadt, a "soft" camp for privileged Jews. Finally, the special police sent direct from Germany to round up the Jews were warned by the SS officers in Denmark that Danish police would probably forcibly resist attempts to take the Jews away by force, and that there was to be no fighting between Germans and Danes. Meanwhile the Jews themselves had been warned and most of them had gone into hiding, helped, of course, by friendly Danes: then wealthy Danes put up money to pay for transportation of nearly six thousand Jews to Sweden which offered them asylum, protection and the right to work. Hundreds of Danes cooperated in ferrying Jews to Sweden in small boats. Half the Danish Jews remained safely in hiding in Denmark, during the rest of the war. About five hundred Jews who were actually arrested in Denmark went to Theresienstadt and lived under comparatively good conditions: only forty-eight of them died, mostly of natural causes.

Denmark was certainly not the only European nation that disapproved more or less of the "solution" which Hitler had devised for the judenfrage. But it was the only nation which, as a whole, expressed a forthright moral objection to this policy. Other nations kept their disapproval to themselves. They felt it was enough to offer the Jews "heartfelt sympathy," and, in many individual cases, tangible aid. But let us not forget that generally speaking the practice was to help the Jew at considerable profit to oneself. How many Jews in France, Holland, Hungary, etc., paid fortunes for official permits, bribes, transportation, protection, and still did not escape!

The whole Eichmann story, as told by Hannah Arendt (indeed as told by anybody) acquires a quality of hallucinatory awfulness from the way in which we see how people in many ways exactly like ourselves, claiming as we do to be Christians or at least to live by humanistic standards which approximate, in theory, to the Christian ethic, were able to rationalize a conscious, uninterrupted and complete cooperation in activities which we now see to have been not only criminal but diabolical. Most of the rationalizing probably boiled down to the usual half-truths: "What can you do? There is no other way out, it is a necessary evil. True, we recognize this kind of action to be in many ways `unpleasant.' We hate to have to take measures like these: but then those at -the top know best. It is for the common good. The individual conscience has to be overruled when the common good is at stake. Our duty is to obey. The responsibility for these measures rests on others . . . and so on."

Curiously, the Danish exception, while relieving the otherwise unmitigated horror of the story, actually adds to the nightmarish and hallucinated effect of incredulousness one gets while reading it. After all, the Danes were not even running a special kind of nonviolent movement. They were simply acting according to ordinary beliefs which everybody in Europe theoretically possessed, but which, for some reason, nobody acted on. Quite the contrary! Why did a course of action which worked so simply and so well in Denmark not occur to all the other so-called Christian nations of the West just as simply and just as spontaneously?

Obviously there is no simple answer. It does not even necessarily follow that the Danes are men of greater faith or deeper piety than other western Europeans. But perhaps it is true that these people had been less perverted and secularized by the emptiness and cynicism, the thoughtlessness, the crude egoism and the rank amorality which have become characteristic of our world, even where we still see an apparent surface of Christianity. It is not so much that the Danes were Christians, as that they were human. How many others were even that?

The Danes were able to do what they did because they were able to make decisions that were based on clear convictions about which they all agreed and which were in accord with the inner truth of man's own rational nature, as well as in accordance with the fundamental law of God in the Old Testament as well as in the Gospel: thou shalt love thy neighbor as thyself. The Danes were able to resist the cruel stupidity of Nazi anti-Semitism because this fundamental truth was important to them. And because they were willing, in unanimous and concerted action, to stake their lives on this truth. In a word, such action becomes possible where fundamental truths are taken seriously.

from "The Nonviolent Alternative" by Thomas Merton, 1980. Merton was a Trappist priest who lived in the Gethsemani Monastery from 1941 to 1968, the year of his death.

The Dutch Resistance
by Peter Ackerman and Jack Duval

One month and one day after German forces took possession of Denmark in April 1940, troops of the Wehrmacht crossed the border into the Netherlands while German planes bombed Dutch airfields. At the same time, Berlin's ambassador in The Hague delivered a note claiming that German forces were entering the country to protect Dutch neutrality and invited the government to place itself under the Reich's protection. Without hesitation Queen Wilhelmina and her ministers rejected the proposal.

As German bombers smashed Rotterdam and other Dutch cities, the royal family escaped to London, which the queen proclaimed the new seat of government, ensuring its legal existence. "I hereby issue a fiery protest against . . . the outrage done to the conduct customary between civilized nations," she declared. But five days later General H. G. Winkelman, the commander-in-chief of the Dutch armed forces, signed articles of surrender. On May 29 Dr. Arthur Seyss-Inquart, the Reichskommissar for the Netherlands, gave his inaugural address. He claimed the Dutch to be Germanic brothers and promised that all Dutch prisoners of war would be released by mid-June. But Nazi plans for the Netherlands were far more drastic: transforming Holland into a National Socialist state, exploiting the Dutch economy for the German war machine, deporting and exterminating over 100,000 Dutch Jews and Gypsies, and suppressing any form of resistance.

The Dutch had a tradition of neutrality and no recent experience with resisting invaders. Like Denmark, the country's flat and open topography made paramilitary resistance problematic. But already on the day of invasion, groups of students and workers came together to offer some measure of defiance. One Amsterdam group, calling itself the Geuzen Action Committee, distributed a message promising that it would gradually develop an organization to fight for Dutch liberty: "one day we will recapture our liberty . . . Our country shall not become a part of Germany!"

On June 29, the birthday of Prince Bernhard, people in

Amsterdam rallied publicly against the Germans. The prince had adopted the habit of wearing a white carnation on all holidays and for every public ceremony. On his birthday, vases filled with carnations could be seen in the windows of every dwelling and storefront. Around midday people started appearing in front of the monument to Queen Wilhelmina's mother. Each person brought a carnation and placed it at the monument's base. By the end of the day, the monument was buried under a sea of blossoms. In response, the Germans arrested two of the demonstration's organizer—and even seized General Winkelman, who had nothing to do with it.

In the fall the Nazis began to go after Dutch Jews, at first firing all Jewish public officials and professors. At the University of Leiden, the dismissals led to a large demonstration that culminated in the singing of the national anthem. At the Technical University of Delft, the students went on strike, forcing the university to shut down. Leiden followed suit. As in Denmark, the Germans were to find that victimizing individual citizens, even Jews, would deepen the hatred of those who had been invaded.

On February 22, 1941, three days after a fierce showdown between Dutch Nazis and armed Jewish citizens in Amsterdam, 600 SS soldiers moved in, sealed off the Jewish quarter, and arrested 400 young Jewish men. They were beaten and then shipped to the Buchenwald concentration camp. News of this spread quickly. Communist workers met late one night and made preparations for a massive strike. With the help of underground printers, they distributed leaflets calling for every worker to join them. Two days later shipyard workers and streetcar drivers were the first to walk off their jobs; they were soon followed by industrial workers. Businesses, workshops, offices, and stores closed their doors, and workers massed in the city center, where they shouted and sang in protest. Over 300,000 out of a population of 800,000 took part in the strike.

The Germans, although stunned, were quick to crack down. Hundreds of German police and SS soldiers moved in with orders to fire without warning at troublemakers. A curfew was imposed, with violators subject to arrest. The threat of reprisals turned out to be too much for Amsterdam's mayor, who ordered city officials to return to work or risk dismissal. Unlike Denmark, the Netherlands had been conquered and its head of state had gone into exile, so Dutch administrators were left to their own devices—and, early in the war, many were constrained to carry out German decrees. This initial collaboration meant that strikers were acting on their own, and the February strike proved unsustainable.

But at the grass roots of Dutch society, resistance became an act of patriotism, and most of the population took part. School-teachers refused to submit their names for approval by the Germans. Artists refused to join the Nazi Kulturkammer (culture guild), even though this denied them income and public appearances. Over 160,000 farmers withheld required payments to the Nazis, and thousands of young men refused to report for the Arbeitsdienst, an occupation corps devoted to reclaiming the land.

The underground press, numbering about sixty papers, also thrived. (One of the most influential papers, Het Parool still exists today and is one of the country's most respected dailies.) During the war everyday greetings and chores became imbued with symbolic pride. The "V" sign replaced the handshake and was painted on walls and kiosks in every major city. The simple greeting "Hallo" became an acronym for "Hang alle landverraders op" (Hang all traitors). Citizens also wore coins bearing the portrait of Queen Wilhelmina.

Seyss-Inquart came to realize that the Dutch were not going to become obedient National Socialists, so German repression intensified. By the end of 1942 over 800 resistance fighters had been arrested and deported to concentration camps in Germany. The country's largest Protestant political parry was abolished, and its members were compelled to join a Nazi-controlled trade union. When the Dutch Catholic Church sent letters and telegrams to the German administration protesting the deportation of Jews, some 700 Catholics of Jewish origin were arrested and sent to Auschwitz.

In less than three years, about 300,000 Dutch were relocated to Germany to work in the Ruhr—a threat to the livelihood of Dutch families that buttressed their will to resist. Around 100,000 deportees managed to escape back to Holland and found safe places to hide with farmers and householders. Vital to this operation was the Landelijke Organisatie (National Organization), comprising nearly 15,000 people, and the National Support Fund, established by a group of bankers who had escaped to England. The Fund also subsidized sabotage squads that damaged Dutch rail lines, stalled weapons transport, and raided German supply convoys.

Perhaps the greatest solidarity was displayed by Dutch doctors, who had been told that they had to join the Artztekammer (doctors guild) and follow Nazi medical guidelines, including screening patients for racial background and genetic defects. Over three-quarters of the country's doctors refused to join the organization and, in response, gave up their practices and removed their name plates from the fronts of their homes and offices. A group of doctors formed the Medisch Contact (Medical Contact) that worked closely with local physicians through eleven district representatives, to help hide doctors who came under attack from German police. By centralizing its direction, the Contact staved ofd a Nazi takeover of their profession.

On April 29, 1943, the Germans announced that all former Dutch army soldiers, who had been captured and released in 1940, were to be recaptured and sent to labor camps in Germany. This startling order affected more than 300,000 men. Instantly workers in the town of Hengelo walked off their jobs. The strike quickly spread through the province of Overijssel and to the major city of Eindhoven, where every Philips factory ground to a halt. In the province of Limburg, over 10,000 miners came up from the pits and went on strike. By the next morning the number swelled to 40,000. Then German police and troops moved in and began shooting indiscriminately. Those arrested were given perfunctory hearings and sentenced to death. Thereafter the strikes diminished in intensity everywhere except in Limburg. A German police force was sent there and violent clashes broke out. On May 5 the Limburg miners finally gave up and returned to work. The strikes had cost over 180 deaths, 400 casualties, and 900 prisoners of war, who were sent to German concentration camps.

In the next months there were more incidents of resistance, but despite perseverance by groups like doctors and factory workers, whose lives had been directly affected by Nazi policies, the overall resistance lacked systematic guidance. As in Denmark, resistance groups had sprung up locally and communication was established slowly. It was not until later in the war that a group known as De Kern (The Core)—made up of union officials, resistance leaders, and editors of underground papers—tried to coordinate a national effort. They met weekly in Amsterdam but never achieved the stature of Denmark's Freedom Council and therefore could not speak for a majority of Dutch workers and resistance fighters. As a result, Dutch resistance never had clear national goals, and a strategic effort to challenge German control of the country never came to pass.

The last major act of resistance came in September 1944, when Dutch railway workers went on strike to obstruct the transport of Jews to concentration camps in the East and also to slow the movement of German troops back home to defend the Fatherland from Allied invasion. As the French had done in the Ruhr twenty years before, and as they had done in Denmark, the Germans imported their own railwaymen to keep the trains running. And in reprisal, the Germans shipped some 50,000 Dutch men from Rotterdam to Germany to help prepare defenses for German cities. In a bitter, unintended consequence of the rail strike, deliveries of coal, gas, and food were halted to Rotterdam and other Dutch cities, and the ensuing winter was unbearable for many. Allied victory the following spring delivered the Dutch from a harsher war than the Danes had seen.

In contrast to events in Denmark, the Nazis had made the Dutch authorities capitulate formally at the war's outset, and they dragooned a half million Dutch workers for service in the German war effort. Given this investment in Dutch submission, the Germans were willing to work much harder to maintain it than they ever did in Denmark, where the carrot-and-stick approach-the same strategy the French used initially against the Germans in 1923-brought mixed results. Morever, German sanctions depleted the ranks of potential resisters and narrowed the space in which they could operate. Able to offer only pockets of opposition, the Dutch were unable to prevent the Nazis from exploiting their labor and from wrenching nearly eight of ten Dutch Jews out of the country and into the Holocaust.

This frightful cost in lives and honor might have been reduced had resistance in the Netherlands been better organized. As it was, although hindered by the early collaboration of some Dutch officials and the lack of any real cohesion, the resistance still prevented Holland from being turned into a Nazi satellite state, which had been the Germans' original intent, and it turned the deportation process into a constant struggle that diverted the Germans' time and resources from other war activities. Having seized both Denmark and the Netherlands through offensive operations, the Nazis nevertheless were forced by nonviolent resistance in both countries to mount rearguard defensive actions to redeem the value of having occupied these countries in the first place. In Denmark, that value was seriously depreciated. In the Netherlands, it was at least diminished.

from "A Force More Powerful: A Century of
Nonviolent Conflict"
by Peter Ackerman and Jack Duval. St. Martin's Press, 2000

Nonviolent Weapons of the Spirit
by Colman McCarthy

In courses on nonviolence that I've been teaching for the past seven years in high schools and colleges, no question arises more frequently than this: Nonviolence is fine as an abstract intellectual system, but do you seriously believe it would have succeeded in the real world against the Nazis?

The question—usually thrown up as a statement wanting to end the discussion, not broaden it—is currently being answered in a low-budget film, now playing at the Key in Georgetown, that is making its modestly advertised way across the country. Weapons of the Spirit, written, directed and produced by Pierre Sauvage, tells the story of Le Chambon, a farming village in central France that nonviolently defied the German Army in the occupation during World War II.

The film-in understated narrative and with simple photography presents surviving villagers whose fearlessness and quality of love in the early 1940s led them to harbor 5,000 Jewish refugees.

Other villages hid Jews, but they were few and did so only reluctantly. Le Chambon deliberately sought refugees by putting out the word that all were welcome. The Chambonnais were Huguenots-Protestants in a Catholic country who had not forgotten centuries of persecution.

Le Chambon was unique for another reason: It did not adopt pacifism as a strategy the day the Gestapo swept into town. Citizens had embraced it as a way of life years before. Saving Jewish refugees was the external fulfillment of the internal commitment to peace through the strength of nonviolence.

In their defiance of Nazis, the villagers, most of them peasants, were led by their pacifist minister, Andre Trocme. When France surrendered to Germany, he called on his people to resist Nazis with "weapons of the spirit."

Trocme and his family came to Le Chambon in 1934. Part of his ministry was establishing a parish supported school where the study of nonviolence and pacifism was emphasized. When the

148

Nazis came, the town had a choice for self-defense: violent or non-violent. It could choose the superior one of nonviolence because it was educated by the pastor in the theories and techniques.

In Weapons of the Spirit, villagers, now in their seventies and eighties, recall their nonviolent resistance and harboring of refugees as exercises in common decency, not uncommon valor. What is life for, they had been taught to wonder, if not to risk for others? What is peacemaking for, if not to do it at the moment of crisis. Anyone can be a pacifist between wars.

Two years after Trocme's death in 1971, some of his essays were collected in Jesus and the Nonviolent Revolution. The writing is as virile as anything found in Gandhi or Martin Luther King,Jr. when they wrote of nonviolence. Trocme addressed the question of how to stop the world's Hitlers:

"People say, ` Our nation is about to be exterminated; or the future of our civilization, of our moral values, of true religion, is threatened; or yet, our institutions violate human rights to save human rights, we must temporarily forget our scruples and use violence, sacrificing men to destroy unjust structures, arid thus saving the poor from oppression.' For centuries both progressive and reactionary camps have been 'temporarily' choosing violence, `temporarily' shedding the blood of millions of victims in the name of a better future. Because each side speculates about `what would happen if we let the enemy win,' they mercilessly sacrifice man, whether friend or enemy ...And every generation is faced with new options time after time considered to be so important that it repeatedly believes itself compelled to use violence. "

In addition to Weapons of the Spirit, the story of Trocme and Le Chambon is told in *Lest Innocent Blood Be Shed* by Philip Hallie. In the 1979 book, Hallie, a professor at Wesleyan University, captures the soul of the pastor much as Pierre Sauvage's film reveals the iron of the villagers: Trocme "believed that decent people who stay inactive out of cowardice or indifference when around them human beings are being humiliated and destroyed are the most dangerous people in the world. His nonviolence was not passive or saccharine, but an almost brutal force for awakening human beings."

After World War II, the historian and military strategist B.H. Liddell Hart interviewed German generals on the different kinds of resistance they met in occupied countries. As practiced in Denmark, Norway, Holland and such places as Le Chambon, nonviolent resistance was effective. The Nazis, Hart writes, had an "inability to cope with it. They were experts in violence, and had been trained to deal with opponents who used that method. But other forms of resistance baffled them ...It was a relief to them when resistance became violent."

By defending themselves with love, the strongest weapon of the spirit, the Chambonnais gave the Nazis no relief.

from Washington Post, February 25, 1990

7

Pacifism or Warism?

You can no more win a war than win an earthquake.
                              Jeannette Rankin

Behind every war there is a big lie ...
The big lie behind all murder, from the random street
killing to the efficient ovens of Auschwitz,
to the even more efficient hydrogen bomb, is that the
victims deserve to die.
                              Jim Wallis

A Warrior Turns Pacifist
by Howard Zinn

There are some people who do not question war. In 1972, the general who was head of the U.S. Strategic Air Command told an interviewer, "I've been asked often about my moral scruples if I had to send the planes out with hydrogen bombs. My answer is always the same. I would be concerned only with my professional responsibility."

It was a Machiavellian reply. Machiavelli did not ask if making war was right or wrong. He just wrote about the best way to wage it so as to conquer the enemy. One of his books is called *The Art of War*.

That title might make artists uneasy. Indeed, artists, poets, novelists, and playwrights as well as musicians, painters, and actors, have shown a special aversion to war. Perhaps because, as the playwright Arthur Miller once said, "When the guns boom, the arts die." But that would make their interest too self-centered; they have always been sensitive to the fate of the larger society round them. They have questioned war, whether in the fifth century before Christ, with the plays of Euripedes, or in modern times, with the paintings of Goya and Picasso.

Machiavelli was being realistic. Wars were going to be fought. The only question was how to win them.

Some people have believed that war is not just inevitable but desirable. It is adventure and excitement, it brings out the best qualities in men—courage, comradeship, and sacrifice. It gives respect and glory to a country. In 1897, Theodore Roosevelt wrote to a friend, "In strict confidence ...I should welcome almost any war, for I think this country needs one."

In our time, fascist regimes have glorified war as heroic and ennobling. Bombing Ethiopia in 1935, Mussolini's son-in-law Count Ciano described the explosions as an aesthetic thrill, as having the beauty of a flower unfolding.

In the 1980s, two writers of a book on war see it as an effective instrument of national policy and say that even nuclear war can, under certain circumstances, be justified. They are contemptuous of "the pacifist passions: self-indulgence and fear," and of "American statesmen, who believe victory is an archaic concept." They say, "The bottom line in war and hence in political warfare is who gets buried and who gets to walk in the sun."

Most people are not that enamored of war. They see it as bad, but also as a possible means to something good. And so they distinguish between wars that are just and those that are unjust. The religions of the West and Middle East—Judaism, Christianity, and Islam—approve of violence and war under certain circumstances. The Catholic church has a specific doctrine of "just" and "unjust" war, worked out in some detail. Political philosophers today argue about which wars, or which actions in wars, may be considered just or unjust.

Beyond both viewpoints—the glorification of war and the weighing of good and bad wars—there is a third: that war is too evil to ever be just. The monk Erasmus, writing in the early sixteenth century, was repelled by war of any kind. One of his pupils was killed in battle and he reacted with anguish:

Tell me, what had you to do with Mars, the stupidest of all the poet's gods, you who were consecrated to the Muses, nay to Christ? Your youth, your beauty, your gentle nature, your honest mind-what had they to do with the flourishing of trumpets, the bombards, the swords?

Erasmus described war: "There is nothing more wicked, more disastrous, more widely destructive, more deeply tenacious, more loathsome." He said this was repugnant to nature: "Whoever heard of a hundred thousand animals rushing together to butcher each other, as men do everywhere?"

Erasmus saw war as useful to governments, for it enabled them to enhance their power over their subjects: "...once war has been declared, then all the affairs of the State are at the merry of the appetites of a few."

This absolute aversion to war of any kind is outside the orthodoxy of modern thinking. In a series of lectures at Oxford University in the 1970s, English scholar Michael Howard talked disparagingly about Erasmus. He called him simplistic, unsophisticated, and someone who did not see beyond the "surface manifestations" of war. He said,

With all [Erasmus's] genius he was not a profound political

analyst, nor did he ever have to exercise the responsibilities of power. Rather he was the first in that long line of humanitarian thinkers for whom it was enough to chronicle the horrors of war in order to condemn it.

Howard had praise for Thomas More: "Very different was the approach of Erasmus's friend, Thomas More; a man who had exercised political responsibility and, perhaps in consequence, saw the problem in all its complexity." More was a realist; Howard says,

He accepted, as thinkers for the next two hundred years were to accept, that European society was organized in a system of states in which war was an inescapable process for the settlement of differences in the absence of any higher common jurisdiction. That being the case, it was a requirement of humanity, of religion and of common sense alike that those wars should be fought in such a manner as to cause as little damage as possible.. For better or worse war was an institution which could not be eliminated from the international system. All that could be done about it was, so far as possible, to codify its rationale and to civilize its means.

Thus, Machiavelli said: Don't question the ends of the prince, just tell him how best to do what he wants to do, make the means more efficient. Thomas More said: You can't do anything about the ends, but try to make the means more moral.

In the 400 years following the era of Machiavelli and More, making war more humane became the preoccupation of certain liberal "realists." Hugo Grotius, writing a century after More, proposed laws to govern the waging of war (*Concerning the Law of War and Peace*). The beginning of the twentieth century saw international conferences at The Hague in the Netherlands and at Geneva in Switzerland which drew up agreements on how to wage war.

These realistic approaches however, had little effect on the reality of war. Rather than becoming more controlled, war became more uncontrolled and more deadly, using more horrible means and killing more noncombatants than ever before in the history of mankind. We note the use of poison gas in World War I, the bombardment of cities in World War II, the atomic destruction of Hiroshima and Nagasaki near the end of that war, the use of napalm in Vietnam, and the chemical warfare in the Iran-Iraq war of the early 1980s.

Albert Einstein, observing the effects of attempts to "humanize" wars, became more and more anguished. In 1932, he attended a conference of sixty nations in Geneva and listened to the lengthy discussions of which weapons were acceptable and which were not, which forms of killing were legitimate and which were not.

Einstein was a shy, private person, but he did something extraordinary for him: he called a press conference in Geneva. The international press turned out in force to hear Einstein, already world famous for his theories of relativity. Einstein told the assembled reporters, "One does not make wars less likely by formulating rules of warfare ....War cannot be humanized. It can only be abolished." But the Geneva conference went on, working out rules for "humane" warfare, rules that were repeatedly ignored in the world war soon to come, a war of endless atrocities.

In early 1990, President George Bush, while approving new weapons systems for nuclear warheads (of which the United States had about 30,000) and refusing to join the Soviet Union in stopping nuclear testing, was willing to agree to destroy chemical weapons, but only over a ten-year period. Such are the absurdities of "humanizing" war.

Liberal States and Just Wars: Athens

The argument that there are just wars often rests on the social system of the nation engaging in war. It is supposed that if a "liberal" state is at war with a "totalitarian" state, then the war is justified. The beneficent nature of a government is assumed to give rightness to the wars it wages.

Ancient Athens has been one of the most admired of all societies, praised for its democratic institutions and its magnificent cultural achievements. It had enlightened statesmen (Solon and Pericles), pioneer historians (Herodotus and Thucydides), great philosophers (Plato and Aristotle), and an extraordinary quartet of playwrights (Aeschylus, Sophocles, Euripides, and Aristphanes). When it went to war in 431 BC against its rival power, the city-state of Sparta, the war seemed to be between a democratic society and a military dictatorship.

The great qualities of Athens were described early in that war by the Athenian leader Pericles at a public celebration for the warriors, dead or alive. The bones of the dead were placed in chests; there was an empty litter for the missing. There was a procession, a burial, and then Pericles spoke. Thucydides recorded Pericles' speech in his *History of the Peloponnesian War*.'

Before I praise the dead, I should like to point out by what principles of action we rose to power, and under what institutions and through what manner of life our empire became great. Our form of government does not enter into rivalry with the institutions of others .... It is true that we are called a democracy, for the administration is in the hands of the many and not of the few .... The law secures equal justice to all alike .... Neither is poverty a bar .... There is no exclusiveness in our public life .... At home the style of our life is refined .... Because of the greatness of our city the fruits of the whole earth flow in upon us .... And although our opponents are fighting for their homes and we on foreign soil, we seldom have any difficulty in overcoming them .... I have dwelt upon the greatness of Athens because I want to show you that we are contending for a higher prize than those who enjoy none of these privileges.

Similarly, American presidents in time of war have pointed to the qualities of the American system as evidence for the justness of the cause. Woodrow Wilson and Franklin Roosevelt were liberals, which gave credence to their words exalting the two world wars, just as the liberalism of Truman made going into Korea more acceptable and the idealism of Kennedy's New Frontier and Johnson's Great Society gave an early glow af righteousness to the war in Vietnam.

But we should take a closer look at the claim that liberalism at home carries over into military actions abroad.

The tendency, especially in time of war, is to exaggerate the difference between oneself and the opponent, to assume the conflict is between total good and total evil.

Liberalism at War

Liberalism at home, however, seems to become corrupted by war waged abroad. French philosopher Jean Jacques Rousseau noted that conquering nations "make war at least as much on their subjects as on their enemies." Tom Paine, in America, saw war as the creature of governments, serving their own interests, not the interests of justice for their citizens. "Man is not the enemy of man but through the medium of a false system of government." In our time, George Orwell has written that wars are mainly "internal."

One certain effect of war is to diminish freedom of expression. Patriotism becomes the order of the day, and those who question the war are seen as traitors, to be silenced and imprisoned.

Mark Twain, observing the United States at the turn of the century, its wars in Cuba and the Philippines, described in *The Mysterious Stranger* the process by which wars that are at first seen as unnecessary by the mass of the people become converted into "just" wars:

The loud little handful will shout for war. The pulpit will warily and cautiously protest at first .... The great mass of the nation will rub its sleepy eyes, and will try to make out why there should be a war, and they will say earnestly and indignantly: "It is unjust and dishonorable and there is no need for war."

Then the few will shout even louder... Before long you will see a curious thing: anti-war speakers will be stoned from the platform, and free speech will be strangled by hordes of furious men who still agree with the speakers but dare not admit it ....

Next, the statesmen will invent cheap lies ...and each man will be glad of these lies and will study them because they soothe his conscience; and thus he will bye and bye convince himself that the war is just and he will thank God for a better sleep he enjoys by his self-deception.

Mark Twain died in 1910. In 1917, the United States entered the slaughterhouse of the European war, and the process of silencing dissent and converting a butchery into a just war took place as he had predicted.

President Woodrow Wilson tried to rouse the nation, using the language of a crusade. It was a war, he said, "to end all wars." But large numbers of Americans were reluctant to join. A million men were needed, yet in the first six weeks after the declaration of war only 73,000 volunteered. It seemed that men would have to be compelled to fight by fear of prison, so Congress enacted a draft law.

The Socialist Party at the time was a formidable influence

in the country. It had perhaps 100,000 members, and more than a thousand Socialists had been elected to office in 340 towns and cities. Probably a million Americans read Socialist newspapers. There were fifty-five weekly Socialist newspapers in Oklahoma, Texas, Louisiana, and Arkansas alone; over a hundred Socialists were elected to office in Oklahoma. The Socialist party candidate for president, Eugene Debs, got 900,000 votes in 1912 (Wilson won with 6 million).

A year before the United States entered the European war, Helen Keller, blind and deaf and a committed Socialist, told an audience at Carnegie Hall:

Strike against war, for without you no battles can be fought! Strike against manufacturing shrapnel and gas bombs and all other tools of murder! Strike against preparedness that means death and misery to millions of human beings! Be not dumb, obedient slaves in an army of destruction! Be heroes in an army of construction!

The day after Congress declared war, the Socialist party met in an emergency convention and called the declaration "a crime against the American people." Antiwar meetings took place all over the country. In the local elections of 1917, Socialists made great gains. Ten Socialists were elected to the New York State legislature. In Chicago the Socialist party had won 3.6 percent of the vote in 1915 and it got 34.7 percent in 1917. But with the advent of war, speaking against it became a crime; Debs and hundreds of other Socialists were imprisoned.

When that war ended, 10 million men of various countries had died on the battlefields of Europe, and millions more had been blinded, maimed, gassed, shell-shocked, and driven mad. It was hard to find in that war any gain for the human race to justify that suffering, that death.

Indeed, when the war was studied years later, it was clear that no rational decision based on any moral principle had led the nations into war. Rather, there were imperial rivalries, greed for more territory, a lusting for national prestige, and the stupidity of revenge. And at the last moment, there was a reckless plunge by governments caught up in a series of threats and counterthreats, mobilizations and countermobilizations, ultimatums and counterultimatums, creating a momentum that mediocre leaders had neither the courage nor the will to stop. As described by Barbara Tuchman in her book *The Guns of August*:

> *War pressed against every frontier. Suddenly dismayed, governments struggled and twisted to fend it off. It was no use. Agents at frontiers were reporting every cavalry patrol as a deployment to beat the mobilization gun. General staffs, goaded by their relentless timetables, were pounding the table for the signal to move lest their opponents gain an hour's head start. Appalled upon the brink, the chiefs of state who would be ultimately responsible for their country's fate attempted to back away, but the pull of military schedules dragged them forward.*

Bitterness and disillusion followed the end of the war, and this was reflected in the literature of those years: Ernest Hemingway's *A Farewell to Arms*, John Dos Passo's *USA.*, and Ford Madox Ford's *No More Parades*. In Europe, German war veteran Erich Maria Remarque wrote the bitter antiwar novel *All Quiet on the Western Front*.

An Eager Bombardier

My own first impressions of something called war had come at the age of ten, when I read with excitement a series of books about "the boy allies": A French boy, an English boy, an American boy, and a Russian boy, who became friends, united in the wonderful cause to defeat Germany in World War I. It was an adventure, a romance, told in a group of stories about comradeship and heroism. It was war cleansed of death and suffering.

If anything was left of that romantic view of war, it was totally extinguished when, at eighteen, I read a book by a Hollywood screenwriter named Dalton Trumbo (jailed in the 1950s for refusing to talk to the House Committee on Un-American Activities about his political affiliations). The book was called *Johnny Got His Gun*. It is perhaps, the most powerful antiwar novel ever written.

Here was war in its ultimate horror. A slab of flesh in an American uniform had been found on the battlefield, still alive, with no legs, no arms, no face, blind, deaf, unable to speak, but the heart still beating, the brain still functioning, able to think about his past, ponder his present condition, and wonder if he will ever be able to communicate with the world outside.

For him, the oratory of the politicians who sent him off to war—the language of freedom, democracy, and justice—is now seen as the ultimate hypocrisy. A mute, thinking torso on a hospital bed, he finds a way to communicate with a kindly nurse, and when a visiting delegation of military brass comes by to pin a medal on his body, he taps out a message. He says: Take me into the workplaces, into the schools, show me to the little children and to the college students, let them see what war is like.

Take me wherever there are parliaments and diets and congresses and chambers of statesmen. I want to be there when they talk about honor and justice and making the world safe for democracy and fourteen points and the self determination of peoples .... Put my glass case upon the speaker's desk and every time the gavel descends let me feel its vibration .... Then let them speak of trade policies and embargoes and new colonies and old grudges. Let them debate the menace of the yellow race and the white man's burden and the course of empire and why should we take all this crap off Germany or whoever the next Germany is .... Let them talk more munitions and airplanes and battleships and tanks and gases and why of course we've got to have them we can't get along without them how in the world could we protect the peace if we didn't have them ....

But before they vote on them before they give the order for all the little guys to start killing each other let the main guy rap his gavel on my case and point down at me and say here gentlemen is the only issue before this house and that is are you for this thing here or are you against it.

Johnny Got His Gun had a shattering effect on me when I read it. It left me with a bone-deep hatred of war.

Around the same time I read a book by Walter Millis, *The Road to War*, which was an account of how the United States had been led into World War I by a series of lies and deceptions. Afterward I would learn more about those lies. For instance, the sinking of the ship *Lusitania* by German submarines was presented as a brutal, unprovoked act against a harmless passenger vessel. It was later revealed that the *Lusitania* was loaded with munitions, intended for use against Germany; the ship's manifest had been falsified to hide that. This didn't lessen the ugliness of the sinking, but did show something about the ways in which nations are lured into war.

Class consciousness accounted for some of my feeling about war. I agreed with the judgment of the Roman biographer Plutarch, who said, "The poor go to war, to fight and die for the delights, riches, and superfluities of others."

And yet, in early 1943, at the age of twenty-one, I enlisted in the U.S. Army Air Force. American troops were already in North Africa, Italy, and England; there was fierce fighting on the Russian front and the United States and Britain were preparing for the invasion of Western Europe. Bombing raids were taking place daily on the continent, U.S. planes bombing during the day, British planes bombing at night. I was so anxious to get overseas and start dropping bombs that after my training in gunnery school and bombing school I traded places with another man who was scheduled to go overseas sooner than me.

I had learned to hate war. But this war was different. It was not for profit or empire, it was a people's war, a war against the unspeakable brutality of fascism. I had been reading about Italian fascism in a book about Mussolini by journalist George Seldes called Sawdust Caesar. I was inspired by his account of the Socialist Matteotti, who stood up in the Italian Chamber of Deputies to denounce the establishment of a dictatorship. The black-shirted thugs of Mussolini's party picked up Matteotti outside his home one morning and shot him to death. That was fascism.

Fascism had to be resisted and defeated. I had no doubts. This was a just war.

I was stationed at an airfield out in the countryside of East Anglia (between the towns of Diss and Eye), that part of England that bulges eastward toward the Continent. East Anglia was crowded with military airfields, from which hundreds of bombers went out every day across the Channel.

Our little airfield housed the 490th Bomb Group. Its job was to make sure that every morning twelve B 17s-splendid-looking, low winged, four-engined heavy bombers—each with a crew of nine, wearing sheepskin jackets and fur-lined boots over electrically heated suits and equipped with oxygen masks and throat mikes—were ready to fly. We would take off around dawn and assemble with other groups of twelve, and then these huge flotillas would make their way east. Our bomb bay was full; our fifty-caliber machine guns (four in the nose, one in the upper turret, one in the ball turret, two in the waist, and one in the tail) were loaded and ready for attacking fighter planes.

I remember one morning standing out on that airfield, arguing with another bombardier over who was scheduled to fly that morning's mission. The target was Regensburg, and Intelligence reported that it was heavily defended by antiaircraft guns, but the two of us argued heatedly over who was going to fly that mission. I wonder today, was his motive like mine—wanting to fly another mission to bring closer the defeat of fascism. Or was it because we had all been awakened at one AM in the cold dark of England in March, loaded onto trucks, taken to hours of briefings and breakfast, weighed down with equipment, and after going through all that, he did not want to be deprived of another step toward his air medal, another mission. Even though he might be killed.

Maybe that was partly my motive too, I can't be sure. But for me, it was also a war of high principle, and each bombing mission was a mission of high principle. The moral issue could hardly be clearer. The enemy could not be more obviously evil—openly espousing the superiority of the white Aryan, fanatically violent and murderous toward other nations, herding its own people into concentration camps, executing them if they dared dissent. The Nazis were pathological killers. They had to be stopped, and there seemed no other way but by force.

If there was such a thing as a just war, this was it. Even Dalton Trumbo, who had written *Johnny Got His Gun*, did not want his book to be reprinted, did not want that overpowering antiwar message to reach the American public, when a war had to be fought against fascism.

If, therefore, anyone wants to argue (as I am about to do) that there is no such thing as a just war, then World War II is the supreme test.

I flew the last bombing missions of the war, got my Air Medal and my battle stars. I was quietly proud of my participation in the great war to defeat fascism. But when I packed up my things at the end of the war and put my old navigation logs and, snapshots and other mementos in a folder, I marked that folder, almost without thinking, "Never Again."

I'm still not sure why I did that, because it was not until years later that I began consciously to question the motives, the conduct, and the consequences of that crusade against fascism. The point was not that my abhorrence of fascism was in any way diminished. I still believed something had to be done to stop fascism. But that clear certainty of moral rightness that propelled me into the Air Force as an enthusiastic bombardier was now clouded over by many thoughts.

Perhaps my conversations with that gunner on the other crew, the one who loaned me *The Yogi and the Commisar*, gave me the first flickers of doubt. He spoke of the war as "an imperialist war," fought on both sides for national power. Britain and the United States opposed fascism only because it threatened their own control over resources and people. Yes, Hitler was a maniacal dictator and invader of other countries. But what of the British Empire and its long history of wars against native peoples to subdue them for the profit and glory of the empire? And the Soviet Union—was it not also a brutal dictatorship, concerned not with the working classes of the world but with its own national power?

I was puzzled. "Why," I asked my friend, "are you flying missions, risking your life, in a war you don't believe in?" His answer astonished me. "I'm here to speak to people like you."

I found out later he was a member of the Socialist Workers party; they opposed the war but believed that instead of evading military service they should enter it and propagandize against the war every moment they could. I couldn't understand this, but I was impressed by it. Two weeks after that conversation with him, he was killed on a mission over Germany.

After the war, my doubts grew. I was reading history. Had the United States fought in World War II for the rights of nations to independence and self-determination? What of its own history of expansion through war and conquest? It had waged a hundred-year war against the native Americans, driving them off their ancestral lands. The United States had instigated a war with Mexico and taken almost half its land, had sent marines at least twenty times into the countries of the Caribbean for power and

163

profit, had seized Hawaii, had fought a brutal war to subjugate the Filipinos, and had sent 5,000 marines into Nicaragua in 1926. Our nation could hardly claim it believed in the right of self-determination unless it believed in it selectively.

Indeed, the United States had observed Fascist expansion without any strong reactions. When Italy invaded Ethiopia, the United States, while declaring an embargo on munitions, allowed American businesses to send oil to Italy, which was crucial for carrying on the war against Ethiopia. An official of the U.S. State Department, James E. Miller, reviewing a book on the relations between the United States and Mussolini, acknowledged that "American aid certainly reinforced the hold of fascism."

During the Spanish Civil War, while the Fascist side was receiving arms from Hitler and Mussolini, Roosevelt's administration sponsored a Neutrality Act that shut off help to the Spanish government fighting Franco.

Neither the invasion of Austria nor Czechoslovakia nor Poland brought the United States into armed collision with fascism. We went to war only when our possession Hawaii was attacked and when our navy was disabled by Japanese bombs. There was no reason to think that it was Japan's bombing of civilians at Pearl Harbor that caused us to declare war. Japan's attack on China in 1937, her massacre of civilians at Nanking, and her bombardments of helpless Chinese cities had not provoked the United States to war.

The sudden indignation against Japan contained a good deal of hypocrisy. The United States, along with Japan and the great European powers, had participated in the exploitation of China. Our Open Door Polity of 1901 accepted that ganging up of the great powers on China. The United States had exchanged notes with Japan in 1917 saying, "the Government of the United States recognizes that Japan has special interests in China," and in 1928, American consuls in China supported the coming of Japanese troops.

It was only when Japan threatened potential U.S. markets by its attempted takeover of China but especially as it moved toward the tin, rubber, and oil of Southeast Asia, that the United States became alarmed and took those measures that led to the

Japanese attack: a total embargo on scrap iron and a total embargo on oil in the summer of 1941.

A State Department memorandum on Japanese expansion, a year before Pearl Harbor, did not talk of the independence of China or the principle of self-determination. It said,

Our general diplomatic and strategic position would be considerably weakened by our loss of Chinese, Indian and South Seas markets (and by our loss of much of the Japanese market for our goods, as Japan would become more and more self-sufficient) as well as by insurmountable restrictions upon our access to the rubber, tin jute, and other vital materials of the Asian and Oceanic regions.

Dresden and Hiroshima

It becomes difficult to sustain the claim that a war is just when both sides commit atrocities, unless one wants to argue that their atrocities are worse than ours. True, nothing done by the Allied Powers in World War II matches in utter viciousness the deliberate gassing, shooting, and burning of six million Jews and four million others by the Nazis. The deaths caused by the Allies were less, but still so massive as to throw doubt on the justice of a war that includes such acts.

Early in the war, various world leaders condemned the indescriminate bombing of city populations. Italy had bombed civilians in Ethiopia; Japan, in China; Germany and Italy, in the Spanish Civil War. Germany had dropped bombs on Rotterdam in Holland, on Coventry in England, and other places. Roosevelt described these bombings as "inhuman barbarism that has profoundly shocked the conscience of humanity."

But very soon, the United States and Britain were doing the same thing and on a far larger scale. When the Allied leaders met at Casablanca in January 1943, they agreed on massive air attacks to achieve "the destruction and dislocation of the German military, industrial and economic system and the undermining of the morale of the German people to the point where their capacity for armed resistance is fatally weakened." Churchill and his advisers had decided that bombing working class districts of German cities would accomplish just that, "the undermining of the morale of the German people."

The saturation bombing of the German cities began. There were raids of a thousand planes on Cologne, Essen, Frankfurt, and Hamburg.

The British flew at night and did "area bombing" with no pretense of aiming at specific military targets.

The Americans flew in the daytime, pretending to precision, but bombing from high altitudes made that impossible. When I was doing my practice bombing in Deming, New Mexico, before going overseas, our egos were built up by having us fly at 4,000 feet and drop a bomb within twenty feet of the target. But at 11,000 feet, we were more likely to be 200 feet away. And when we flew combat missions, we did it from 30,000 feet, and might miss by a quarter of a mile. Hardly "precision bombing."

There was huge self-deception. We had been angered when the Germans bombed cities and killed several hundred or a thousand people. But now the British and Americans were killing tens of thousands in a single air strike. Michael Sherry, in his study of aerial bombing, notes that "so few in the air force asked questions." Sherry says there was no clear thinking about the effects of the bombing. Some generals objected, but were overruled by civilians. The technology crowded out moral considerations. Once the planes existed, targets had to be found.

It was terror bombing, and the German city of Dresden was the extreme example. (The city and the event are immortalized in fiction by Kurt Vonnegut's comic, bitter novel, Slaughterhouse Five.) It was February, 1945, the Red Army was eighty miles to the east and it was clear that Germany was on the way to defeat. In one day and one night of bombing, by American and British planes, the tremendous heat generated by the bombs created a vacuum, and an enormous firestorm swept the city, which was full of refugees at the time, increasing the population to a million. More than 100,000 people died.

The British pilot of a Lancaster bomber recalled, "There was a sea of fire covering in my estimation some forty square miles. We were so aghast at the awesome blaze that although alone over the city, we flew around in a stand-off position for many minutes before turning for home, quite subdued by our imagination of the horror that must be below."

One incident remembered by survivors is that on the afternoon of February 14, 1945, American fighter planes machine-gunned clusters of refugees on the banks of the Elbe. A German woman told of this years later: "We ran along the Elbe stepping over the bodies."

Winston Churchill, who seemed to have no moral qualms about his policy of indiscriminate bombing, described the annihilation of Dresden in his wartime memoirs with a simple statement: "We made a heavy raid in the latter month on Dresden, then a center of communication of Germany's Eastern Front."

At one point in the war Churchill ordered thousands of anthrax bombs from a plant that was secretly producing them in the United States. His chief science adviser, Lord Cherwell, had informed him in February 1944: "Any animal breathing in minute quantities of these N (anthrax) spores is extremely likely to die suddenly but peacefully within the week. There is no known cure and no effective prophylaxis. There is little doubt that it is equally lethal to human beings." He told Churchill that a half dozen bombers could carry enough four-pound anthrax bombs to kill everyone within a square mile. However, production delays got in the way of this plan.

The actor Richard Burton once wrote an article for *The New York Times* about his experience playing the role of Winston Churchill in a television drama:

In the course of preparing myself ..I realized afresh that I hate Churchill and all of his kind. I hate them virulently. They have stalked down the corridors of endless power all through history .... What man of sanity would say on hearing of the atrocities committed by the Japanese against British and Anzac prisoners of war, "We shall wipe them out, everyone of them, men, women, and children. There shall not be a Japanese left on the face of the earth"? Such simple-minded cravings for revenge leave me with a horrified but reluctant awe for such single-minded and merciless ferocity.

When Burton's statement appeared in the "Arts and Leisure" section of *The New York Times*, he was banned from future BBC productions. The supervisor of drama productions for BBC said, "As far as I am concerned, he will never work for us again.. Burton acted in an unprofessional way"

It seems that however moral is the cause that initiates a war (in the minds of the public, in the mouths of the politicians), it is in the nature of war to corrupt that morality until the rule becomes "An eye for an eye, a tooth for a tooth," and soon it is not a matter of equivalence, but indiscriminate revenge.

The polity of saturation bombing became even more brutal when B29s, which carried twice the bomb load as the planes we flew in Europe, attacked Japanese cities with incendiaries, turning them into infernos.

In one raid on Tokyo, after midnight on March 10, 1945, 300 B29s left the city in flames, fanned by a strong northwest wind. The fires could be seen by pilots 150 miles out in the Pacific Ocean. A million people were left homeless. It is estimated that 100,000 people died that night. Many of them attempting to escape leaped into the Sumida River and drowned. A Japanese novelist who was twelve years old at the time, described the scene years later: "The fire was like a living thing. It ran, just like a creature, chasing us."

By the time the atomic bomb was dropped on Hiroshima (August 6, 1945) and another on Nagasaki (three days later), the moral line had been crossed psychologically by the massive bombings in Europe and by the fire bombings of Tokyo and other cities.

The bomb on Hiroshima left perhaps 140,000 dead; the one on Nagasaki, 70,000 dead. Another 130,000 died in the next five years. Hundreds of thousands of others were left radiated and maimed. These numbers are based on the most detailed report that exists on the effects of the bombings; it was compiled by thirty-four Japanese specialists and was published in 1981.

The deception and self-deception that accompanied these atrocities was remarkable. Truman told the public, "The world will note that the first atomic bomb was dropped on Hiroshima, a military base. That was because we wished in this first attack to avoid, insofar as possible, the killing of civilians."

Even the possibility that American prisoners of war would be killed in these bombings did not have any effect on the plans. On July 31, nine days before Nagasaki was bombed, the headquarters of the U.S. Army Strategic Air Forces on Guam (the take-off airfield for the atomic bombings) sent a message to the War Department:

*Reports prisoner of war sources not verified by photo give loca-
tion of Allied prisoner-of-war camp, one mile north of center of city of
Nagasaki. Does this influence the choice of this target for initial Center-
board operation? Request immediate reply.*

The reply came, "Targets previously assigned for Center-
board remain unchanged."

The terrible momentum of war continued even after the
bombings of Hiroshima and Nagasaki. The end of the war was a
few days away, yet B29s continued their missions. On August 14,
five days after the Nagasaki bombing and the day before the actual
acceptance of surrender terms, 449 B29s went out from the
Marianas for a daylight strike and 372 more went out that night.
Altogether, more than 1,000 planes were sent to bomb Japanese
cities. There were no American losses. The last plane had not yet
returned when Truman announced the Japanese had surrendered.

Japanese writer Oda Makoto describes that August 14 in
Osaka, where he lived. He was a boy. He went out into the streets
and found in the midst of the corpses American leaflets written in
Japanese, which had been dropped with the bombs: Your government has surrendered; the war is over.

The American public, already conditioned to massive
bombing, accepted the atomic bombings with equanimity, indeed
with joy. I remember my own reaction. When the war ended in
Europe, my crew flew our plane back to the United States. We
were given a thirty-day furlough and then had to report for duty to
be sent to Japan to continue bombing. My wife and I decided to
spend that time in the countryside. Waiting for the bus to take us,
I picked up the morning newspaper, August 7, 1945. The headline
was "Atomic Bomb Dropped on Hiroshima." My immediate reaction was elation: "The war will end. I won't have to go to the
Pacific."

I had no idea what the explosion of the atomic bomb had
done to the men, women, and children of Hiroshima. It was abstract and distant, as were the deaths of the people from the bombs
I had dropped in Europe from a height of six miles; I was unable to
see anything below, there was no visible blood, and there were no
audible screams. And I knew nothing of the imminence of a Japanese surrender. It was only later when I read John Hersey's

Hiroshima, when I read the testimony of Japanese survivors, and when I studied the history of the decision to drop the bomb that I was outraged by what had been done.

It seems that once an initial judgment has been made that a war is just, there is a tendency to stop thinking, to assume then that everything done on behalf of victory is morally acceptable. I had myself participated in the bombing of cities, without even considering whether there was any relationship between what I was doing and the elimination of fascism in the world. Thus a war that apparently begins with a "good" cause stopping aggression, helping victims, or punishing brutality ends with its own aggression, creates more victims than before, and brings out more brutality than before, on both sides. The Holocaust, a plan made and executed in the ferocious atmosphere of war, and the saturation bombings, also created in the frenzy of war, are evidence of this.

The good cause in World War II was the defeat of fascism. And, in fact, it ended with that defeat: the corpse of Mussolini hanging in the public square in Milan; Hitler burned to death in his underground bunker; Tojo, captured and sentenced to death by an international tribunal. But forty million people were dead, and the elements of fascism, militarism, racism, imperialism, dictatorship, ferocious nationalism, and war were still at large in the postwar world.

Two of those forty million were my closest Air Force friends, Joe Perry and Ed Plotkin. We had suffered through basic training and rode horses and flew Piper Cubs in Burlington, Vermont, and played basketball at Santa Ana before going our own ways to different combat zones. Both were killed in the final weeks of the war. For years afterward, they appeared in my dreams. In my waking hours, the question grew: What did they really die for?

We were victorious over fascism, but this left two superpowers dominating the world, vying for control of other nations, carving out new spheres of influence, on a scale even larger than that attempted by the Fascist powers. Both superpowers supported dictatorships all over the world: the Soviet Union in Eastern Europe and the United States in Latin America, Korea, and the Philippines.

The war machines of the Axis powers were destroyed, but

the Soviet Union and the United States were building military machines greater than the world had ever seen, piling up frightful numbers of nuclear weapons, soon equivalent to a million Hiroshima-type bombs. They were preparing for a war to keep the peace, they said (this had also been said before World War I) but those preparations were such that if war took place (by accident? by miscalculation?) it would make the Holocaust look puny.

Hitler's aggression was over but wars continued, which the superpowers either initiated or fed with military aid or observed without attempting to halt them. Two million people died in Korea; two to five million in Vietnam, Cambodia, and Laos; one million in Indonesia; perhaps two million in the Nigerian civil war; one million in the Iran-Iraq War; and many more in Latin America, Africa, and the Middle East. It is estimated that, in the forty years after 1945, there were 150 wars, with twenty million casualties.

The victorious and morally righteous superpowers stood by in the postwar world while millions—more than had died in Hitler's Holocaust—starved to death. They made gestures, but allowed national ambitions and interpower rivalries to stand in the way of saving the hungry. A United Nations official reported, with great bitterness that:

In pursuit of political objectives in the Nigerian Civil War, a number of great and small nations, including Britain and the United States, worked to prevent supplies of food and medicine from reaching the starving children of rebel Biafra.

Swept up in the obvious rightness of a crusade to rid the world of fascism, most people supported or participated in that crusade, to the point of risking their lives. But there were skeptics, especially among the nonwhite peoples of the world—blacks in the United States and the colonized millions of the British Empire (Gandhi withheld his support).

The extraordinary black writer Zora Neale Hurston wrote her memoir, *Dust Tracks on a Road*, at the start of World War II. Just before it was to come out, the Japanese attacked Pearl Harbor, and her publisher, Lippincott, removed a section of the book in which she wrote bitterly about the "democracies" of the West and their hypocrisy. She said:

All around me, bitter tears are being shed over the fate of Hol-

land, Belgium, France and England. I must confess to being a little dry around the eyes. I hear people shaking with shudders at the thought of Germany collecting taxes in Holland. I have not heard a word against Holland collecting one twelfth of poor people's wages in Asia. Hitler's crime is that he is actually doing a thing like that to his own kind ....

As I see it, the doctrines of democracy deal with the aspirations of men's souls, but the application deals with things. One hand in somebody else's pocket and one on your gun, and you are highly civilized .... Desire enough for your own use only, and you are a heathen. Civilized people have things to show to their neighbors.

The editor at Lippincott wrote on her manuscript, "Suggest eliminating international opinions as irrelevant to autobiography." Only when the book was reissued in 1984 did the censored passages appear.

Hurston, in a letter she wrote to a journalist friend in 1946, showed her indignation at the hypocrisy that accompanied the war:

I am amazed at the complacency of Negro press and public. Truman is a monster. I can think of him as nothing else but the Butcher of Asia. Of his grin of triumph on giving the order to drop the Atom bombs on Japan. Of his maintaining troops in China who are shooting the starving Chinese for stealing a handful of food.

Some white writers were resistant to the fanaticism of war. After it was over, Joseph Heller wrote his biting, brilliant satire *Catch-22* and Kurt Vonnegut wrote *Slaughterhouse Five*. In the 1957 film *Bridge on the River Kwai*, the Japanese military is obsessed with building a bridge, and the British are obsessed with destroying it. At the end it is blown up and a British lieutenant, barely surviving, looks around at the river strewn with corpses and mutters: "Madness. Madness."

There were pacifists in the United States who went to prison rather than participate in World War II. There were 350,000 draft evaders in the United States. Six thousand men went to prison as conscientious objectors; one out of every six inmates in U.S. federal prisons was a conscientious objector to the war.

But the general mood in the United States was support. Liberals, conservatives, and Communists agreed that it was a just war. Only a few voices were raised publicly in Europe and the

United States to question the motives of the participants, the means by which the war was being conducted, and the ends that would be achieved. Very few tried to stand back from the battle and take a long view. One was the French worker-philosopher Simone Weil. Early in 1945 she wrote in a new magazine called *Politics*:

Whether the mask is labeled Fascism, Democracy, or Dictatorship or the Proletariat, our great adversary remains the Apparatus-the bureaucracy, the police, the military .... No matter what the circumstances, the worst betrayal will always be to subordinate ourselves to this Apparatus, and to trample underfoot, in its service, all human values in ourselves and in others.

The editor of *Politics* was an extraordinary American intellectual named Dwight MacDonald, who with his wife, Nancy, produced the magazine as an outlet for unorthodox points of view. After the bombing of Hiroshima, MacDonald refused to join in the general jubilation. He wrote with a fury:

The CONCEPTS "WAR" AND "PROGRESS" ARE NOW OBSOLETE ...THE FUTILITY OF MODERN WARFARE SHOULD NOW BE CLEAR. Must we not now conclude, with Simone Weil, that the technical aspect of war today is the evil, regardless of political factors? Can one imagine that the atomic bomb could ever be used "in a good cause"?

But what was the alternative to war, with Germany on the march in Europe, Japan on its rampage through Asia, and Italy looking for empire? This is the toughest possible question. Once the history of an epoch has run its course, it is very difficult to imagine an alternate set of events, to imagine that some act or acts might set in motion a whole new train of circumstances, leading in a different direction.

Would it have been possible to trade time and territory for human life? Was there an alternative preferable to using the most modern weapons of destruction for mass annihilation? Can we try to imagine instead of a six-year war a ten-year or twenty-year period of resistance; of guerilla warfare, strikes, and non-cooperation; of underground movements, sabotage, and paralysis of vital communication and transportation; and of clandestine propaganda for the organization of a larger and larger opposition?

Even in the midst of war, some nations occupied by the

Nazis were able to resist: the Danes, the Norweigians, and the Bulgarians refused to give up their Jews. Gene Sharp, on the basis of his study of resistance movements in World War II, writes:

During the second World War in such occupied countries as the Netherlands, Norway and Denmark patriots resisted their Nazi overlords and internal puppets by such weapons as underground newspapers, labor slowdowns, general strikes, refusal of collaboration, special boycotts of German troops and quislings, and non-cooperation with fascist controls and efforts to restructure their societies' institutions.

Guerrilla warfare is more selective, its violence more limited and more discriminate, than conventional war. It is less centralized and more democratic by nature, requiring the commitment, the initiative, and the cooperation of ordinary people who do not need to be conscripted, but who are motivated by their desire for freedom and justice.

History is full of instances of successful resistance (although we are not informed very much about this) without violence and against tyranny, by people using strikes, boycotts, propaganda, and a dozen different ingenious forms of struggle. Gene Sharp, in his book The *Politics of Non-Violent Action*, records hundreds of instances and dozens of methods of action.

Since the end of World War II, we have seen dictatorships overthrown by mass movements that mobilized so much popular opposition that the tyrant finally had to flee in Iran, in Nicaragua, in the Philippines, and in Haiti. Granted, the Nazi machine was formidable, efficient, and ruthless. But there are limits to conquest. A point is reached where the conqueror has swallowed too much territory, has to control too many people. Great empires have fallen when it was thought they would last forever.

We have seen, in the Eighties, mass movements of protest arise in the tightly controlled Communist countries of Eastern Europe, forcing dramatic changes in Hungary, Czechoslovakia, Poland, Bulgaria, Rumania, and East Germnay. The Spanish people, having lost a million lives in their civil war, waited out Franco. He died, as all men do, and the dictatorship was over. For Portugal, the resistance in its outlying African Empire weakened control; corruption grew and the long dictatorship of Salazar was overthrown without a bloodbath.

There is a fable written by German playwright Bertolt Brecht that goes roughly like this: A man living alone answers a knock at the door. When he opens it, he sees in the doorway the powerful body, the cruel face, of The Tyrant. The Tyrant asks, "Will you submit?" The man does not reply. He steps aside. The Tyrant enters and establishes himself in the man's house. The man serves him for years. Then The Tyrant becomes sick from food poisoning. He dies. The man wraps the body, opens the door, gets rids of the body, comes back to his house, closes the door behind him, and says, firmly, "No."

Violence is not the only form of power. Sometimes it is the least effective. Always it is the most vicious, for the perpetrator as well as for the victim. And it is corrupting.

Immediately after the war, Albert Camus, the great French writer who fought in the underground against the Nazis, wrote in Combat, the daily newspaper of the French Resistance. In his essay called "Neither Victims Nor Executioners," he considered the tens of millions of dead caused by the war and asked that the world reconsider fanaticism and violence:

All I ask is that, in the midst of a murderous world, we agree to reflect on murder and to make a choice .... Over the expanse of five continents throughout the coming years an endless struggle is going to be pursued between violence and friendly persuasion, a struggle in which, granted, the former has a thousand times the chances of success than has the latter. But I have always held that, if he who bases his hopes on human nature is a fool, he who gives up in the face of circumstances is a coward. And henceforth, the only honorable course will be to stake everything on a formidable gamble: that words are more powerful than munitions.

Whatever alternative scenarios we can imagine to replace World War II and its mountain of corpses, it really doesn't matter any more. That was is over. The practical effect of declaring World War II just is not for that war, but for the wars that follow. And that effect has been a dangerous one, because the glow of rightness that accompanied that war has been transferred, by false analogy and emotional carryover, to other wars. To put it another way, perhaps the worst consequence of World War II is that it kept alive the idea that war could be just.

Looking at World War II in perspective, looking at the world it created and the terror that grips our century, should we not bury for all time the idea of just war?

Some of the participants in that "good war" had second thoughts. Former GI Tommy Bridges, who after the war became a policeman in Michigan, expressed his feelings to Studs Terkel:

It was a useless war, as every war is .... How gaddamn foolish it is, the war. They's no war in the world that's worth fighting for, I don't care where it is. They can't tell me any different. Money, money is the thing that causes it all. I wouldn't be a bit surprised that the people that start wars and promote 'em are the men that make the money, make the ammunition, make the clothing and so forth. Just think of the poor kids that are starvin' to death in Asia and so forth that could be fed with how much you make one big shell out of.

Higher up in the military ranks was Admiral Gene LaRocque, who also spoke to Studs Terkel about the war:

I had been in thirteen battle engagements, had sunk a submarine, and was the first man ashore in the landing at Roi. In that four years, I thought, What a hell of a waste of a man's life. I lost a lot of friends. I had the task of telling my roommate's parents about our last days together. You lose limbs, sight, part of your life-for what? Old men send young men to war. Flag, banners, and patriotic sayings..

We've institutionalized militarism. This came out of World War Two ....It gave us the National Security Council. It gave us the CIA, that is able to spy on you and me this very moment. For the first time in the history of man, a country has divided up the world into military districts .... You could argue World War Two had to be fought. Hitler had to be stopped.

Unfortunately, we translate it unchanged to the situation today ....

I hate it when they say, "He gave his life for his country." Nobody gives their life for anything. We steal the lives of these kids. We take it away from them. They don't die for the honor and glory of their country. We kill them.

Granted that we have started in this century with the notion of just war, we don't have to keep it. Perhaps the change in our thinking can be as dramatic, as clear, as that in the life of a French general, whose obituary in 1986 was headed: "Gen. Jacques

Paris de Bollardiere, War Hero Who Became a Pacifist, Dead at the age of 78."

He had served in the Free French Forces in Africa during World War II, later parachuted into France and Holland to organize the Resistance, and commanded an airborne unit in Indochina from 1946 to 1953. But in 1957, according to the obituary, he "caused an uproar in the French army when he asked to be relieved of his command in Algeria to protest the torture of Algerian rebels. In 1961 he began to speak out against militarism and nuclear weapons. He created an organization called The Alternative Movement for Non-Violence and in 1973 participated in a protest expedition to France's South Pacific nuclear testing site."

It remains to be seen how many people in our time will make that journey from war to nonviolent action against war. It is the great challenge or our time: How to achieve justice, with struggle, but without war.

"Declarations of Independence:
Cross-Examining American Ideology"
Harper Collins 1990

The Challenge for Pacifists
by Michael Farrell

In 1916, someone in the U.S. Army launched an investigation: "Why do men go to war?" When news of this reached Gen. Pershing, he ordered the study stopped because he already knew the answer. "Men go to war because they enjoy it. "

Such evasion is not new. In 416 B.C., when Euripides' "The Trojan Women," one of the world's greatest antiwar plays, was first produced, the Athenians were deeply shaken by its tragedy, to such a degree that something had to be done. They had a war going on at the time. But they did not stop the war. Instead, they sent Euripides into exile.

A new book, *The Psychology of War: Comprehending Its Mystique and Its Madness*, by Lawrence LeShan, promises to bring to bear "a new concept, recent to scientific thought."

LeShan, a psychologist, first outlines history's explanations for war. His review adds up to a depressing analysis of the human condition. Some said wars happen because people have an insatiable desire for power. Others threw greed into the bellicose brew. For others the cause was more radical: "Man is born evil."

These, at least, presume war was a blight. Adding insult to injury, however, was an insane strain insisting war is good. Many of those, alas, were poets and philosophers. Hegel, for example: "War has the higher meaning that through it . . . the ethical health of nations is maintained."

And if it's not good, it's at least enjoyable, LeShan goes on. May Sarton is one of many to highlight its insidious attraction: "The fact is, unfortunately, that hatred in the public sense makes people's eyes bright, starts the adrenaline flowing, as love in the public sense does not. People feel fine when they are full of anger and hatred against someone else."

A medieval document, the Zohar, puts it another way: "When men are at war, even God's anger does not frighten them." This is borne out by the medieval church's efforts to restrict warfare to certain days of the week and to prohibit the crossbow as inhumane. Although much more powerful then than now, the church failed on both counts.

And while the church has had its antiwar moments, history shows that, in practice, it usually had a belligerent wing to match the pacifist theory. And not only the churches.

The best and brightest have as often as not been on the side of war.

With the exception of Bertrand Russell, no first-rate philosopher in our history has consistently advocated peace. In all major wars of this century, the educated classes voted for war policies and enlisted in the army as readily and enthusiastically as did their less-educated compatriots.

This penchant is all the more extraordinary in light of the fact that lower nature does not engage in mutual mass destruction. The only animals that wage war are human beings and harvester ants - which doesn't say much for harvester ants.

Something in the life-and-death joust, it seems, touches a part of humans that few other human experiences do. In *War and Peace*, Tolstoy wrote: "Every general and every soldier was conscious of his own significance, feeling himself but a grain of sand in the ocean of humanity, and at the same time was conscious of his might, feeling himself a part of the whole."

A woman who survived the London Blitz said, "It was a marvelous time. You forgot about yourself and you did what you could and we were all in it together .... You worried about getting killed, but in some ways it was better than now. Now, we're all just ourselves again."

Among the daunting tasks confronting pacifists is to compete with this hankering for the extraordinary and sublime, which so few human activities or conditions offer, including the banal condition of ordinary old peace. After the recent Super Bowl, the Dallas Cowboys coach reminded his triumphant players that what was important and worth remembering was not the ring or the money but the solidarity and even love they generated in order to achieve this important goal.

Perhaps the crafty coach had been reading Erich Marie Remarque's *All Quiet on the Western Front*: "The body with one bound is in full readiness .... Perhaps it is our inner and most secret life that falls on guard. We sit opposite one another ... . We don't talk much, but 1 believe we have a more complete communion with one another than even lovers have."

But why do they not, after the carnage is over, as they pick up the body pieces and survey the destroyed cities—why do they not realize it was all less than lovers have? Because, LeShan indicates, there is no energy left: "It is all better forgotten, and when Johnny comes marching home with a chronic disability from his wounds, we all try to forget our recent bout of psychological illusion."

The "psychological illusion" is at the heart of *The Psychology of War*. LeShan's research led him to divide reality into four modes, of which the "sensory" and "mythic" are relevant here. These are pretty much what the reader might expect. "Sensory" wars bear a striking resemblance to objective reality: Blood is blood and pain hurts and those whose guts are blown sky high are mostly the poor and ignorant and innocent.

In the "mythic" mode, blood is the red wine of tomorrow's utopia, the other guy is an evil empire and our soldiers are pure heroes fighting gloriously for a nation of saints and geniuses back home.

This book does not deliver the breakthrough it promised at the outset—most well-read people are likely to have stumbled across its main insights in one shape or another. Even so, there is enough wisdom here to stop any war—if the world were to take it seriously (which of course could also be said of the Bible and many other books).

The most striking thing is what we have done to our own and each other's minds to make war seem normal at worst and glorious at best. There is nothing humans couldn't do if they applied to life's nobler projects the secrets so successfully used in priming people for war.

Peace activists bemoan the fact that the same money and resources and person power devoted to war is not also invested in peacemaking. This is true and lamentable. But more powerful than the Pentagon's money and materiel are the ideas that have made war mythical and popular.

Lester Pearson, in his 1957 Nobel Peace Prize address, said: 'The grim fact is that we prepare for war like precocious giants and for peace like retarded pygmies."

Where is the peace myth? Where is even the church that can bring to its message and ministry the fervor that a few good men can bring to a war?

It will be argued that something must be done with the Hitlers or the Pol Pots. Perhaps war is the answer to the Hitlers. That would still leave unanswered the question of war's popularity. And even in the case of Hitler, it was the culture of war that led the contending sides to the only compelling solution the history of the world up to that time had prepared them for.

Suppose, instead, that Pope Pius XII invited every Catholic on earth, tens of millions, on a pilgrimage to Hitler's Germany. And suppose the Catholics, because this was what their Catholicism taught them, started marching, and driving, and sailing, a hundred million and more, never mind what they would do when they got there, never mind that some would doubtless be slaughtered—sure, it's a bit unusual, but now compare it for common sense with what actually happened.

It is totally illogical, intangible, but it's there - the urge to something inhuman, whether subhuman or supra, because humans have made the ordinary intolerable. Said a woman who fought in the French resistance, 15 years later. "My life is so unutterably boring nowadays .... I do not love war or want it to return. But at least it made me feel alive."

And historian Bruce Catton wrote of the Civil War veterans in this country: "They seemed to speak for a certainty, for an assured viewpoint, for a standard of values which did not fluctuate, that put such things as bravery, patriotism, confidence in the progress of the human race, and the belief in a broadening freedom for all men, at the very basis of what men moved by."

Was it who they were inside, or the fact that they fought? Was there no one else with a philosophy—or a theology to match theirs in that little town?

Philosopher Alfred North Whitehead wrote an encomium in swelling cadences for the young dead of World War II, ending: "They are dying for the worth of the world."

Nice sentence, but it's baloney. What did the young men think as their lives ebbed away in foreign trenches? "This one's for the worth of the world"?

And the irony continues: This all-too-human activity is so insane that the human mind can't figure it out.

The National Catholic Reporter Feb. 19, 1993

Gen. George Patton Said "Americans Love War."
He's Right.
by Donald Kaul

We are a peace-loving people everybody says so. Well, maybe not everybody, but we sure say so. Hardly a week goes by without one of our national leaders referring to Americans as a peace-loving people.

What can they be thinking of?

In the past 50 years, we have fought four major wars; that is, wars that fully engaged the national attention. In addition, we have invaded Panama, Grenada and the Dominican Republic; sent troops to Lebanon (twice); given naval escort in wartime to ships in the Persian Gulf; bombed Libya; provided clandestine military support to various regimes and rebel groups in Central America; conspired in the assassination of at least three foreign heads of state; launched war planes to help thwart a coop in the Philippines and nurtured a military assault on Cuba. Those are mealy the adventures that come readily to my aging mind; I'm sure there are others.

None of these wars, invasions, incursions, police actions and punitive expeditions, I hasten to point out, involved the defense of our soil (although, to be fair, World War II might qualify in that regard since it began for us with the bombing of Hawaii).

No other country in the past half-century can match our record for embracing armed conflict as a foreign policy tool.

Nor have we, for the most part, gone into these battles reluctantly. American presidents are never more popular than when they take us to war. It is only when we are perceived as losing the war that public opinion turns on them.

Ronald Reagan is credited with restoring our good opinion of ourselves largely through the mechanism of waging war on small, weak nations that couldn't fight back.

George Bush has been president two years and he's gotten us into two wars. Despite a recession, he's running an 80 percent approval rating in the polls. Already Republicans are aiming their campaign guns at Democrats who counseled delay of the present hostilities.

The fact is, we are a war-like people. I remember being shocked when Gen. George Patron said as much. "Americans love war," he said in a famous address to his troops on the eve of battle.

He was right.

I'm not sure the soldiers involved are enthralled with war, but the people at home are invariably enthusiastic about it. They decorate the streets with ribbons and flags, as if in celebration. They say it's to show support for the troops, but it's the war that gets supported.

In theory, we conduct our wars in a civilized manner, adhering scrupulously to the rules, laid down by the Geneva Convention; no targeting of civilians, no poison gas, no abuse of prisoners. In practice, we are less fastidious.

It is somewhat ironic that our bombing of that civilian bunker in Baghdad should have taken place virtually 45 years to the day after the World War II firebombing of Dresden. It was a grim reminder of one of the darkest moments of our past.

The British, that other peace-loving people, conducted the first raids on Dresden, reducing one of the most beautiful cities of Europe to kindling. Then they came in with incendiary bombs to light the kindling. Then our bombers showed up to make sure the survivors couldn't fight the fires.

The result was a huge firestorm that killed more than 35,000 people—virtually all civilians. Dresden had no military significance to speak of. Most of the dead suffocated to death in their shelters.

There is a difference between herding civilians into rooms for the purpose of gassing them and bombing them into shelters for the propose of suffocating them, but I'm not sure it's a moral one.

Even as we bomb Iraqi troops to pulp we are outraged at the thought that Saddam Hussein might use chemical weapons against us. He is "without a shred of human decency," we are told.

Have you heard about our air-fuel bombs? They explode above the ground, sending out a fine mist of petroleum jelly which then ignites, creating a firestorm that sucks up the oxygen over an area the size of four or five football fields, suffocating its victims, Dresden-style.

Why is that not a chemical weapon? What makes it more ethical than poison gas? You say that the difference is that air-fuel bombs are not banned by the Geneva Convention.

Oh, I see.

We are many things, some of them good, but peace-loving we are not. We are, instead, war-like creatures of self-delusion, able to convince ourselves of the nobility of our cause, no matter what means we use to pursue it.

Syndicated column distributed by
Tribune Media Services, Feb. 22, 1991

Proud To Be a Soldier
by Midshipman Tara Lee

Dear Mr. McCarthy:

There are two reasons for this letter. First, I have for some time followed your columns and have developed quite a respect for your abilities as a writer. That respect recently increased considerably when I opened my newest textbook to find a reproduction of your 2 January, 1987 column. I read, instantly copied, and almost as quickly memorized your list of 10 writing guidelines, promoted you to "mentor" from "writer-to-admire" and resolved to write you a letter gushing with praise and gratitude. I didn't write it because I soon doubted my ability to do so without violating one or more of the rules, and because there wasn't much to say except to announce myself as an amateur/admirer who aspires in her secret dreams to one day do what you do.

Well, that's one day. Today I am a midshipman at the United States Naval Academy, aspiring to the service of my country, and that, combined with a more recent column, is why I am writing now.

Sir, you have some crazy ideas about women and war. Guideline # 11—"say what you mean." In your 14 January column you said:

War is a male ritual based on a hyper-masculine ethic that violence is rational. Linda Bray in Panama was less a victory for female rights than for male wrongs She bought into traditional masclinism: Fists, guns, armies and killing are sensible solutions to problems.

As far as I can determine, the main thrust of your column is that "war is bad." Sir, I certainly do not disagree. I completely respect your right to be as anti-war and as anti-military as you like. However, as a woman in the military, I take great offense at your using the premise that "war is bad" as a launching pad from which to attack and criticize Capt. Bray for doing her job. I agree that her role in the conflict—and the fact that she performed her job in a "combat" capacity—has been overplayed. But I would hardly accuse her of "leading the charge up Mt. Equality." She followed her orders, nothing more.

I cannot speak for Capt. Bray, or for all women in the military; I only speak for myself. And you made several assumptions about me that I would like the opportunity to correct. By being in the military wearing a uniform and serving my country-I am not "buying into traditional masculinism," as you put it. I do not believe any more than you do that "Fists, guns, armies, and killing are sensible solutions to problems." And no, I do not believe that Capt. Bray simply accomplishing her given mission provides eternally irrefutable proof that men and women should be side by side in the trenches forevermore. I am, however (unlike you), very much in support of Rep. Pat Schroeder's legislative proposal. Her proposed bill would allow a period of testing for combat roles for women. The issue of women in combat is not going to disappear, and Rep. Schroeder's bill is the first positive step I have seen anyone take toward resolving it.

I don't know the answers. The arguments you and several others have presented against women in combat are valid ones. But the "license to rape" issue that you mention is a problem of war and not a problem of women in war. The solution you offer in your column is the "abolition" to war, and frankly I'm all for that. However, while you columnists and politicians in Washington are working on that one, as a young woman about to become a military officer, I'd like to see more constructive work toward resolving our continuing problems of integration, and less pointless prattle about the inequality of the sexes.

There are combat roles that women can do as well as men. I can learn to fly an F-14 as effectively as any of my classmates, but at the same time I am under no illusions about my physical limitations in other roles. I appreciate that my male counterpart can run faster and jump higher with a 20-pound pack on his back, and is therefore much better suited to certain combat roles. I am not asking for that kind of "job equality"; like most women in the military I would not want a job that physical limitations would prevent me from doing well. On the contrary, I only hope that when the time comes, Congress does not prevent me from doing the job I have been trained to do, as Capt. Bray did in Panama. It can no longer be a question whether or not women are capable of firing the guns, flying the planes, driving the ships, and leading the troops.

The question remaining is whether or not America is ready to accept that equality and begin to take advantage of the full resources of military women.

I'm honestly not sure if this country is ready. I am however, more than ready to find out, and so is Rep. Schroeder. Why aren't you?

Proud To Know a Soldier
by Colman McCarthy

Dear Tara:

Half a ton of thanks for your letter, and a full ton for its impassioned language. When I was in college I dreamed, as you do now, of earning a living as a writer. Plenty of room is available for you in this calling, even if you have to call yourself, which is fine because usually no one else will or should.

You're right that the "main thrust" of my column was, in your words, "war is bad." If you agree with that, as you say you do, why are you in a school dedicated to war preparation? The Naval Academy has its portion of quality professors, some of whom I came to know when I was invited occasionally to speak to writing classes. Many of the students have as high ideals as those in the classes I teach at the University of Maryland and Georgetown Law.

None of that alters what you are being trained to do: kill people and destroy property if the order is given. "Aspiring to the service of my country" is a pseudo-patriotic slogan. When commissioned, you won't be serving your country, you'll be serving those who run your country. In "The Kingdom of God Is Within You," Leo Tolstoy wrote, "Government is an association of men who do violence to the rest of us." Why serve those men? Government-sanctioned slaughter, otherwise known as war, has caused the deaths of 8 million people in this century. Some 40,000 are killed a month in current wars and conflicts. Last December, between 1,000 and 4,000 people were killed in the U.S. invasion of Panama. The Pentagon doesn't know or care how many Panamanian civilians were killed, hence the estimates of between 1,000 and 4,000. Instead of a national debate on the morality of sending any U.S. soldier-male or female-to slaughter Panamanians, the triviality of women's role in combat has been the preoccupation.

It's beneath both of us to be sucked into it. What we should be doing, instead, is examining our consciences to be as certain as possible that we are using our time and energy to decrease the violence of war. How is that done? By acting, in our personal and professional lives, on what David Dellinger said on entering prison for draft resistance in 1943: "Very few people choose war. They choose selfishness and the result was war. Each of us, individually and nationally, must choose: total love or total war."

We are what we choose. Perhaps my choices are flawed, and someday I will come to my senses and abandon what you call my "crazy ideas." I've been tempted often, except that occasionally events affirm theories. Twenty years ago Gene Sharp wrote in "The Politics of Nonviolence": "The essence of power is not in military might. People are ruled by the state to the degree that they cooperate with the state. The state loses its power to the degree that the people withdraw or sever their cooperation."

Yeah, I was told by the knowledgeable and wordly-wise, try selling that in Eastern Europe. Now that the dictatorships from Poland to Romania have fallen, Gene Sharp, is seen to have been right. Such pacifists as Lech Walesa are cheered in Congress, but his philosophy is ignored. He said: it is due "to nonviolence that I am where I am now. I'm a man who believes in dialogue and agreement. I strongly believe that the 21st century will not be a century of violence. We've already tried and tested every form of violence, and not once in the entire course of human history has anything good or lasting come from it." But we still don't get it. American politicians go on with our war preparation economy and arming the world. Weapons sales to Third World governments increased 66 percent in 1988 over the previous year. Yes, some parts of our system are worth working and fighting for, but how do we fight? Again, choices. There's George Patton: "I want you to remember that no bastard ever won a war by dying for his country. He won it by making the other poor dumb bastard die for his country."

Or Albert Einstein: "Our schoolbooks glorify war and conceal its horrors. They indoctrinate children with hatred. I would teach peace rather than war, love rather than hate . . . (People) should continue to fight, but they should fight for things worthwhile, not imaginary geographical lines, racial prejudices and private greed draped in the colors of patriotism. Their arms should be weapons of the spirit, not shrapnel and tanks."

Thanks for your letter. The Naval Academy is lucky to have you: I wish it served you better by offering courses on nonviolence. But the militarists who run your school, and the military-supporting Congress that lavishly bankrolls it, fear academic freedom and intellectual choices. You'll have to study on your own, which takes us back to where I began. The study of peace is a calling, and we end up calling ourselves.

Washington Post

April 10, 1990

8

The Vietnam War Is Not Over

Every senator in this chamber is partly responsible for sending 50,000 young Americans to an early grave. This chamber reeks of blood. Every senator here is partly responsible for that human wreckage at Walter Reed and Bethesda Naval [hospitals] and all across our land—young men without legs, or arms, or genitals, or faces, or hopes.

There are not very many of these blasted and broken boys who think this war is a glorious adventure. Do not talk to them about bugging out, or national honor, or courage. It does not take any courage at all for a congressman, or a senator, or a president to wrap himself in the flag and say we are staying in Vietnam, because it is not our blood that is being shed. But we are responsible for those young men and their lives and their hopes.

Senator George McGovern, September 1, 1970
Senate speech calling for an end of funding for the Vietnam War

I'm Gordon Livingston. I went to West Point to become a soldier. Tired of learning to kill, I became a doctor. At a military ceremony in Vietnam in 1969 I handed the commanding general a satirical prayer I had written: 'Lord, forget not the least of thy children as they hide from us in the jungles. Bring them under our merciful hand that we may end their suffering.' Before I was discharged from the Army as 'an embarrassment,' I adopted an Amerasian child of the war. Michael is 30 now. When I look at him I remember what I was in the moment I chose life over death.

Washington Post, Jan. 1, 2000

Who Will Apologize for Vietnam?
by W. D Ehrhart

In the spring of 1966, at the age of 17, 1 enlisted in the U.S. Marine Corps. Lyndon Johnson had only recently warned the American people that if we did not stop the communists in Vietnam, we would one day have to fight them on the sands of Waikiki, and the words of John Kennedy were still reverberating in my heart as if he'd spoken them directly to me: "Ask not what your country can do for you; ask what you can do for your country." I was going to serve my country in Vietnam.

I had never heard of Archimedes Patti or Christian de Castries, Edward Lansdale or the Binh Xuyen—key figures in the early stages of the Vietnam conflict. I did not know that China had occupied Vietnam for a thousand years, or that Ho Chi Minh had sought and been refused an audience with Woodrow Wilson at Versailles.

I knew only what was necessary to do my job: How to fire and clean my rifle, how to apply a pressure bandage to a sucking chest wound, how to make a stove from an empty C-ration can.

Whether the United States should have been in Vietnam or not was a question I never asked myself before I arrived there. That was not part of my job. That was the job of men like Lyndon Johnson, Dean Rusk, Robert McNamara, McGeorge Bundy and Walt Rostow, and I trusted my government leaders, elected and appointed, to do their job just as I was doing mine.

There is an implicit but sacred bargain struck between those who ask others to put their lives at risk and those who do the risking, and for those sacrifice. I accepted that bargain willingly, proudly, because those who put me at risk assured me and my country that the cause was worthy.

During the long and painful passage of the 13 months I fought in Vietnam, however, I found myself less and less confident that either I or my government knew what we were doing. In a world of free fire zones and "Bouncing Betty" mines, punji pits and Zippo raids, it became increasingly difficult to believe in anything but my own survival. In a world where helpless old men were

194

beaten bloody and small children were included in the body count of Viet Cong dead, it became impossible to avoid the conclusion that I was fundamentally, perhaps pathologically, evil.

By the time I left Vietnam in the waning days of the Tet Offensive and the battle for Hue, I had become acutely aware that something had gone horribly wrong in Vietnam. But I didn't know what.

I thought maybe it was me. Men like Dean Rusk and McGeorge Bundy and Walt Rostow were still insisting that the cause was worthy. They would soon be replaced by men like Richard Nixon and Henry Kissinger, but they, too, would insist the worthiness of their cause right up to the very moment North Vietnamese tanks crushed the gates of the Presidential Palace in Saigon, achieving at an incalculable cost in human suffering what might have been achieved without the loss of a single life 30 years earlier.

I paid a terrible price for the bargain I struck with the people who sent me to wage war on Vietnam: more than a decade of nightmares and alcohol and self-loathing; a white-heat fury, shapeless and unpredictable, that seared anyone who came too close; a loneliness profound as the Silence beyond the stars. And I was lucky.

I have friends whose names are caved into that ugly black slab in Washington, D.C. I have friends who were dumped into wheelchairs at 19 and won't be taken out again until they are laid into their coffins. I have friends who still can't see an Asian face without trembling. I have friends whose wives are afraid to touch them while they are sleeping.

OK. My friends and I made a mistake, and we paid the price. I've learned to accept my share of responsibility for that mistake, I can live with myself. But where now are the people who asked us to take the risk? Where have they been these past 20 years?

Willy Crapser spent 17 years in and out of psychiatric wards, and Robert McNamara became president of the World Bank. Ron Kovic never had the chance to have children before he was paralyzed for life, and McGeorge Bundy became president of the Ford Foundation. Kenney Worman and Randy Moore have been dead longer than they got to live, and Walt Rostow and Dean Rusk are professors at respected universities.

Not once—not once in all these years—have I ever heard a single high-level policymaker of the Vietnam war apologize for what he did, ever admit that he made a mistake, ever show the slightest sign of remorse for all the havoc and misery, the shattered lives and shattered families and shattered nations left gasping in the wake of his decisions.

There is no regret, no sorrow, no shame. Some of these men merely skulked off the public stage quietly. Others continue to this day to insist that their cause was worthy, and always will be.

Honorable men, they asked my friends and me to get down and dirty in the rice fields only to abandon us under fire. We did the killing and the dying, and then they left us to find our own way back while they went on with their honorable lives as if nothing at all were out of order.

They struck a bargain with us, and then they broke it. And they have refused ever after to admit that it was broken.

I have often wondered how these men live with themselves. How do they get up each day and look themselves in the eye? How do they go on pretending that God's in His heaven, all's right with the world? Or are there private doubts, private demons, that they are simply too proud or too ashamed to admit?

I'd like to believe these honorable men are not evil, but only human. I'd like to believe these honorable men didn't just walk away from the wreckage they created without a second thought. I'd like to believe they have nightmares too. But nothing that has happened in the last 20 years has given me any cause to think so.

The Philadelphia Inquirer
July 4, 1989
W.D. Ehrhart received the Purple Heart, two Presidential Unit Citations and the Cross of Gallantry for his service in Vietnam. He teaches at Germantown Friends School.

Remembering Paul
by George Swiers

During the middle watch, in the eerie midnight hour, every sound in the Vietnamese jungle seemed horribly intensified. Every shadow gave the appearance of death coming to call. If you were lucky, very lucky, it was merely your fatigue and anxiety and nothing more. But luck, in March's last week in 1969, was the lover that had fled the ninth Marines, leaving us with that collective foreboding familiar to the infantry in every war. The awful wisdom that something terrible was about to happen. Soon.

So I was grateful for the company that night when Paul, who was unable or unwilling to sleep, came and sat beside me on my watch. No company, in good times or bad, was better company than Paul Baker. That night, a night suffocating with apprehension, he actually sang. Sang in this ridiculous tone-deaf whisper—not Hendrix, the Doors, the Temptations, or any other secular grunt anthems—but this wonderfully corny song called "High Hopes." Sang this inspirational melody about ants moving rubber tree plants until we laughed so hard he had to clamp a hand over my mouth.

Of all the mysteries of the mind, the greatest is how it faithfully protects us. A quarter of a century later, whenever I hear "High Hopes" I burst into spontaneous laughter, and that night long ago, courtesy of my friend Paul, I forgot that I was a hostage to tomorrow. "Stay close tomorrow," whispered Paul, after a long, mournful silence, "It'll be OK."

My son, Paul, is three now. Innocent enough to see life as a daily, delightful adventure. Bold enough so that the adventure is boundless. Among his favorite adventures are the once in awhile visits to the comfortable North Troy neighborhood where John and Marion Baker raised their four children. Marion Baker, he knows, will tirelessly produce toys, books, and juice to indulge him, will laugh lovingly at his silly attempts at conversation, will tenderly take his hand when he wishes to explore her home.

As I watch this warm, dignified woman enjoying my son, I wonder if she thinks about her own Paul. Perhaps proudly recalling the class president, gifted athlete, valedictorian at Troy's Catholic Central. Perhaps painfully recollecting the helplessness she surely felt that evening when he called to say that he'd quit college, joined the marines, and had volunteered for Vietnam because, he insisted, so many less fortunate were required to serve. And I wonder, too, about the bond, forged by chance, that we share. She had been with him when he came into this world, and I was with him when he left it.

I was beside Paul that afternoon, staying close, part of a long horizontal line moving up the wooded hillside—moving up in the relentless heat, against an objective we knew could never be taken. Then, just in front of Paul and me, the khaki blur of a North Vietnamese soldier and the distinct pops of an AK-47 rifle. That quickly. Leaving me to forever wonder why he chose my friend, not me, leaving me with the most profound, instant loneliness I ever knew.

I look at my son through his open doorway. Each night he looks the same. Smiling the sleep that only children can know. His blankie, worn more thin and ragged by the day's adventure, is balled in a tiny pillow.

In frequent moments of moral outrage, I promise myself that he will never go to war. In calmer moments, I know that if he always acts on principle and follows his conscience, as I hope he will, the path will sometimes lead there anyway. The fact is, I have not yet learned myself whether the greater madness lies in war or in the casual indifference to it.

"Stay close tomorrow." I whisper to him each night. "It'll be OK."

Then the khaki blurs were everywhere, and the rest of the horizontal line began to die. Died all that afternoon. Mostly teenagers. Sometimes in twos or threes. White, Black, Red, and Brown. At nightfall, isolated and devastated, we formed a circle around our dead and dying friends and hoped for morning. That night I lay beside Doc Tom, our hospital corps-man, and told him about the song Paul had sung the night before. Tom wept unashamedly for the friend he loved and missed, then said something extraordinary. He said he was thankful that Paul had been the first to die, that seeing what had happened would have broken his heart.

Some people go to war and lose their lives. Others go to

war and find that life has given them a second chance.

Each night when I look in on my son, usually in the mid-night hour, I adjust the lighting in the hall just so, and let a sooth-ing circle of light drip.

The Daily Gazette
Scenectacty, NY
May 29, 1994

When Hearts and Minds Didn't Follow
by William Blum

"If you grab 'em by the balls, the hearts and minds will follow" ... "Give us your hearts and minds or we'll burn down your goddamn village" ... the end result of America's anticommunist policy in Vietnam; also its beginning and its middle.

There was little serious effort to win the hearts and minds of the Vietnamese people, even less chance of success, for the price of success was social change, of the kind that Diem was unwilling to accept in Vietnam, the kind the United States was not willing to accept anywhere in the Third World. If Washington had been willing to accept such change which they have always routinely and disparagingly dismissed as "socialist"—there would have been no need to cancel the elections or to support Diem, no need for intervention in the first place. There was, consequently, no way the United States could avoid being seen by the people of Vietnam as other than the newest imperialist occupiers, following in the footsteps of first the Chinese, then the French, then the Japanese, then the French again.

On 27 January 1973, in Paris, the United States signed the "Agreement on Ending the War and Restoring Peace in Vietnam". Among the principles to which the United States agreed was the one stated in Article 21: "In pursuance of its traditional policy, the United States will contribute to healing the wounds of war and to postwar reconstruction of the Democratic Republic of Vietnam [North Vietnam] and throughout Indochina."

Five days later, 1 February, President Nixon sent a message to the Prime Minister of North Vietnam reiterating and expanding upon this pledge. The first two principles put forth in the President's message were:

(1) The Government of the United States of America will contribute to postwar reconstruction in North Vietnam without any political conditions. (2) Preliminary United States studies indicate that the appropriate programs for the United States contribution to postwar reconstruction will fall in the range of $3.25 billion of grant aid over 5 years. Other forms of aid will be agreed

upon between the two parties. This estimate is subject to revision and to detailed discussion between the Government of the United States and the Government of the Democratic Republic of Vietnam.

For the next two decades, the only aid given to any Vietnamese people by the United States was to those who left Vietnam and those who were infiltrated back in to stir up trouble. At the same time, the US imposed a complete embargo on trade and assistance to the country, which lasted until 1994.

Are the victims of the Vietnam War also to be found in generations yet unborn? Tens of millions of gallons of herbicides were unleashed over the country; included in this were quantities of dioxin, which has been called the most toxic man-made substance known; three ounces of dioxin, it is claimed, in the New York City water supply could wipe out the entire populace. Studies in Vietnam since the war have pointed to abnormally high rates of cancers, particularly of the liver, chromosomal damage, birth defects, long-lasting neurological disorders, etc. in the heavily-sprayed areas. Other victims were Americans. Thousands of Vietnam veterans fought for years to receive disability compensation, claiming irreparable damage from simply handling the toxic herbicides.

After the Second World War, the International Military Tribunal convened at Nuremberg, Germany. Created by the victorious Allies, the Tribunal sentenced to prison or execution numerous Nazis who pleaded that they had been "only following orders". In an opinion handed down by the Tribunal, it declared that "the very essence of the [Tribunal's] Charter is that individuals have international duties which transcend the national obligations of obedience imposed by the individual state."

During the Vietnam war, a number of young Americans refused military service on the grounds that the United States was committing war crimes in Vietnam and that if they took part in the war they too, under the principles laid down at Nuremberg, would be guilty of war crimes.

One of the most prominent of these cases was that of David Mitchell of Connecticut. At Mitchell's trial in September 1965, Judge William Timbers dismissed his defense as "tommyrot" and "degenerate subversion", and found the Nuremberg principles to be "irrelevant" to the case. Mitchell was sentenced to prison. Conservative columnist William F. Buckley, Jr., not celebrated as a champion of draft resistance, noted shortly afterward:

"I am glad I didn't have Judge Timbers' job. Oh, I could have scolded Mr. Mitchell along with the best of them. But I'd have to cough and wheeze and clear my throat during that passage in my catechism at which I explained to Mr. Mitchell wherein the Nuremberg Doctrine was obviously not at his disposal."

In 1971, Telford Taylor, the chief United States prosecutor at Nuremberg, suggested rather strongly that General William Westmoreland and high officials of the Johnson administration such as Robert McNamara and Dean Rusk could be found guilty of war crimes under criteria established at Nuremberg. Yet every American court and judge, when confronted by the Nuremberg defense, dismissed it without according it any serious consideration whatsoever.

The West has never been allowed to forget the Nazi holocaust. For 40 years there has been a continuous outpouring of histories, memoirs, novels, feature films, documentaries, television series ... played and replayed in every Western language; there have been museums, memorial sculptures, photo exhibitions, remembrance ceremonies ... Never Again! But who hears the voice of the Vietnamese peasant? Who has access to the writings of the Vietnamese intellectual? What was the fate of the Vietnamese Anne Frank? Where, asks the young American, is Vietnam?

From "Killing Hope: U.S. Military and CIA Interventions Since World War II"

The Myth of the "Uncensored War"
by Jeff Cohen

Of the many myths that mushroomed from the carnage of the Vietnam War, perhaps none is more specious than the fable about how a bold, aggressive mainstream media turned America against the war.

Let's begin with the My Lai massacre of March 1968, where hundreds of Vietnamese civilians were executed by American soldiers. My Lai would later be cited as proof of a mainstream press bent on sensationalizing U.S. atrocities in Vietnam.

The reality was just the opposite. Beginning months after My Lai, evidence of the massacre was presented to top national news media by Vietnam veteran Ron Ridenhour and others, but not one outlet would touch the story. It wasn't until November 1969, more than a year and a half after the My Lai slaughter, that the story was finally published by the small, alternative Dispatch News Service and dogged investigative reporter Seymour Hersh.

In the middle of the 20-month period of media silence on My Lai, an inexperienced lieutenant named Kerrey and his team of Navy Seals were sent into a "freefire zone" at Thanh Phong, under rules of engagement that had just been loosened. One wonders if the lives of Vietnamese civilians there or elsewhere could have been spared if mainstream U.S. journalists had been aggressive about My Lai, instead of burying the story for so long.

Myths and empty cliches flourish if unexamined. Professor Daniel Hallin of the University of California at San Diego conducted perhaps the most thorough study of U.S. media coverage of Vietnam, in light of the standard rhetoric that Vietnam had been an "uncensored war" showing its "true horror."

What Hallin found was a war, especially on TV, that was largely sanitized, as a result of media coziness with government and military sources and network TV policies against airing footage that might offend soldiers' families. Pictures of U.S. casualties were rare, Vietnamese civilian victims almost nonexistent.

It wasn't the mainstream media that turned the public against the war. Quite the contrary: It was the public—especially the ever-growing anti-war movement fortified by Vietnam veterans who spoke out against the war—that prodded mainstream media toward more skeptical coverage.

In February 1968, the Boston Globe (2/18/68) surveyed the editorial positions of 39 leading U.S. dailies with a combined circulation of 22 million and found that not one advocated withdrawal from Vietnam. But that was the position of millions of Americans who'd educated themselves about the war—not through the nightly news or Time magazine, but via alternative media or attending protests or talking to returning vets. Campus teach-ins on Vietnam began in 1965.

Walter Cronkite is often remembered for his uncharacteristic on-air commentary in 1968 (2/27/68) calling the war a "stalemate" and urging negotiations. But by 1968, a half-million U.S. troops were already in Vietnam. Professor Hallin's study found that, with few exceptions, network coverage prior to 1968 was "strongly supportive" of the war.

As for the country's turning against the war, Hallin concluded: "Television was more a follower than a leader of public opinion." And the mainstream media debate that intensified in 1968 tended to focus narrowly on the war's winnability not on the war's morality or its effect on the Vietnamese population, 2 million of whom were ultimately killed.

Though not a veteran, I played a minor role in the Winter Soldier hearings, which Vietnam vets convened in Detroit in January 1971 to try to communicate directly to the American people the horrors they'd experienced. In three days of testimony open to the press and public, dozens of veterans described—often tearfully—atrocities against Vietnamese they'd witnessed or participated in, events similar to and even more grisly than the killings at Thanh Phong.

The national hearings were dramatic and visual, but few major U.S. media bothered to cover them. Many of the veterans expressed hostility toward the media, blaming gung ho, pro-war coverage for deceiving them into going to Vietnam in the first place.

During particularly gripping testimony, one of the few mainstream camera crews present turned off its lights and packed up; the crew's exit sparked boos and jeers from the vets. That was the moment I became a media critic.

Extra!, the Bimonthly Newsletter of FAIR
130 W 25th St., New York, NY
Jeff Cohen is the founder of FAIR, a non-profit that reports on the media.

Saving Lt. Kerrey
by Colman McCarthy

As the lead officer of a seven-man Navy SEAL squad in Vietnam's Mekong Delta on the night of Feb. 25, 1969, Lt. Bob Kerrey obeyed orders to "eliminate the local political leadership of the South Vietnamese communists" said to be in the village of Thanh Phong. Thirty-two years later, Kerrey, elected to the U.S. Senate in 1988, calls that mission of elimination "a tragedy." Between 13 and 20 unarmed civilians—mostly women and children—were killed.

"I have been haunted by it for 32 years," Kerrey says.

As a low-level twenty-five-year-old field worker carrying out the military policies of the Johnson-Westmoreland McNamara-Rostow-Bundy-Nixon-Kissinger cabal, Kerrey takes responsibility for the slaughter, saying that the civilians were mistakenly killed as the squad returned fire. One squad member has claimed that the civilians were rounded up and killed, which Kerrey and the rest of the squad deny. The dead of Thanh Phong were part of the overall toll of 2.6 million Vietnamese killed from 1959 to 1974.

It is astonishing that three decades later—ample time presumably for reflection and reevaluation—Kerrey continues to endorse war making. "When contemplating war," he said in a speech to tomorrow's officers at the Virginia Military Institute April 18, "we must abandon euphemism and answer the question does the cause justify sending young men out to kill other human beings?"

It's only the occasional messiness of military violence Kerrey opposes. Efficient killing yes, sloppy killing no. Operation Just Cause, not Operation Bad Cause. Obey the rules of war, while regretting when war is unruly.

As a senator, Kerrey was not known as a critic of America's well-funded war machine. As a combat veteran, he has kept far away from the thinking of former warriors such as Howard Zinn, Phillip Berrigan, Garry Davis, Heinrich Boll, Jacques de Bollardiere, Tolstoy and Francis of Assisi. All returned home to become pacifists.

Zinn, describing himself as "an eager bombardier" in World War II, became a voice for nonviolence: "I had moved away from my own rather orthodox view that there are just wars and unjust wars, to a universal rejection of war as a solution to any human problem."

Berrigan, also a World War II veteran, is currently imprisoned for anti-war actions. He writes: "There will be no healing for veterans, myself included, until we disavow war completely, until we disarm the bomb and the killing machine and ourselves. Why are we alive except to unmask the Big Lie of war? Where are veterans from all the empire's wars in the struggle for disarmament, for justice and peace? They should ask themselves, 'Can I remedy my violence, can I heal myself until I try to heal the body of humankind from the curse of war?'"

As the haunted Bob Kerrey expresses remorse about his deeds at the Thanh Phong, for which he received the Bronze Star, the former warrior is receiving supportive words from fellow Vietnam veterans now in the Senate. In the April 29 Washington Post, Max Cleland, Chuck Hagel and John Kerry sound the bugle: War is "a serious proposition and should never be undertaken lightly or without the highest regard for those who bear the ultimate burden."

Such militaristic cant means that the people killed in Vietnam, on whatever side, were duped then and are dishonored now. It also means that members of the peace movement, from the War Resisters League to Pax Christi, need to double their efforts, not only to condemn military violence in the some 35 wars or conflicts now raging globally but to educate the young that other ways exist—moral, effective and nonviolent ways—to solve conflicts than by fists, guns, armies and bombs. If the Bob Kerreys of the 1960s had had the chance for that kind of education, perhaps they would have answered the call to resist, not comply.

From The National Catholic Reporter May 11, 2001

9

Racing to End Racism

The man said, "I believe they are shorthanded, but I don't believe they're employing any colored boys in the reconversion jobs.

I said, "What makes you think I'm colored? They done took such words off of jobs in New York State by law."

I know he wanted to say, "But they ain't took the black off of your face."

Langston Hughes, The Best of Simple 187
(1961)

Satchel Paige Is My Main Model
by Roger Wilkins

I don't believe in the perfectibility of white people anymore. I used to think that there was no more thrilling story in all
of human history than that by virtue of the American Constitution, the decency of some whites and the valor of blacks that a
people were being raised out of slavery into equality in the greatest nation the world had ever seen. God, how I loved America in
1950, when that was the essence of my understanding of this place!
I thought then that prejudice was an individual thing that would
die in heart after heart after the Constitution and the true humanity of black people were demonstrated to the people of our country.

I didn't know about the pervasive nature of racism then or
about the bitterness of competition, about the genocide practiced
on native Americans or about how the worst aspects of Calvinism
had come to influence the worst instincts of a whole people.

And, I hadn't the faintest inkling of the essence of racism,
which is the evasion of individual responsibility by finding scape-
goats for disappointment, failure and bad behavior and is also the
imposition of a white fantasy upon peoples who look different and
who have a different culture. For instance, even I thought for a
long time that all Mexicans, with big sombreros on their heads,
sat in the sun, cuddling their knees and saying "Mañana." I was an
American before I knew it.

White people in this country insist on telling those of us
who are not white exactly who we are, though they don't have a
clue about what they are talking about. One of the great Justices,
Roger Taney, told blacks that the Constitution said we couldn't be
citizens. The American government told us in World War II that
we weren't good enough to fight for democracy, except in segregated units and usually behind the lines. White Americans told us
that we were shiftless, unclean and licentious. In the heyday of
affirmative action they told us that we were unqualified. And now,
the neoconservatives are telling us that we are free. All of that is
bullshit. The clearest thing I was ever told by an outsider was by

that stewardess on the Air India flight—that I was a man and an American. And I have fought off the fantasies that white people have tried to impose on me ever since.

And, there was one man outside the circle of my own family who helped me to do that more than any other. There were lots of beacons of course. W.E.B. DuBois, Martin Luther King, Jr., Malcolm X, Mary McLeod Bethune, Joe Louis and Adam Clayton Powell were among them. But, Jack Roosevelt Robinson was my main man.

Now, Satchel Paige is my main model. A baseball historian once told me that in one of those interrcolor all-star games that they had before organized baseball decided that black men were good enough to play a children's game with white men, that a newcomer slammed a home run off Paige. Paige asked his shortstop who the newcomer was and was told that the man's name was Ralph Kiner, and that he had been rookie of the year and had led the National League in home runs. "Remember, Satch," the shortstop said, "he can hit the fast ball." The next time Kiner came up, Paige, against the advice of his catcher, threw three fast balls past Kiner and then said to his shortstop, "Nobody can hit Satch's fast ball."

That's the game I know. Two guys take turns on the mound firing their best blazers. The one who's still out there firing when the sun goes down wins. That's my game.

But, if it hadn't been for Jackie Robinson, I probably wouldn't have gotten a chance to play my game. Jackie changed the way we all think of ourselves. As an American, I grew up believing in heroes the Lone Ranger, for instance.

Jackie put human dimensions on heroism. He was as fiercely competitive a man as ever lived, as far as I can tell. But when conditions for the race called for it, he reined in his fire under the most severe provocations—as when he couldn't stay with the Dodgers in segregated St. Louis, or when some "bush" ball players put black cats on the field to taunt him—and just played superb baseball. He was humble and quiet that year, as the needs of his people required him to be. But after he had proved himself in his rookie year and had paved the way for others to come, he became his full competitive, slashing self and he seemed to be saying, "No white folks going to cut me down ever again."

There were others after that. Bill Russell of the Celtics, for instance, who was proud, fierce, superb and a winner. And there was Jimmy Brown, a runner unlike any we have ever seen, who was proud enough to walk away at the top of his game. But, Jackie was the first and the fullest human being. He and the other black athletes engaged white people on fields and courts where there were rules and umpires and where white people had to play fair. Fields of play became human proving grounds where blacks had a reasonable shot at disproving the white fantasy about their inferiority. Watching Jackie, somehow I decided that I would do that on the sloping grounds of government, philanthropy and journalism, where there are no umpires and where white people cheat and demean blacks every day. I took my fast ball to those fields because Jackie had taught me that a black man need never again submit his psyche to the cruelties of white people's racist fantasies. Jackie also helped teach me that I was an American. Jackie was a fish.

President Ronald Reagan called me up here at the lake one day to complain about something I had written in the Star. If I were he, I would have complained too. Any fair reading of that column would reveal that I had called him an ignorant bigot and any fair reading of my mind would reveal that that is exactly what I think. Blacks used to laugh at white people who would deny bigotry by asserting, "One of my best friends is a Negro." But people haven't been that crude for years. But Ronald Reagan called to say that he knew about bigotry, because he had had a black teammate in college; he and his white teammates had been so offended by racial epithets thrown at the black by the other team that they had turned a 14-14 half-time tie into a 43-14 rout. He also talked about his Catholic father, who wouldn't sleep in a place that wouldn't admit Jews.

Well, "Pretty is as pretty does," as Gram used to say, so I argued with the President about his policies, which are sure to hurt the poor and the minorities. I was polite to the President, but I didn't back off. We had no more agreement at the end of our civil conversation than when we started talking.

When I got off the phone, Patricia said: "I'm so proud of

212

you. There you are, talking to the President of the United States and you didn't give up one inch of your honor."

I thought about that last night when I read something else I wrote in the Star arguing, on the basis of a trip to Mississippi, that the Voting Rights Act shouldn't be gutted, as Senator Strom Thurmond and a lot of other politicians seem to want to do.

A few days after I got back from Mississippi, I took my daughter, Amy, to visit with Uncle Roy before she goes off on her first real job ....

Uncle Roy is old now and he bends over in his chair. He sees best to his left and Amy sat on the floor holding his hand and kissing his arm. He loves her so. When she would move away, he would put out his left hand, looking for her and she would come back and that fine old man would smile at her and that splendid young woman would smile at him.

Looking at them, loving them, I realized something. Because some white people are so resistant to chapge and some powerful white people dissemble and misuse power so, Uncle Roy believes that we will achieve America's constitutional promises more than I do and I believe more than Amy does.

That is not a promising trend, so I would say to Senator Thurmond—and others who would destroy the Voting Rights Act: Let my people vote or there is apt to be great American sorrow in the time of my grandchildren and also yours.

But, gut away though they will, there will always be honorable black people to come back and to fight another day. I've always thought that if I have fifteen lucid moments before I die, I'll want to look back and see that I tried to act with honor, fifteen minutes by fifteen minutes throughout my life. The struggle of life is not won with one glorious moment like Reggie Jackson's five straight home runs in a recent World Series-wonderful and thrilling though that was-but a continual struggle in which you keep your dignity intact and your powers at work, over the long course of a lifetime."

"A Man's Life: an Autobiography"
Simon & Shuster 1982

From Prisoner to Peacemaker
by Carl Upchurch

It is long past time for African-Americans to take their future into their own hands: to protest the slaughter of black males in urban settings, to be outraged at the unprecedented number of black children who live in poverty, to stem the exploding prison population and the epidemic of HIV among black men, and to acknowledge that the unbridled killing of poor people in America's death chambers is a national disgrace.

We can generalize forever about how "they" see us, treat us, and feel about us. Such grumbling may satisfy some conditioned reaction in us to be victims and therefore not responsible, but it does nothing to change our circumstances or improve our children's lives. The hard truth. as it relates to race and class, is that most people, black and white, who live outside of poor communities don't care about how poor people live as long they don't impinge on their lives. If we continue to wait for "them" to fix "us," it will never happen. We won't achieve equality until we respect ourselves, and we won't respect ourselves until we take responsibility for our lives.

There is a predictable pattern to the lives of most black inner-city boys. I say boys only because I was one, with no authority to give you a first-person account of the lives of black inner-city girls except to tell you that both begin in poverty, and both are surrounded by drugs, violence, and gangs. The pattern of young black urban males is that they are destined, for the most part, to grow up to be drug users and/or sellers, to become proficient with street weapons, and to end up either dead by age twenty-one or cycling through the criminal justice system, or both.

My formative years were spent on the streets. I used weapons and drugs, joined gangs, served time in prison. My life was a textbook example of the pattern—until I reached Western State Penitentiary. It was there, because of timing, maturity, and the people I met, that I was able to challenge those patterns and begin my recovery process.

I arrived at Western a cynical, angry smartass. My reputa-

214

tion was that of a dangerous man, and I played it for everything it was worth. I made weapons and collected scars and never thought beyond my own survival.

I started taking classes for the flimsiest of reasons: They got me out of other responsibilities. But as time passed, I found myself interested in what I was hearing in those classrooms. Looking back, it's clear that the opportunity to go to school came along just when I was ready to understand that education is a gift.

In my jail cell at Western, teased by self-discovery, I began to see the world in a new way. In the context of the stories, biographies, autobiographies, poetry, and history that I read, I began to evaluate my own life and my many shortcomings. I was challenged by a wide range of authors to examine the behaviors that had brought me to this place of despair. And eventually I glimpsed my humanity, small fragments of my connectedness to a wider universe of common decency. This connectedness served as a powerful reminder of the potential salvageability of self. It was in me at birth but was buried by poverty, racism, social inequities, anger, and hopelessness.

In solitary confinement I started consciously to re-create myself. Twenty-five years later, I'm still trying to reconcile life's inevitable contradictions and be a better human being. This endless struggle transcends all social barriers. including race and class. Yet for people born into an environment rife with social disadvantages, the questions are monumental: How do we transcend and then transform such environments while simultaneously protecting the inalienable rights of those who, for whatever reason, are unable to protect themselves? How do we connect across those social gaps that segregate our efforts?

I believe these are the critical questions of our day. And I believe we accomplish precious little by consistently moaning about the inequities instead of taking actions to rectify them.

My goal, therefore. is to challenge Black America—especially poor Black America—to awaken to the possibilities that unfold once we take responsibility for our own lives. This is not to deny that society bears responsibility for our condition. It does. But first we must decide, one by one, that we will not be victims any longer. We will not be niggers any longer.

Change comes from within, and before we can change the world around us, we must change ourselves one by one. We must look in our mirrors and acknowledge our responsibility for our lives: "I'm the one carrying a gun." "I'm the one shooting dope into my arm." "I'm the one getting drunk every day." "I'm the one who dropped out of school." "I'm the one who would rather steal than work." "I'm the one who uses violence, or threats of violence, to make my way through the world." "I'm the one setting an example for the children around me." "I'm the one killing my brother." "My behavior contributes to my niggerization.'"

As African-Americans, we can neutralize niggerization by relying on ourselves, our ingenuity, our history, our church, our faith, and our intelligence. But we must do it together, as a people, rejecting the mantle of inferiority, settling for nothing less than total equality. There are too many young Carl Upchurches out there suffering from a sense of worthlessness. Too many of us are wasting vital moments of our future on self-destructive, abusive, pointless activities that are speeding us to our graves. Those of us who are already engaged in the lifelong process of recovering from this disease of self-hatred must take the lead if we are to eradicate the existence of a second-class citizenry mired in poverty and racial hatred.

Two things, at least, must happen to break the cycle. First, we who inflict the wounds must acknowledge our racial biases and our role in the all-too-frequent eruptions of overt violence. Second, the poor must use the lessons of history to empower themselves to demand that they be treated with the innate dignity to which they are entitled.

Social change has always bubbled up from the bottom. Those on top—the ones who have attained the power and grabbed the money appear little inclined to change the status quo voluntarily. Change can't occur until the poor unite to articulate and support each other's struggle for justice—to refuse to tolerate injustice.

Education is one of the keys to our cultural empowerment. The time is upon us to seriously consider education-education of our selves, education especially of our children and of those ineareerated as an essential ingredient for lifting ourselves out of this morass.

The greatest gift an education gives is perspective. By now you should understand how remarkable it was for me to discover that someone, somewhere, was thinking as I thought, feeling what I felt, hurting as I hurt. Just knowing that was empowering. It validated me somehow, gave me a sense of self-worth-and the courage to persevere in the face of monumental obstacles.

We have to stop thinking of education as the simple accumulation of facts. Education is power. That is what we have to give to ourselves and our children. No less important, we have to give it to our brothers and sisters who are trapped in prisons because they've never learned they have the power to change their lives.

It's more complicated, though, than just preaching to our children to stay in school. Since we've passed our own attitudes on to our children, it's no wonder they believe that school is something they're stuck doing until the rest of life comes along. We, and they, need to rethink, reprogram, reposition these old attitudes. A broad spectrum of African-Americans have used education to deniggerize themselves. Malcolm X; Martin Luther King, Jr.; Maya Angelou; Carter G. Woodson; W.E.B. Du Bois; Cornel West; and many others. All these men and women hold the road map for change. They tell us in every way that education is essential to any movement toward freedom. Even in our most desperate hours—during slavery—we understood one fundamenal truth: that we must become educated to make progress in this culture. Whether at Harvard or Howard, at Princeton or the penitentiary, education is our key.

Maya Angelou's words sent me the clearest message: "It doesn't natter what you read. Just read something." I live by that today. Our iistory, our journey toward freedom, our abilities to alleviate our burdens, all can be challenged with an education. And if there is one thing that we have consistently outlined, it is that without knowledge, without knowing, without learning, we're dead.

I was a nigger in the womb. Not just black, not just male--& nigger. Centuries of contempt for my race were laid on my infant shoulders the instant I was born. But God's grace was there too, at the center of my soul. No matter how hard I tried to kill it, my humanness, my innate need to connect never disappeared. And when I finally went looking for it, starting in my cell at Western, it was there waiting.

Every single one of us must stop participating in our own oppression. No matter what our life circumstances are, we must assume the responsibility to improve them. We must stop living passive lives, content to be herded around like cattle. Deniggerization is meaningless unless we acknowledge our role in perpetuating niggerization. It's long past time for us to declare that the racial damage that we have inherited through generations of cultural assault will stop with us.

Where we begin does not necessarily represent where we will end. Indeed, many of us are born into circumstances that do not lend themselves to an easy, comfortable journey. Some have a political ideology that promotes the rather simplistic and racist notion that some intrinsic quality accounts for our negative behavior. These folks accuse us of deserving our plight at every level. Others essentially disagree with that theory but still demean us by asserting that we need special help to overcome our unfortunate circumstances. Both approaches conspire to maintain a status quo that perpetuates the misery we endure.

This book is meant for all those who are living as I once lived. If you get nothing else from it, get this: I would not be where I am today, who I am today, had I waited for "society" to rescue me. The history you have read here marks me as a blessed man. Blessed to have survived. Blessed to have realized that I held the keys to my own future. Blessed that the right people crossed my path at the right time, when I was ready to hear what they had to say and act on it.

South Philly used to be the center of my world. It seemed to have an inescapable gravitational pull, like a cosmic black hole into which I would eventually have disappeared. Some special people helped me realize that I could escape that deadly gravity and pushed me to work hard enough to break free. If I could do it, so can countless other "lost" youths. But somebody has to tell them that. Somebody has to lift their eyes to a wider horizon. Somebody has to inspire hope within them.

I finally understood that, in the end, I may not be responsible for what I was, but I am responsible for what I am, what I hope to become, and what I hope my children will become. I'm the role model now. I cannot possibly demand moral behavior from others, demand 'integrity and forthrightness, if my own life does not exemplify it.

from "Convicted in the Womb"
by Carl Upchurch

On the Streets of Black Washington DC
by David Nicholson

Maybe things would have been different if instead of only being born to the culture I'd grown up in it as well. But I spent much of my childhood in Jamaica, and when my parents separated and my mother returned to America with her four children, this middle-class boy, whose dentist father and high school teacher mother had sent him to the Queen's Preparatory School in Kingston, was completely unprepared for what he found on the predatory streets and playgrounds of black Washington, D.C. .

I had no sense of rhythm and I couldn't dance. I couldn't and still can't dribble well enough to play basketball. For years the purpose and the verbal agility of "the dozens" (which we called joneing) eluded me.

The worst, though, was the casual violence—everybody seemed to want to fight. Someonb pushed someone else in line waiting to go out to the playground. Someone said something about someone else's mother. Someone said someone had said something about a third someone else's mother. Sex didn't matter (some girls terrified all but the most fearless boys) and neither did the pre-text. If a serious enough offense had been committed, or even merely alleged, push soon came to shove as books were dropped and fists raised and the aggrieved partiessurrounded by a crowd gleefully chanting "Fight! Fight!" circled each other with murder in their eyes.

Raised to believe gentlemen obeyed two essential com-mandments—they did not hit girls, and they did not hit anyone who wore glasses—I would have been fixed in an insoluble moral quandary if a glasses-wearing girl had dared me to fight. But some-how it was arranged that I would fight another boy in the fifth grade class of Mrs. Omega P. Millen (so named, she'd told us, be-cause her mother had forsworn more children after her birth). I don't remember how it happened, but someone probably offered the usual reasons—Furman had said something about my mother or I'd said something about his. The truth, though, was that Furman, fair-skinned and freckled, with curly, ginger-colored hair, was as much of an outsider because of his color as I was because of my accent. A fight would decide which of us belonged.

We met in an alley near school. When it was over, the spectators who'd gathered, jamming the mouth of the alley so that Furman and I had to be escorted in, must have been as disappointed as ticketholders who'd mortgaged their homes for ringside seats at the Tyson-Spinks title fight. Furman and I circled each other warily until he pushed me or I pushed him or someone in the crowd pushed us into each other. After a moment or two of wrestling on the dirty brick paving, rolling around on the trash and broken glass, I shoved Furman away and stood.

Memory plays tricks, of course, but I don't think I was afraid. Not as afraid as I would be later, when, coming home from the High's Dairy Store on Rhode Island Avenue with a quart of ice cream on Sunday, some bigger boy, backed by two or three of his cronies demanded a nickel. If I said I didn't have one, they'd leave me to choose between two humiliations—having my pockets searched or fighting all three, one after the other. And I certainly wasn't as afraid as I would be when, as I walked home alone, four or five boys jumped me because I'd strayed into a neighborhood where outsiders had to be ready to fight just to walk down the street.

So what I remember feeling in the alley was not fear but puzzlement. The fight with Furman had seemed like a joke right up to the moment we'd squared off against one another. I hadn't taken it seriously, and now it felt like a piece of foolishness that had gone too far. No one else seemed to have enough sense to call a halt, so it was up to me. I found my glasses, put them on, and announced I wasn't going to fight. I'd done nothing to Furman. He'd done nothing to me. And, besides, one of us might get hurt.

There was a moment of silence and then a low grumbling of disappointment as the boys and girls who'd come expecting to see a fight realized there wasn't going to be one. I went home, one or two friends walking with me, assuring me that it was all right, I didn't have to fight if I didn't want to.

But I knew they were wrong. And I knew they knew it too.

It is a terrible thing to be condemned by others as a coward, but it is even worse to condemn yourself as one. For that reason, I brood about that time in the alley more often than is probably healthy, even given that I'm a writer and my stock in trade is memories and the past. Lately, however, I've been thinking about it as I read, or read about, the new violence-laden autobiographies by black men—Nathan McCall's Makes Me Wanna Holler, Kody Scott's Monster. I don't listen to rap music (the phrase has always struck me as an oxymoron), but I'm aware that the genre has become one of art-imitating-life-imitating-art as entertainers like Tupac Shakur are arrested and charged with crimes ranging from sexual assault to murder. And then, if all that wasn't enough, there were the Tshirts and sweatshirts featuring Mike Tyson's face and the ominous legend "I'll be back," and those bearing the legend "Shut Up Bitch, or I'll O.J. You."

More and more it's begun to seem, as we enter the middle of the 1990s, that violence and black men go together as well as the fingers of the hand make up the fist. What's most troubling is that not only has the media seized on America's enduring bogeyman, the bad nigger, as an object of fear and pity, but that black men and women have also gleefully embraced that image. It's as if a generation, soured by disappointment in the post-civil rights era, has given up all hope of achievement and decided that it's almost as good to be feared as it is to be respected.

And so where does that leave me, who long ago eschewed violence, whether from fear or cowardice or simply because I couldn't see the point of it? Feeling at forty-three much the same as I'd felt facing Furman in the alley—that I'd been given a choice that really wasn't a choice. If I fought, I'd become like the rest of the boys. If I didn't, I'd be a sissy. What I really wanted was just to be me.

Perhaps I'm making too much out of all this. Perhaps that afternoon in the alley was part of some perfectly normal rite of passage. Perhaps all boys test each other to find Out who will fight and who will not. And perhaps by not fighting Furman or, later, any of a number of bullies and thugs, I threw away the opportunity to earn their respect. Perhaps.

All I knew then was that the rules were different from those I'd learned growing up in Jamaica, and that while almost all of the children I'd known there were also black, violence was of mystifying importance to the black boys of Washington, D.C. One reason for the difference, I see now, was poverty. My school chums in Jamaica were all middle-class, but most of us in Mrs. Millen's (and later Miss Garner's) classroom were poor enough to relish our mid-morning snack of government-issue oatmeal cookies, soft and sweet at their centers, and half-pints of warm, slightly sour milk. On winter days, windows closed and the radiators steaming, the stale air in the classroom smelled faintly of sweat and dust and urine and unwashed clothes. I remember it as the smell of poverty and of crippling apathy.

Small wonder, then, that because so many of the boys had precious little except their bodies with which to celebrate life, violence became part of that celebration. It offered them a way of feeling masculine as well as the chance to be feared, to feel important.

But I never understood the tribal nature of the violence, the randomness and the gratuitousness of it, until I saw how they'd probably been introduced to it before they were aware of what was happening, before they were old enough to understand there might be other choices. I was driving past a public housing project one gray winter afternoon when I saw two boys facing each other on the brown lawn. Each boy howled, runny-nosed in fear, as the man towering over them directed their tiny fists at each other. They couldn't have been much older than three.

Years after my abortive fight with Furman in the alley, I had a summer job downtown in the District Building, working for an agency of the city government. Five of us, all high school or college students, were summer help. We spent the day sorting building plans and building permits in a narrow, dusty back room lined with filing cabinets and ceiling-high wooden shelves. Sometimes we had to deal with citizens seeking copies of plans or permits, but most of the time we were left alone to work by ourselves, only nominally supervised.

One of the other buys (I'll call him Earl) was a freshman or sophomore at Howard. Under other circumstances—if we'd met, say, in one of the integrated church coffee houses or drama groups I'd begun to frequent because they allowed me the freedom to be black and myself in ways segregated situations did not—perhaps Earl and I might have been friends. Skinny and bespectacled, we looked enough alike to be brothers. We read books and valued them. We spoke standard English. All of that, of course, set us apart from the other boys. For that reason, instead of becoming friends with Earl, I decided to hate him.

The other boys encouraged me, aiding and abetting, but they were only accomplices, because I had made up my own mind. We goaded Earl. We taunted him. Finally, one of the other boys told me Earl had dropped some of my files and picked them up without putting them back in order. Earl hadn't, of course, and I knew it. But I also knew my choice was to fight him or become identified with him. And Earl, with his suspiciously effeminate air of striving for refinement, was not someone I wanted to be identified with.

What happened was worse than if I had beaten him, worse than if he had fought back and beaten me. Earl simply refused to fight. He crumpled, stood crying, holding his glasses, begging me to leave him alone. I didn't hit him, but I joined with the others in making him do my work as well as his own while the rest of us sat drinking sodas or coffee, watching and making jokes.

I wish now I'd done something else. That I'd refused to fight Earl. That I'd suggested we join forces to resist the others. That I'd gone, on his behalf, to complain to our supervisor. But I didn't. And, sickened, I learned a lesson—it felt no better to threaten violence against someone incapable of resisting than it had been to be the one threatened and equally incapable of resistance.

What's missing here is the kind Ellisonian epiphany—I am who I am, and no one else—that might have long ago allowed me to let go of all this. Instead, I've had to make do with patchwork realizations and small comforts.

One evening a few years ago I was standing on the street I grew up on, talking with a man I'd known since we were both children. He is younger than I am, so I hadn't known him well. Still, I knew him well enough to know he'd been comfortable on that street in ways I had not. So I was surprised when all of a sudden he told me he had always admired me. Puzzled but curious, I asked why, and he said it was because I hadn't stayed in the neighborhood; I'd left it to live other places and see other things.

For a moment I was speechless. I knew, of course, that there were qualities the apparent cool and the readiness to deal that we call an ability to hang—that he possessed and I lacked. I envied him those. But it was inconceivable he might also envy me.

Hard on the heels of that realization came another. Life was a series of stages and I'd passed through one, but precisely because I'd long ago left that street I hadn't known it: violence was a function of age, even for black men (like the one I was talking to) who weren't middle-class and who lacked intellectual pretensions. A wishful capacity for it might remain one of the ways we defined ourselves, and were defined; however, the truth was that after a certain point even the bad boys were forced to realize they were no longer boys and that suddenly but almost imperceptibly they'd become one step too slow to continue in the game. It's then that, for all but the most stubborn, violence becomes a matter of ritual and voyeurism: football on Sundays, heated arguments in the barbershop, the heavyweight championship on pay-per-view.

During that same sojourn in the old neighborhood, I was walking to church one winter Sunday morning. I was almost there when I heard them, and then I rounded the corner and saw a man and a woman screaming at each other beside the iron fence in front of the churchyard while a little boy watched. A few late parishioners walked past, conscientiously ignoring them.

It's been long enough now so that the details are hazy. But I remember that he pushed her, and then she pushed him, and that they were screaming at each other. And I remember their faces, his young and still beardless, adorned with that practiced air of aggrievement I remembered from my childhood after one boy had sucker-punched another and gotten caught by Mrs. Millen or Miss Garner, an insolent glare that said, "Why you lookin' at me for? I ain't did shit." The girl's face would have been pretty except that it was twisted with tears and anger. The little boy stood a little away, looking at them, and what was terrifying about it was that his face showed no expression at all.

I stepped into it, right between them, begging them to

calm down, circling with them, hands out to keep them apart. He was bigger than I am, and younger. He may have pushed me once, trying to reach past to get at her. She bent to pick up a brick and lunged after him. I held her back.

Finally the police came.

An hour or so later, when I was finally home, I started to shake, thinking about what I'd done, thinking about what could have happened if he'd had a gun or a knife, or if the two of them had turned on me. Mostly, though, I thought about the little boy, looking up at me from under the hood of his parka when I stooped to ask if he was all right. He'd nodded, almost diffidently, nothing in his eyes at all that I could read. And I had thought, as I patted him on the shoulder and said, "Everything's going to be okay," that I was lying, that it wasn't going to be okay at all.

Because in that moment I could see the past-and the futures-of so many of the boys I'd first encountered on the streets and playgrounds around First Street and Rhode Island Avenue. They'd all had the same look in their eyes, the same distancing of themselves from what was happening around them. In time, I thought, this boy, too, would go on to acquire the same wariness, a quality of disguised hurt, a quality of removal and disavowal. In some important way he, like them, would cease to care. It wasn't just that these boys had come to expect to be blamed when they really had done nothing, although that was part of it. No, what was really important was that they'd made it so that it didn't matter any more. Because they'd long ago discovered that the way to survive was to hide their real selves from the world. And no matter what happened, they would never, ever, let anything touch them.

I write this now for the boy I once was who almost had his love of books and poetry beaten out of him. I write it for Earl, wherever and whoever he is, as a way of asking his forgiveness for having humiliated him in a vain attempt to avenge my own humiliations. I write it for the boy whose parents fought in front of the church that winter morning, hoping he made it whole into manhood despite the odds against him. And I write it for the boys whose names I never knew or can't remember, the ones whose eyes in elementary school were deader than any child's should ever be. Now I understand, I feel the pain they could not admit. In this way perhaps I can also one day forgive them.

"On the Streets of Washington DC"
by David Nicholson

True Heroes: Black Male Teachers
by Colman McCarthy

Of the 27 faculty members teaching 549 minority students at Garrison Elementary School in the Shaw neighborhood of Washington D.C., two are black males. Darryll Vann has 26 boys and girls in his kindergarten class, Hassan Abdullah 21 in his first grade class.

In the educational and moral lives of their children, the two teachers stand, even loom, as much more than educators. They are among the few stable black males with whom the children have consistent contact. Vann and Abdullah are among the few black males regularly delivering gifts of compassion and discipline. The two men are educationally successful, both as teachers and citizens, and enter the doors at Garrison everyday knowing that, for the children, a lot—perhaps everything—is riding on the early elementary years. To the 47 boys and girls in their classes, Vann and Abdullah are the role models about whom the children can reflect, "If I become like my teacher one day, I'll have turned out well."

How Vann and Abdullah are using their professional and personal energies to stir the minds of some of the poorest children in one of the nation's most administratively chaotic school systems is a story of two idealists pitting their compassion against such entrenched forces as low pay, conventional educational thinking and, often enough, disastrous home and neighborhood environments.

Garrison Elementary, named after William Lloyd Gaprison, the 19th century pacifist and abolitionist, is at 12th and S Streets, NW, about a mile north of the White House and two miles west of the U.S. Capitol. Geography is about the only link to power and wealth. Ninety-six percent of the students are eligible for free or reduced price lunches. More than 90 percent live in fatherless households. Despite the social-reform successes of some local churches and civic groups, every urban blight—high unemployment, crime, street violence, drug addiction—is in the Shaw neighborhood.

One result of these combined negatives shows up annually in the Garrison reading scores. Of the 109 District elementary schools, Garrison children had the 9th lowest: 48.8 percent were reading below the basic level, with 37.7 at basic. Twelve percent were proficient and 1.5 advanced. Seventy nine D.C. schools had a higher number of advanced readers. The Stanford 9 reading achievement tests were given in May 1997 to first through sixth graders.

As males in a traditionally female profession, Vann and Abdullah are in the conspicuous minority. In the faculties of America's 61,165 public elementary schools, only 11 percent are men. In high schools, the number quadruples to 44 pet-cent. Being black males, Vann and Abdull1ali are minorities within a minority, and a vanishing one at that. Robert Chase, president of the National Education Association, reports that within a decade the percentage of minority public school teachers "is expected to shrink to an all-time low of five percent, while 41 percent of American students will be minorities ....Classrooms everywhere are starved for good teachers of color, particularly black and Hispanic men." Late in 1997, the NEA awarded grants to 11 affiliates to recruit minority teachers.

My personal involvement with Garrison began in the early 1990s when, through the Center for Teaching Peace, a non-profit my wife and I began in 1985, we funded an after school program in nonviolent conflict resolution. Many of my students at the University of Maryland and Bethesda-Clievy Chase High School served as tutors. In 1994, my son John McCarthy began Elementary Baseball, a federally funded literacy and sports program that brings in Superior Court judges, college and high school students to tutor Garrison children. More than 40 of my students have served in the program.

On one of my first visits to Garrison, I learned that the principled principal, Andrea Robinson, had been laboring mightily to recruit male teachers, especially black males. Vann and Abdullah are two rarities that resulted.

When all the politicians end their speeches on school reform, when all the editorial writers are through praising or damning vouchers, when all the task forces finish recommending one cure-all or another, it's the lone elementary school teacher six or seven hours a day with the children who must cut through the baloney and educate. Even then, children in kindergarten have already been taught, either for good or ill, by the adults at home and by the television. Psychologists report that about 80 percent of a person's character is shaped by the age eight.

Ebullience marks the teaching style of Darryll Vann, in his fourth year at Garrison. While speaking animatedly to his students, and with dreadlocks swinging long and loose, he moves around the room athletically. Naturally enough. He was a professional mountain biker who won prize money on the trails. At 46, and a husband for 20 years and the father of a teenager, he came to kindergarten teaching in mid-career, after doing financially well as a fashion photographer for 12 years.

One recent afternoon, while the last of his charges had found a lost lunch pail and was out the door, Vann sat near the classroom aquarium and spoke of his teaching. He is convinced that "there needs to be a positive male influence in the early grades, for the kids to see a man who nurtures. A lot of them don't have that at home."

Aware that the children see him as different because he is a man, Vann teaches them by example that masculinity means being passionate about reading. Everyday, large amounts of time are set aside for books: " I call parents to give them comments about their children and they tell me, `Mr. Vann, my son wants to get a gerbil but he's more interested in reading a book because you do that in class. He wants me to go out and buy books.' In these households, there might be five books total. Now parents are being forced by the children to get books, which is what I want to have happen.

"I want children to make the demand. Reading has to be interesting. If it's a labor, no one's going to read. I read newspapers to my children. And they see me reading the newspaper. They want to know what I'm reading. Then we sit and read it together. When they see adults reading, internally they say, `that must be something I need to do.' If they're around adults yelling at each other, they say, `that's what I should be doing, so I need to yell.'"

In the four years I've known Darryll Vann—seeing his

classroom liveliness, observing him coaching for Elementary Baseball, listening to his views on education—he has been the model of a loving teacher. How loving? Vann estimates that he spends several hundred dollars a year of personal money on his students: bargain hunting for books, supplies and equipment. He loads up at garage sales in the affluent neighborhoods of Washington. His salary is well under $30,000, that sum being the bonus that several D.C. public school officials—including double dipping retired generals—received last year on top of their $100,000-plus salaries. Vann, who works part-time at a bike shop to supplement his income, is only passingly rankled by the scandal of that.

It is much the same for Hassan Abdullah. He is 48, in his fifth year at Garrison and 13th of elementary school teaching. Raised in a Baptist family in the District, he embraced the Muslim faith in 1974 after graduating from the old D.C. Teachers College. "I'm a teacher," he said during a lunch break down the corridor from his second floor classroom, "because it's God's will. For a long time, I tried to avoid going into grade school teaching. I thought that it just wouldn't look right for a man to be in a classroom with little children."

After earning a masters degree in early childhood education and working some 10 years as a consultant to state and federal school programs, Abdullah, obedient to God, was in the classroom. "From what parents have shared with me," he says, "and from my own observations, male teachers—particularly AfricanAmerican males—are making a dramatic difference in the lives of young developing children. It's because so many come from one-parent homes, and that parent is the mother. A lot of our boys—and girls, too—have not had a nurturing relationship with a male. As a result, my students tend to listen to me. They try to adhere to the classroom rules. There's a difference between boys and girls. If you ask girls to attend to a task, they go right away. With boys, you have to watch them all the way, or they'll deviate. Most of the boys don't seem to respect women, not the way I was raised."

Abdullah—like Darryll Vann, he is athletic, having been a three letterman in high school—tells stories about his own male teachers who were positive influences. He knows it is likely he will be remembered that way, too, by many of his Garrison children. It is unimaginable that his first-graders aren't aware that Abdullah is a special person. "I really enjoy my work," he says. "Some days I can't wait to get to school so I can start teaching. God has blessed me to be an elementary school teacher. I tried my best not to! I've had some wonderful experiences helping children to grow and begin to learn how to think."

Few societal rewards go to elementary school teachers. The plums are reserved for college and university professors. They are well paid, they are asked by newspaper editors to review the latest books on education, often written by other professors. They are asked to write op-eds on school reform. They are given teaching assistants to handle the lowly chores of grading papers. They enjoy paid sabbaticals. Yet little of the professorial life compares with the daily arduousness of what Darryll Vann, Hassan Abdullah and most elementary school teachers go through. Under the name of "classroom teaching," they are expected to discipline, entertain, correct, nurse, motivate, grade, call parents, fill out attendance sheets, tell kids not to run in the hall, and tell them again the next day, and the next, look for lost raincoats and rubbers, put chairs back in place, order books, hustle for more book shelves, and then go home to turn on the evening news to behold still another expert blasting "the schools" for failing.

Asked if he expects more black males to be coming into elementary schools, Abdullah states firmly, "No, I do not. It's sad. If only black males knew how valuable they are in an elementary school, they would be flying here."

Why aren't they? "Coming out of a college with a bachelor's degree to teach in the public school system doesn't pay much. The starting salary [in the mid-$20,000s in most systems] is pathetic. You can't blame the young men. They probably come from a household where they were the first college graduate. And now they're asked to work hard for four or five years and still make only $24,000 a year, while other industries—even the government—are paying much more. Something has to be done."

If the doers are the nation's political leaders, it's uncertain how much help is on the way. In his State of the Union speech last year, President Clinton announced his "Call to Action for American Education" based on ten principles. No. 2: "To have the best schools, we must have the best teachers ...We should challenge more of our finest young people to consider teaching as a career."

Clinton's call included raising standards, raising teaching accountability and raising student achievement. Darryll Vann and Hassan Abdullah would have been more heartened had they also heard a call for raising salaries. They'll keep listening.

from The Reporter
published by the Alicia Patterson Foundation, 1999

10

Resisting State Homicide

The death penalty is a confession of failure. When you say as a society that you have to kill people, then that means that you have no other way to deal with them. So it is really an admission of failure. It is also a lie, because there are other ways of dealing with murder. I mean, look at all the European nations. Somehow they manage to deal with people who commit murder without executing them and it certainly hasn't sent them back into the twelfth century.

Joseph Ingle

I have yet to find a case where there wasn't a red flag thrown up years ago—in grammar school or somewhere—where a kid said, 'I'm in trouble, help me.' He gave us the message loud and dear and we didn't pay any attention. And he ended up, years later, going down and down and killing someone. Let me tell you something. I resent the hell out of that as a member of a murder victim's family... These governors, these prosecutors, Ronald Reagan and George Bush all getting up and saying, 'I care about victims, I want the death penalty.' If they care about victims, they would have taken care of that victimized kid when he was six years old and prevented a homicide later.

Marie Deans

The World's Only True False Quiz on Legalized Killing

1.   Of the 38 death penalty states, 25, including Texas and Virginia, allow executions of mentally retarded people.

2.   Five methods of killing are used in one state or another: gassing, hanging, drugging,shooting and electrocuting.

3.   The electric chair in South Carolina is called "Old Sparky," as was the chair in Florida.

4.   The Association of Government Attorneys in Capital Litigation, which strongly favors executions, is known as "The Fryers Club."

5.   In 1992 Gov. Bill Clinton flew to Arkansas during the New Hampshire primary for the execution of a brain-damaged man whose last meal included a piece of pie as dessert. On leaving his cell to be lethally injected, he told a guard that he didn't eat the pie because he wanted to save it for after the execution.

6.   The 1996 Anti-Terrorism and Effective Death-Penalty Act makes it more difficult for prisoners to obtain federal review of claims that their constitutional rights have been violated.

7.   St. Thomas Aquinas, among other Roman Catholic saints, was an ardent supporter of the death penalty.

8.   Louisiana executed a black teenager whose body was so small that two phone books were put under him so his head could reach the electric chair cap.

9.   At a Southern execution, the prisoner's last words were, "I'm about to learn a lesson."

10.   In 1997 in Florida after a man's head caught fire while he was being electrocuted, State Attorney General Bob Butterworth said, "People who wish to commit murder, they better not do it in the state of Florida because we may have a problem with our electric chair."

11. Prison guards on death row are told to watch out for suicidal inmates, to keep them from killing themselves before their executions. More than 45 death row inmates have killed themselves since 1973.

12. At a recent execution, the prisoner asked to be allowed to take his Bible with him to the electric chair. He request was denied because the Bible might catch fire.

13. In the early 1980s, the warden of California's San Quentin prison placed a newspaper ad saying that any one wishing to witness an execution should phone to reserve a seat. The switchboard was swamped with calls. Fifty requests were granted. Any higher number would create a fire hazard, ruled the fire marshal.

14. In 1981, the French minister of justice, Robert Badinter, ended capital punishment in France. He gave one of the country's two guillotines to the national museum in Paris. The second was sold at an auction. The buyer was a Texas millionaire who put it in his game room.

15. When a six-year-old shot and killed a classmate in Michigan, the Sun, a British newspaper, speculated that American ingenuity would come up with a solution: build a kiddie-size electric chair.

16. Senator Orrin Hatch of Utah and in 2000 the Republican chair of the Judiciary Committee said: "Capital punishment is our society's recognition of the sanctity of human life."

17. While governor of California, Ronald Reagan favored lethal injection as the ideal means of killing condemned prisoners. He said that's how horses on his ranch were put down: "The horse goes to sleep. That's it."

18. The Texas death row holds several men whose lawyers fell asleep during their trials. In October 2000 the U.S Court of Appeals for the Fifth Circuit denied the appeal of man whose lawyer slept. The court cited a Supreme Court finding that the prisoner must prove that his lawyer's napping impacted on the trial.

19. In September 1988, a California newspaper reported that Vice President George Bush received "wild applause"

from high school students for stating that he strongly believed in the death penalty.

20. A 1995 Hart Research poll of U.S. police chiefs found that the majority do not believe that the death penalty is an effective law enforcement tool.

21. The day before Velma Barfield was executed in North Carolina, Billy Graham phoned her: "Velma, you're going to beat us home. Tomorrow night you'll be in the arms of Jesus."

22. Seven members of Pennsylvania Abolitionists United Against the Death Penalty were arrested in Oct. 1997 outside Philadelphia's Criminal Justice Center for distributing informational fliers. The charges included "obstructing the application of justice through picketing." One of the fliers was titled "How Racism Riddles the U.S. Death Penalty."

23. A Sept. 2000 Justice Department report stated that nearly 80 percent of federal prisoners are minorities. They account for 74 percent of the cases in which federal prosecutors seek the death penalty.

24. In 1994, Congress expanded the number of crimes eligible for capital punishment to more than 40.

25. Eighty-two percent of those put to death since 1987 had been convicted of murdering a white person even though people of color are the victims in more than half of all homicides.

26. Since 1976 the South has had 80 percent of the nation's executions and the highest murder rate of any region.

27. A Duke University study found that the cost executing a person in North Carolina was $2.1 million. If applied nationally to all executions, the cost of the death penalty since 1976 penalty exceeds $1 billion.

28. At least 381 homicide convictions have been overturned since 1963 because prosecutors concealed evidence of innocence or presented evidence they knew was false.

29. Over 90 percent of those tried on capital charges had court-appointed lawyers. Not one state meets the American Bar Association's standard for the appointment of

counsel for poor people.

30.   When the Texas Senate passed a bill to overturn a law that allowed executions of profoundly retarded people, and the House was about to concur, Gov. George Bush stopped further action by saying "I like the law the way it is right now."

31.   Three hours before his scheduled execution in Texas, Johnny Paul Penry, whose IQ is below 60, was told by the warden that the Supreme Court gave him a stay. The warden—accompanied by the chaplain--—came to the cell to read aloud the Court's wording. Of the warden, Penry said: "He couldn't read it to me, so he gave it to Father Walsh to read. The warden didn't understand the Catholic language, and it was in Catholic. Father Walsh read it to me because he understands Catholic."

from The Center for Teaching Peace Newsletter Sept. 2001

Abolish Capital Punishment
by Kerry Kennedy Cuomo

I was eight years old when my father was murdered. It is almost impossible to describe the pain of losing a parent to a senseless murder. And in the aftermath, it is similarly impossible to quiet the confusion: "Why him? Why this? Why me?" But even as a child one thing was clear to me: I didn't want the killer, in turn, to be killed. I remember lying in bed and praying, Please, God. Please don't take his life, too." I saw nothing that could be accomplished in the loss of one life being answered with the loss of another. And I knew, far too vividly, the anguish that would spread through another family—another set of parents, children, brothers, and sisters thrown into grief.

That was an instinctive reaction, not a tutored one. But tutored ones are not hard to find. In the past twenty years, capital punishment has been abolished and reinstated, and after more than one hundred executions under the resuscitated death penalty, the reasons to abolish it anew are as clear as ever. Abolish it because it does nothing to deter crime. Abolish it because after decades of legal tinkering it remains as random and as capricious as it was in 1972 when Justice Stewart first likened it to lightning. Abolish it because it costs us more than life imprisonment, not less. Because it exacts its toll unevenly, sending to the chair only the poor and never the rich; and those who kill whites much more often than those who kill blacks. Because it brings forth the demeaning spectacles of mobs who stand outside prisons and cheapen life by celebrating death. Because it guarantees that we'll claim innocent lives through our mistakes. Abolish capital punishment because America, alone among Western democracies, clings to its empty promise, and America is better than that.

Those opposed to the death penalty may find the argument for abolition familiar. In this book, Ian Gray and Moira Stanley provide a look at the people behind the arguments, the modern-day abolitionists who are devoting their lives to saving the lives of others. They are a varied lot and a surprising one—nuns and priests, yes; and lawyers; and scholars; and politicians;

and the victims of crime, as well. Their testimony takes this issue of death out of its sloganeering setting on editorial pages and helps us locate it where it actually exists, in real people's lives.

They are people like Marie Deans, who has found her way into the anti-death penalty movement after the murder of her mother-in-law fifteen years ago. She describes the all-night wait with a prisoner scheduled for execution at dawn: "Like a campfire, and the conversation between the three of us was like throwing logs on the fire to keep away the darkness and the terror."

People like Shabaka Waqlimi, who spent eleven years on death row in Florida before convincing a court he had been wrongfully convicted -a story we've seen repeated in the past year with James Richardson in Florida and Randall Dale Adams in Texas.

People like David Bruck, a South Carolina attorney, who describes the banality of the execution chamber's evil: "It's so quick and antiseptic. I suppose it would be better to say that the actual killing was incredibly disgusting, painful, gruesome; and gory to see someone electrocuted. But, to me, the truth is it was not as bad as that, and at the same time it was much worse . . . It is a completely incomprehensible miracle how a human being comes into this world—but to snuff one out is nothing."

The desire to impose the death penalty is an understandable reaction to the anger, fear, and frustration that follow a murder. Individual families, and society at large, turn to the death penalty, if not as a solution then at least as a salve. But it has become common, and politically opportune, to equate opposition to the death penalty with being "soft on crime." Opposition to the death penalty need be no such thing. Life imprisonment—real life imprisonment, without parole—answers our need to punish and our need to protect.

Though my abhorrence of capital punishment at the time of my father's murder was instinctive, I was gratified as I grew older to learn that it was shared by someone I hold in great esteem: my father. "Whenever any American's life is taken by another unnecessarily," said Robert Kennedy, "whether it is down in the name of the law or in defiance of law, by one man or a gang, in cold blood or in passion, in an attack of violence or in response to violence-whenever we tear at the fabric of life which another man has painfully and clumsily woven for himself and his children, the whole nation is degraded."

I work now in the field of international human rights. That means I am constantly forced to recall the evil of murder. It also means this: I am frequently privileged to witness responses of courage and of faith on the part of people who meet violence with non-violence.

from "A Punishment in Search of a Crime:
Americans Speak Out Against the Death Penalty"
Edited by Ian Gray & Moira Stanley for Amnesty
International USA. Avon Books

Choosing Mercy
by Antoinette Bosco

The headlines in an editorial in the *Bigfork Eagle*, the weekly paper of a small town in northwest Montana, on August 25, 1993, literally screamed out the warning: "Era of Unlocked Doors Ending."

The editorial began, "Murder in Bigfork. A grim reminder that as remote and quiet as Bigfork seems, real world, big-time problems have reached into our backyards.

"Last week, the bodies of John and Nancy Bosco were found, shot to death in their Ferndale home. An intruder, apparently intent only on death, cut the phone lines and electricity, then crept into the Boscos' house through a basement window, climbed stairs to the master bedroom and shot John and Nancy to death . . . . "

All too often when we read a story that begins this way, the victims come across as statistics, two people murdered. John and Nancy were not statistics. They were my son and daughter-in-law.

I got the news of the brutal murders on August 19, and that day I learned a new definition of torment. I had had to accept much death in recent years—my father, my sister-in-law, my son Peter. Death from almost any cause, even from accident, can somehow be dealt with rationally. But if the death is caused by murder, there is a collapse in the heart and soul that cannot be described.

For murder is the entrance of the worst evil imaginable into your home, into all the safe places of your life, forever shattering any illusion you might have had that good can protect you from evil. Evil becomes all too real to you and never again can you even for an instant question its power. My beloved son and his beautiful wife were dead at the hand of someone I could only believe to be, at that moment, an agent of Satan.

I found myself screaming, sometimes aloud, sometimes with silent cries tearing at my insides. I tormented myself, wanting to know who was the faceless monster that had brought such permanent unrelenting pain into my family. I wanted to kill him with my own hands. I wanted him dead.

But that feeling also tormented me, for I had always been opposed to the death penalty. I felt now I was being tested on whether my values were permanent, or primarily based on human feelings and expediency. With God's help, I was able to grasp the truth again, that unnatural death at the hands of another is always wrong, except in a case of clear self-defense. The state is no more justified in taking a life than is an individual. And so armed, I found myself speaking out on a national platform, pleading against the death penalty for anyone.

In the year 2000, the death penalty debate in America began to surface with a new urgency as voices against official killings were raised in legislatures, on news broadcasts, in professional legal and medical associations, and in virtually every religious community in the country. With the truth about the inequities and mistakes on death row starting to emerge, Americans, in mid-2000, were beginning to feel some discomfort as they heard such facts as these: over 3,600 people are currently on death row; more than 675 persons have been killed in the past twenty-four years—some surely innocent—by legally sanctioned gassings, electrocutions, hangings, lethal injections, or firing squad bullets; 88 death row inmates have been freed in this time, some after new trials, some with convictions overturned on appeal, some having new DNA proof of innocence; more than 65 inmates whose crimes were committed when they were juveniles are on death row; Texas has executed 8 juvenile offenders since 1985; 26 states have allowed the execution of mentally retarded defendants; application of the death penalty is skewed racially and by income.

The new concerns about this deadly "solution" for ridding the country of murderers were well expressed by Professor Anthony G. Amsterdam at a conference discussing "Global Movements towards a Moratorium on the Death Penalty," held in October 1999 at Columbia University:

"Some of us are concerned with what the death penalty does to societies and systems of law that use it—with how it distorts and erodes the fabric of our moral and our legal norms as those must be twisted and emptied of meaning in an effort to justify taking human life on the basis of procedures that we know to be fallible, error-prone, and inescapably responsive to the urgings of vengeance, prejudice and primal rage.

"Some of us simply are sick of the insidious hypocrisy that is the necessary price of pretending that imperfect human institutions are good enough to make decisions about who should live and who should die and get them right."

The new millennium began with another strong voice when Pope John Paul II appealed to the entire world, urging all nations to abolish the death penalty. He cited the year 2000, which he proclaimed a Holy Year, to be a "privileged occasion" for promoting universal respect for life and the dignity of every person. Ninety countries still hold on to capital punishment,, and, sadly, one of these is the United States, the only Western industrialized country to practice this barbaric punishment. The Holy Father was certainly directing his appeal for ending the death penalty to our nation, which in 1999, with ninety-eight killings, ranked third worldwide in the number of executions carried out.

Death penalty mania has been sweeping the country for over two decades, ever since the Supreme Court reinstated this ultimate punishment in July 1976, holding that "the punishment of death does not inevitably violate the Constitution."

Yet, in the first nine months of the new millennium, some major developments took place which indicate the climate may be beginning to change for the better when it comes to American attitudes toward the death penalty. What has come to light is the truth about the failures of this deadly system, particularly that innocent people have been put to death even when there is viable evidence that they may not have committed the crime. The American Bar Association, citing that the judicial process is seriously flawed, called for a moratorium on executions on February 3,1997, until the process is overhauled. Then, in January 2000, Illinois governor George Ryan, a traditional supporter of the death penalty, put a halt to executions in his state. Appalled by the fact that thirteen death row inmates in Illinois had been found to be innocent since 1977, he declared a moratorium until there is reform legislation that can fix the volumes of errors that accompany convictions in capital cases. With this first sign of hope, people who have worked for years to abolish the death penalty have begun a "Moratorium Now!" coast-to-coast campaign to get all the thirty-eight states that allow the death penalty to follow the example of Illinois. While their true goal would be the end of executions, moratoriums would at least be an action now that could stop the killings, while, hopefully, more Americans would begin to see the wrongness of executions and this perhaps would lead to a strong national voice demanding these end, period.

The Massachusetts Council of Churches has put out a five-sentence statement which best sheds light on why people are beginning to be uncomfortable with our escalating murders in the death chambers of our prisons: "Capital punishment is subject to error by fallible judges and juries. It is not a demonstrated deterrent to violent crimes. In fact, the society that sanctions official vengeance may be setting an example of the brutal devaluation of life that it wants to deter. One of our most serious concerns about the death penalty is the well-documented fact that the color of one's skin, the size of one's bank account to purchase legal services, and the skills of legal counsel, often have much to do with who actually is executed. This discrimination against ethnic minorities and the poor is a chief reason for eliminating capital punishment."

While this statement addresses matters that seriously should be examined in the realm of conscience, it does not deal with a major argument for keeping the death penalty: that without this extreme punishment for brutal killers, families of murder victims will not receive justice. Nothing could be further from the truth. The pain of losing a loved one by the horrible act of murder is not lessened by the horrible murder of another, not even when it is cloaked as "justice" and state-sanctioned. It is only a delusion to believe that one's pain is ended by making someone else feel pain.

Some may quickly criticize me as being some kind of Pollyanna because I am opposed to the death penalty and also believe that murder victims' families should seek to be merciful, not vengeful. Not true. The murder of my son and daughter-in-law plunged me into a position where I have had to examine—really examine—the gains and ills of the death penalty. I had to confront my soul when I learned that they were murdered by an eighteen-year-old named Joseph Shadow Clark, who after confessing to this horrible crime faced the death penalty. I had always been opposed to the death penalty, as I stated before, but where did I stand now when cold-blooded murder had so permanently crashed my life? Let me tell you that when you are in that pit, alone with your searing pain, you can't play cat and mouse with honesty. With tears and prayer and begging the Lord to tell me where I should stand, I found my way and was given to know that to want more unnatural death by the hands of humans would be wrong. I could say that Shadow Clark, who ended the earthly lives of my son and daughter-in-law with a nine-millimeter semi-automatic gun, must be punished for life, but I could not say, Kill this killer.

I am in a minority position. The latest polls show that the majority of Americans still favor the death penalty. I know, especially from antideath penalty talks I've given, that far too many people of many different faiths are in league with pro-death penalty advocates. Many may agree with the pope on abortion, but they're not with him when it comes to this issue of life and death for violent criminals. Not long ago I was asked by a Catholic pro-life group to give a talk, and when I said, yes, but I would also include the need to respect life when it comes to convicted criminals, they withdrew the invitation.

No one can deny that capital punishment is a question that causes confusion and pain. Even dedicated human rights advocates struggle with the arguments for and against—because brutal murder can challenge all of us in a way that puts our heads and our hearts at odds. I've had to look deep inside myself and ask, am I so noble, so altruistic as to still believe that Shadow Clark, this taker of innocent life, deserves to live?

That's why the death penalty puts us on the edge of a sword. The uncertainty, confusion, and anguish it generates offer strong testimony that the death penalty may be the most wrenching moral dilemma of our time. For the issue can't really be dealt with from our human perspective, but only through finding our higher selves.

Advocates of the death penalty say that a murderer forfeits his or her right to life. Maybe that's true, but I don't believe we can be the ones to make that judgment.

I know the claim that vengeance can make on your soul when you are devastated by the injustice of losing a love at the hand of a murderer. It fills every part of you, with rage tearing the very molecules of your existence. Yes, you feel like destroying the person who has so permanently clawed away a vital part of your life. This rage puts you on the point of a defining moment that will determine who you will become and what will happen to your relationship with God.

There are many victims of homicide who become self-righteous in their demand for the death penalty and say, as did Richard Thornton, the husband of the woman murdered by Daniel Ryan Garrett and Karla Faye Tucker, who was executed in Texas in February 1998: "I want to say to every victim in this world, demand this, this is your right." And he repeated, the night she was executed, in raging self-righteousness, that we victims have a right to hate, to demand death for the murderer and call it "closure" when the death house deed is done.

Advocates for death cannot assume that all victims will be ready and anxious to jump on their bandwagon. It is not surprising, however, that in this era of rah, rah death-penalty advocates, a victim who is opposed to this kind of terminal solution is sometimes seen as a traitor.

I know that criticism. It has often been poured on me. All I ask is that people listen to the powerful lesson some of us have learned when murder enters our door—that unnatural death is an evil, no matter whose hand stops the breath.

from "Choosing Mercy:
A Mother of Murder Victims
Pleads to End the Death Penalty"

They Tried To Kill Shabaka
An interview by Ian Gray and Moira Stanley

*Shabaka Sundiata Waqlimi knew the drill on death row at Florida's
death prison, Starke, only too well. During his thirteen years of
incarceration under the name of Joseph Green Brown, he'd seen his
friends sent to the electric chair, so when the guards came to measure
him for his burial suit he decided to put up a fight.*

*He lost the fight, but he managed not only to stay out of the chair,
but to prove his innocence and gain his freedom.*

*There are many injustices in this world, some slight, some gross,
but on a scale of one to ten, what happened to Shabaka is at least an
eleven, maybe more. To this day Shabaka has not received a single
cent in compensation from the state of Florida.*

This is his story.

February 18, 1988.

I was born in Charleston, South Carolina, only a few miles
from here. I went to school there, and in 1966 went to Orlando,
Florida, where I lived most of my life.

Are you angry about what happened to you?

I am bitter, I am angry, and I am frustrated. Not only about
what happened to me but-I can deal with anything that happens
to me but when those whom I love and who love me are made to
suffer unjustly, I take that as a personal offense.

*From your viewpoint, what happened in your case? What were
you arrested for?*

Murder, rape, and robbery of a white woman in Tampa in
1973. The victim, Earline Barksdale, was the wife of a very prominent attorney in Tampa. This attorney had connections straight
up to Tallahassee, the state capital. I am, of course, saddened by
her murder and hope that one day the killer will be brought to
justice.

Nonetheless I was charged with the crimes against Ms.
Barksdale.

I have always maintained, and I'm still quite sure, that my being charged and convicted was a deliberate and intentional thing, brought about by the Tampa police department and the Hillsborough County State Attorney's Office simply to frame me. They needed a murderer, and since I was young and black, in their eyes, I was perfect for the part.

The victim's husband was tight with the chief homicide detective. The leading prosecutor on the case and his assistant are [now] both sitting judges in Hillsborough County. All these people were real buddy buddies.

Anyway, I was charged with murder and I didn't have the finances to hire my own lawyer, which you have to in America—or forget about it. I went to trial, virtually alone, with a court-appointed attorney just three years out of law school. He had only tried three previous cases before a jury, and none of them was a capital case. He was up against an experienced prosecutor who had forty trials behind him, some of which were capital. Where were you tried?

In Tampa.

What was the composition of the jury?

(*Laughs*) A very representative jury of my peers. Twelve white citizens! Average age thirty-five, maybe more.

The trial lasted four and a half or five days. The jury went out seven o'clock that Friday and came back at eleven-thirty, quarter to twelve that night, with a verdict. Guilty.

What was your defense?

Alibi . . . just about everything. The prosecution didn't have a thing. How could they? I was innocent. They didn't have prints, blood, hair or anything that could be matched to me—no physical evidence of any kind. They had this gun, a .38-caliber Smith and Wesson that belonged to me. Now the gun that killed Earline Barksdale was a .38. But the slug they took from her body was a .38 *special*. Not only were the ballistics different, the bullet wouldn't even *chamber* the gun!

What went wrong?

There was this FBI ballistics expert who was listed as a prosecution witness so my attorney didn't bother to subpoena him. He assumed that when the prosecutor called the guy, he'd

250

prove my innocence during the cross-examination. Of course the prosecution didn't call him. Right at the end of the trial he let the FBI guy go back to some fishing holiday somewhere. So, he was gone before my attorney could call him to the stand.

That's dreadful, but surely wouldn't the judge allow a continuance?

Hey this is Tampa, Florida. They don't allow a little thing like the truth to upset a good trial. This judge refused to recall the FBI expert.

The following Monday they set a date for the sentencing portion. I was given death for the murder, and consecutive life sentences for the rape and robbery. It was the judge's contention that if I beat the death sentence, I would never see the street as long as I was alive. I was taken to Florida State Prison, Starke. I was twenty-four years old when I went to death row; I was twenty-three when I was arrested.

What was your state of mind?

Anger. They just took me there and put me in the cell. I didn't realize I was on death row. I was so angry. You could say that for the first two years I survived primarily on my hatred. The strength I received from that hatred was from all the people that were involved. I even felt that the court-appointed attorney had something to do with it. But then I found out that he was just dumb, he did no less than he could.

Were you appointed another attorney for the appeals?

No. Under the Florida law, the same attorney handles the appeal to the Florida Supreme Court. Then in 1977 the attorney left my case and I had to find another one. During this process, I hit the books. I started to study, and from July 1977 until November of 1981, when a lawyer was found for me, I handled my own appeals. I kept myself alive with the help of Deborah Fins of the Legal Defense Fund [NAACP] in New York. We became friends. I trusted her and wanted her to handle the case, but she couldn't devote the time to it that was needed. She found an attorney, the one who eventually got me out.

If I was paying, I would not have chosen this attorney. He had just resigned as the U.S. Attorney for the state of Connecticut, had never handled a capital case. He was a prosecutor and believed in the death penalty. *(Laughs)* He had all these things going against him and, like I say, he was not a person I would choose. I wrote Debbie and said, "You must be kidding." She said, "Let him come down and talk to you, just talk to the man." He came to see me and I liked him; we had good rapport. I had one important question to ask him, though. Could he fight? And he didn't respond to it, he just sort of smiled. And I liked that; there was something in that smile.

He said, as a prosecutor, that when the transcript of my trial was given to him, he was just in awe of the injustices that he saw. So he took the case and we went through the process. He went through the filing to Tallahassee to "Barbecue Bob" Graham [governor of Florida at that time] for clemency. That failed, needless to say.

Then, in 1983, Graham signed my death warrant and I was scheduled to be killed on October 18. I think it was during this stage that Dick [Richard Blumenthal, the attorney] became a convert. It was when I was on death watch that he got a chance to actually see how the death penalty works. He was expecting a stay about three days before I got it. The judge couldn't get to my case that weekend. Dick became so enraged that I had to sit over there on death watch that he said to me, "Shabaka, I don't care what it costs me, my family, or my law firm, but I'm going to get you out of here." And he did.

We got the stay fifteen hours before I was scheduled to be killed.

What was going on in your mind at that time?

Well, you are in a cell that is located about thirty feet from the chair. You stay in that cell an average of twenty-three days. There are two ways out of that cell. One if you receive a stay of execution. The other to take that thirty-foot walk.

During the twenty-three days you are there, you are given what on death row is called the "presidential treatment." The presidential treatment means that you are subjected to the chair being tested. And knowing that the chair is being tested in your honor. You hear it. You are right next to it. It's only thirty steps away. Several times a week. Like I say, you know it's being done in your honor. Then, a week before your scheduled death, you go down to what is known as a second stage.

At the second stage you are measured for your "burial suit." And I think it was at that point, for the first time in all the years I was there I really blew my cool, because the process is like a ritual, it is so mechanical. I was being treated like I was an inanimate object. I was determined that I was not going to let this be just another ritual, so I resisted. Well, I responded very actively because, as I say, I was determined not to let this be another ritual. I am a living, breathing human being. If they wanted to measure me for a burial suit, they are not going to be doing it in this manner. Well, I responded physically, and they responded physically, and they kicked me until I shut up.

How did you manage to evolve as a man and remain sane during all those years in that kind of environment?

I realized that I had a job at hand and that the job at hand was to keep some sick people from killing me.

How did you get out?

Through the action of the Eleventh Circuit Court of Appeals in Atlanta. For my appeal my attorney cited the *Giglio v. United States* and Chief Judge [John C.] Godbold said, "Good— that's what we are interested in." That deals with the issue that the prosecutor knowingly and intentionally used false and perjured testimony. We zeroed on that issue and had enough proof to get the conviction reversed. The state of Florida had eighteen days to appeal, and they never did. The reversal came March 17, 1986, and on April 30 I was moved from death row back to Hillsborough County to await a decision as to whether I would be retried. I did eleven months waiting in the county jail in Tampa.

We were now dealing with a new state attorney, Bill James, who was elected into office by promising that he was not only interested in convicting the guilty but that he was going to make sure the innocent were not going to be caught in the web. We filed some court orders and found a lot of suppressed or unheard evidence from the 1973 trial. Like I said before, the ballistic reports from the FBI showed that the bullet that was removed from the body did not physically match the chamber of the gun that I had. We thought we had the original autopsy report, but we did not. We had the report of the medical examiner first on the scene, and this report stated that the assailants, and they used the plural, assailants, were of the blood groups AB and B + . I am A+. And the state knew this because a court order was granted in September 1973 for me to give certain tests and the blood test was one of them, as well as fingernail scraping, pubic hair, all this. They also had fixed the time of death at between 5:30 and 8:00 in the evening. During the trial the state maintained the crime took place between noon and 1:00 p.m., since this timetable paralleled with certain witness testimony as to their whereabouts during this period. We also found the initial police investigative report on witnesses who were near the place of the murder at the same time the state said the crime was committed.

None of these things were given to us at the original trial. There were people who were supposed to be at the scene of the crime, as the prosecution had stated, who were elsewhere, actually in their places of business. And we found also statements from inmates in the jail who were coerced to testify at my trial, but who did not. Also, one real interesting fact is that the key witness who did testify at my trial, not only didn't know anything about the crime, but was taught and trained by the police and prosecution to recall details. He was taken out of the county jail daily. He was led around the scene of the crime, shown pictures of the crime and shown pictures of where the body lay inside the place.

And he was a chief witness against you?

Yes. He was taught. Anyway, evidence supporting all this was found by us, and I turned to Tom [Thomas McCoun, local counsel] and I said, "Tom, I want to say something. What I like about you white people is that you always like to write things down! Yes, man, you always write things down and they come back to haunt you."

We presented this to the state, and in their own investigation they made a polygraph test on these people and found out that what we had been saying for fourteen years was true. They had tried, convicted, condemned, and almost killed an innocent man.

So they dismissed all charges. They filed a complete dismissal.

Are they going to do anything to compensate you for all of

254

this?

There's the irony. You see Florida, like other states, has a law. If anyone spends any time, whether it's a day, a year, whatever, in any state institution, when you are released you are given a hundred dollars, a suit of clothing, an I.D., and a ticket back to a county that you want to go to. Now, since I was released from the Hillsborough County Jail rather than the state prison I did not qualify. I didn't get a thing. In the jail I think I had about $14. I gave it all away except 75 cents to make three telephone calls. I gave away all my law books. I kept all my transcripts and I left that county jail with just the clothes on my back, my legal papers, and 75 cents in my pocket.

Seventy-five cents for fourteen years in jail?

Yeah, and I used that on the phone. I had no idea how I was going to get out of Tampa, so I called Tom, my lawyer, who is based in St. Petersburg, and asked him to come over and pick me up and take me back to St. Pete so I could get a ride to Gainesville, where I had friends.

What did you find you missed most when you were incarcerated? What did you want to do when you got free?

I always had this vision that when I got out I was gonna look up in the sky, give a prayer to the Heavenly Father, and then take a deep breath and let it out. But I did not do this because when I walked out of the door I was blinded by camera lights from the TV station out there waiting.

But you were free?

Well I, of African descent, am not a free person in this country and never was. It is not my country. When they say that I am free, I say it is because I am no longer restrained by bars, but that's as far as it goes, because they are still killing a lot of my brothers and sisters and they are doing it for the wrong reasons, and I don't think I could be free until I control my own development. I am still growing.

We heard a very tragic story about your brother.

You see, we talk about capital punishment and we talk about victims. As I said earlier, what has been done to me I can deal with, but when you touch those I love and care about, I take offense. Back in 1979 my oldest brother Willie needed a kidney transplant. He lived in Georgia, and a doctor came to Florida State Prison and examined me about a kidney match. For security reasons Florida Department of Corrections refused to allow me to go to Lyons, Georgia. So the doctor said they would transport Willie to Gainesville, which is close to the prison. Again the Florida officials denied me permission, giving security as the reason. Nine days later my brother died because he couldn't get a transplant. As far as I'm concerned, the state of Florida killed my brother as clearly as if they had put a gun to his head and pulled the trigger. If I had been in general prison population I could have given him the kidney, but because I was on death row, I was denied that.

There are victims all the way around. Society teaches that when something violent happens to us we should seek revenge, but I always ask the question about who is out there who will volunteer themselves to be a sacrificial lamb for me, so I can release fourteen years of anger and frustration? I get no volunteers. Society tells me I shouldn't act that way and I should suppress it. So I have to suppress my outrage because, you see, they have no program in society for people like myself.

Thank you, Shabaka. Anything you'd like to say in conclusion?

Do this for me. Just help abolish the death penalty.

from "A Punishment in Search of a Crime"
Avon Books.

Marie Deans, Truthteller

An interview by Ian Gray and Moira Stanley

Everyone said there is no one quite like Marie Deans; a one-woman coalition for the state of Virginia. She is in her forties, long-limbed and slender. Her hair is dark and curly, flecked with gray, her eyes dauntless, heavy-lidded.

She laughs off the harassments she has had to endure since becoming the director of the Virginia Coalition on Jails and Prisons and founder of Murder Victims' Families for Reconciliation, including obscene telephone calls and well-stuffed body bags dumped in her yard.

As the daughter-in-law of a murder victim, she understands the pain brought about by violence. She once said, "Perhaps it would surprise you to know that every time I am about to meet a man, woman, or child on death row for the first time, I am thrown back into Penny's (Marie's mother-in-law) murder, and that I identify so strongly with the victims and their families that I spend days calling on God to help me remember that the man or woman I am about to meet is my brother or sister. I am thankful that God has answered every one of those prayers."

When asked why she goes on doing this kind of work, she answered, "There are many reasons. I have the need to understand why we are so good at passing on violence and so poor at passing on love."

It is true, there is no one quite like Marie Deans.

February 23, 1988

We understand your mother-in-law was a murder victim. Would you mind telling us about it?

When I was thirty-two and pregnant my mother-in-law, Penny, was murdered. This was the worst year of my life. I was really close to my father-in-law and my mother-in-law. Jabo, my father-in-law, had died just a year before Penny was killed. After he died, Penny was very depressed until she found out that I was pregnant and then it was like a new life for her, a new life for all of us. First we did a lot of shopping and talking and planning for the baby, then she went to North Carolina to tell all my father-in-law's family.

She came home early because she missed us. We were living in South Carolina. Somewhere along the road this guy saw her and followed her all the way home. The guy came into the house and there was a struggle and he shot her twice. A neighbor called the police and my brother-in-law called us. Just before we got to the house, cops had arrived and there were already reporters there. They told us Penny had been shot.

(Marie was very emotional at this time)

We wanted to see Penny, but the cops told us we couldn't go into the house but that paramedics were with her. We waited for a while and then realized that my husband's younger sister didn't know what had happened, so we left to get her, and on our way back we passed an ambulance with no lights on.

When we got back to Penny's house, we asked the police if she was in that ambulance and they said, "Yes, she's been taken to the hospital for an autopsy." And that's how we found out she was dead.

What a terrible story. Did you hold your abolitionist views at that time?

We were opposed to the death penalty, or perhaps a better way to put it is that we had not been for it. Somewhere along the line during the investigation someone asked us if this was going to change our minds. It was the first time we had really even thought about the idea that this man could get the death penalty.

They were trying to bring back the death penalty in South Carolina at the time, so we tried to get some information from the prosecutor, and they just kept telling us that was not our responsibility. We even talked to our minister and he told us the same thing. So we decided we would oppose any effort to sentence the man to death.

About that time I started hemorrhaging.

Did you lose the baby?

No. The "baby" is my fifteen-year-old treasure, Robert.

Did they catch the murderer?

Yes. The man had escaped from a prison in Maine. During the escape he had killed a woman and taken her car. I believe it was my hemorrhaging and the possibility of losing our baby that triggered my husband's going to the prosecutor and telling him we'd fight extradition. He'd got a life sentence in Maine, there is no death penalty there. So they never did extradite him back to South Carolina. He is still in prison in Maine.

His sister turned him in. She called down to South Carolina, I didn't talk to her, but she was utterly distraught about what had happened. She wanted to know about us and if we were all right.

We found out that the guy had been in prison three times before, each time for progressively more violent attacks on women. His family and his attorneys had asked for treatment for him and he had gotten no treatment whatsoever. He was just warehoused and released over and over again. I really felt like Penny had paid for our society's inability to face its problems and deal with them effectively. We are more interested in satisfying our emotional needs than we are in finding real solutions to our problems.

How did you get involved with jails and prisons?

I joined Amnesty in 1973. I made one trip to see Rose Styron and some others from Amnesty. Then a man in South Carolina [J. C. Shaw] dropped his appeals and the Alston Wilkes Society (a prison reform organization in South Carolina) called me and asked if I would come out and talk to him. I called the Commissioner of Corrections and made the arrangements to see this inmate.

I never felt so inept in all my life. I didn't know what to say to the prisoner. I didn't know what happened to him; I didn't know what his crime was. All I knew was that he had dropped his appeals primarily from remorse, because he felt the victim's family would be helped by his death. Nevertheless, I returned to visit him again.

J. C. had been mute during his trial, before his trial and for a long time after his trial. But one day, he suddenly started talking. I asked if he knew why I was there and he said, "No, not really," and I said, "I am here just because I don't want you to die, I don't want you to be executed." He asked me why and I said, "I don't know, your life is sacred that's all I know. I don't have any good reasons except that." So he asked me if I would come back to see him, and I did. Between me, a priest, and another friend, we were able to persuade him to pick up his appeal. Then he asked me

259

if I would see another guy on the row who was sitting crouched up in his cell, in the corner of his bunk, and not talking to anybody. So I went to see him, and the next thing I knew I was visiting all the men on the South Carolina death row and working with their attorneys.

Why were you so concerned about vicious murderers?

From the moment Penny was killed, I never understood it. Why she was killed. I came to the conclusion that we would not find out why unless we talked to the people who had done these things and find out from them. Of course they can't tell you why. You have to dig a lot deeper than that. I learned the answers to my "whys" through working with J. C. Shaw and others on death row. But they killed Shaw in 1985.

Tell us about him.

He had asked me to be with him at the end and I went; however, I left before the execution.

I was trying to get J. C. to pick up his appeals. He had said to me several times, "Stop, you are torturing me," so when he was sitting in the death house, I asked him about that, and he said, "Oh no, no, these have been the best years of my life, the best years, because I changed, I came back to God. I really would not have wanted to die back then."

How long was he on death row?

Five years after he picked up his appeals. All told, he was there about seven years.

J. C. Shaw was my first client, my first contact with death row. J. C. was real shy and he would come up when I was doing general visits and would just stand beside me.

It is strange to hear that. J. C. Shaw was always portrayed as the older psychotic, dangerous killer, drug addict, sadistic ex-military policeman.

He was certainly in a psychotic state when he killed. His family could not believe the change in him. J. C. could not believe it either. He had been on Lithium as a youngster, but when he was in the Army, he stopped taking it. He had been diagnosed as a schizophrenic. He had gone to the military hospital two or three times pleading that he be committed. The last time they were having a hot dog party in the backyard and they told him to come back the next day. That was just an afternoon before the murders happened.

He would tell me, "I have lived this crime," and he named a number that was over a thousand, I think. The warden said that was the exact number of days since the murders. He had relived the murders every night since he had committed the crimes.

He told me that going to the electric chair was not a problem for him. The problem for him was what it was doing to his family and his loved ones. So we cried together, and he told me, "I don't want you here if you are afraid you may come to hate these people." I don't think it would have happened, but I was afraid it might.

By the time J. C. Shaw was executed I had moved to Virginia.

Have you been harassed because of your work?

You know the intimidation has been pretty good here in Virginia. I walked out of my house one time and found a body bag, well stuffed, on my doorstep. They painted the outline of a dead body where I parked my car. Came home from work one day and there was this "dead body" I was supposed to park over. People continue to send hate mail and make threatening phone calls.

Who are they?

I don't know who they are. I don't know. They stay anonymous. I suppose because they are as full of fear as they are of hatred.

We read about a case in Virginia where a representative, during a debate, advocated letting condemned men bleed to death so their organs could be used for transplants.

That's true. When that kind of debate can go on in our legislature, we are in more trouble than we want to admit.

I know David Bruck has told you something about being in the execution chamber. I haven't been in the chamber itself. But I have been in the death house with eight people now who have been killed and a number who have gotten stays at the last minute. I have seen two men go crazy right before my eyes in the death house. I have seen us kill Morris Mason, a man-child with a sixty-two IQ who was diagnosed by the state of Virginia as a paranoid schizophrenic [executed June 25, 1985]. Morris said to me

261

before I left, "You tell Roger Coleman [a death row inmate who is a very good basketball player] that when I get through here, I am going to come back and show him that I can play basketball as good as he can." Morris knew he was going to the electric chair but he didn't know he wasn't coming back—that he was going to die. He didn't know what that was. I mean he even asked one of the guards what he should wear to his funeral! And we killed him like we killed all those other people. . . like Richard Whitley, who was seriously brain-damaged.

I have this intellectual concept of God. I believe that God is life and love, and those things that move toward life are good things and godly things and sacred things, and those things that move toward unnatural death are evil, in my mind. Joe Ingle calls the death chambers the "Vortex of Evil" and you feel that when you are in the death house because it is so banal, it is incredibly banal.

There is a ritual, you see, and the American people need ritual. If you deal with something straight up you don't need a ritual. In the death house, ritual is the engine that drives the death machine and it encompasses the most absurd things.

There is a chef at the state penitentiary, who generally wears work clothes but when he serves the last meal in the death house, he wears a suit, a chef's hat, and pulls on white gloves! Even if he's serving french fries. I have to tell the guys not to ask for french fries because every piece of food has to be inspected in front of the execution squad. They go through the french fries in case there is a razor blade or the like. So finally when they get their food, it's cold.

Now Richard Whitley wanted ice tea and he wanted tea for everybody, so they brought a jug of ice tea. I am sitting near the bars close to Richard and they put the jug down and it says on the side "Cider Vinegar" and without thinking I said, "Oh my God. `And our Lord thirsted and they gave him vinegar.' "

Before I left Richard, when the execution squad said, "Marie, you have to go now," Richard had hung onto me. As long as I was there, he was okay, but as soon as I began to leave, he started shaking and he said, "I can't make it without you," and I said, "Yes, you can, you can make it." Then I said, "Where is God,

Richard?" and he raised his hand and he pulled his hand in a downward movement between the two of us. And I said, "Yes, I can feel Him, I know that God is with us, here, and when I go out there Richard, I am going into Babylon but you are staying with God."

I just knew he would be all right. I just knew it. You know, you can feel it. People come in and out of there and you can tell who that Presence is with and who stays in the "Vortex of Evil."

Richard was all right and I did go back out into Babylon. And that's where I live. And that's where I work. And that's where I stay.

Sometimes I am afraid to tell that because Christians can be warped enough to say, "Then it's okay if we kill them because God takes them, they are delivered."

What do you think the death penalty does to the society that executes?

I honestly believe that we are steadily eroding the Constitution in order to kill people. I can see that in the cases. Justices [Thurgood] Marshall and [William S.] Brennan see that, too. We are coming to the point in this country where we must choose between whether we want to kill people or whether we want the Constitution.

I believe we owe a duty to the American public to explain what is happening . . . what they are doing. If they choose to give up their Constitution to kill people, then they have made the same kind of conscious choice that the people in Nazi Germany made. That may sound harsh but when there is a problem and you are not doing anything to stop it, if you know the problem is there and you know it's wrong, then you are making, in my ethics, a conscious choice.

You talk of the Constitution. Which constitutional principle, in your opinion, is being violated?

Equal rights and due process protections. A lot of people say it's the Eighth Amendment because it's cruel and unusual punishment, but we have killed an awful lot of people. It may be *cruel*, but clearly, in American history, it's not *unusual*. What makes it cruel and unusual is the arbitrary manner in which we choose who will get the death sentence and who will be executed. I know

263

that Justice Brennan believes that it is against the Constitution because of the evolving standards of the Eighth Amendment. The standards that clearly have evolved and continue to evolve are international standards of punishment. The death penalty in the United States demonstrates atrophying standards and creates an enormous tension in our Constitution.

The death penalty is something that is destroying the soul of our people. If people don't know that, it just tells me how quickly it is destroying us.

from "A Punishment in Search of a Crime" Avon Books.

Joe Giarratano Waits For Justice
by Colman McCarthy

Among the 87 prisoners freed from America's death rows since 1972, four Virginians stand out: Joseph Giarratano, Earl Washington Jr., Herbert Bassette and Joeph Payne. Beginning with Giarratano in 1991 and ending with Payne in 1996, each won release because a Virginia governor examined the evidence for innocence and ruled that reasonable doubts about guilt were compelling.

When the four men left death row, they didn't go far. They were shackled and dispatched to other state prisons where they are caged today. What holds them is Rule 1.1 of the Supreme Court of Virginia—the 21-day rule. Airtight, it decrees that if a capitally convicted prisoner has post-conviction evidence of innocence, bring it to court within 21 days of the sentencing. After that, don't bother. Proof could exist that the accused was in Antarctica playing with penguins on the day of the crime in Virginia. After 21 days, it wouldn't matter. Nor would old evidence discredited by new DNA testing or other improved forensic methods. For Giarratano, Washington, Bassette and Payne, Rule 1.1 means that they will likely die in prison—effectively a death sentence outside death row.

Driven either by conscience or edginess about what this rule says about Virginia justice, some state politicians have been stirring themselves to corrective action. In late February, the House of Delegates voted 73-25 on a bill that would lethally inject the 21-day rule. The 41 Democrats and 32 Republicans supporting the change believed that, finally, Virginia would no longer be the only one of the nation's 38 death penalty states denying appellate relief for possibly innocent people. The effort came to nothing. In mid-March, the state Senate refused to consider the bill, which would have given three years, not three weeks, to offer new evidence for innocence.

While Virginia stagnates, shiftings are seen elsewhere. Preacher-politician Pat Robertson is the latest pro-death penalty conservative to call for a moratorium. He followed Illinois Gov.

George Ryan, who could no longer ignore that 13 men have been freed from his state's death row since 1977, one more than the number of men executed. Six other states have called for a timeout, now that the mathematics are in: with 87 men freed and some 630 gassed, injected, electrocuted, hung or shot, it's one out of eight prisoners who escaped death row.

It could be asked about the freed men: Why aren't sentencing judges and prosecutors arrested for attempted homicide? With slim chance of that happening, another question is within range of reasonableness: Why are so few details about the incompetent lawyering and erratic judicial decisions from the bench disclosed to the public and to the people victimized by the wrongful convictions?

The case I'm most familiar with is Joseph Giarratano's. Since 1988, I have been in regular contact with him. I visited him four times on death row, including an interview the day before his scheduled execution in February 1991. Since then, I made a half-dozen more visits. On each, I brought students from my classes at Georgetown Law School, the University of Maryland and Bethesda Chevy Chase High School.

Giarratano, a one-time drug addict who turned his life around on death row by reading law, theology and philosophy, was allowed by his progressive warden to give seminars on criminal justice to my students. On legal issues, he had credibility. He had written articles for the *Yale Law Review* and the *Los Angeles Times*. His legal research led to several successful suits on behalf of fellow prisoners. He was the only person on death row ever to write a brief argued before the Supreme Court—on behalf of Earl Washington Jr., his illiterate cellblock friend.

Giarratano, now 43, was convicted of killing two Norfolk, Va., women in February 1979 in a rooming-house apartment he shared with them. The case presented against him during a four-hour trial was so flimsy—five coerced dissimilar confessions; conflicting autopsy reports; bloody shoe prints in the apartment not matching Giarratano's boots; the stabbing and strangulation of the women were done by a right-handed person, while Giarratano is left-handed—that conservative pro-death penalty newspapers throughout Virginia began calling for a new trial. They

266

were joined by Amnesty International and other groups that examined the case in detail. By February 1991, then Gov. L. Douglas Wilder freed Giarratano from death row.

The day before this life-sparing decision, I asked Giarratano the obvious question: If it's so certain that you have a claim for innocence, why haven't the courts, after 10 years of considering well-crafted appeals, agreed?

He answered: "It isn't that the courts weren't convinced one way or the other, but that they're bound by the procedural rules they created. It's a court rule that if the defense attorney didn't make proper objections during the trial, then the error cannot be raised on appeal. The second procedural rule states that any new evidence must be raised within 21 days of the trial's conclusion, otherwise the review is forever barred. Federal courts must defer to state procedural rules. Because of all this, no court has ever ruled on the merits of my case."

Giarratano currently lives in the Red Onion State Prison in Pound, Va., caged 23 hours a day in an 11-by-8-foot cell in the isolation wing. Red Onion, in rural Southwest Virginia, a seven hour drive from Washington, is a supermax facility where inhumane treatment of prisoners is routine. The *Washington Post* reported in April 1999 that "in Red Onion's first nine months, shots have been fired (at inmates) 63 times." The paper quoted Ronald Angelone, the state's director of prisons and a champion of supermax pens, on his views about Red Onion: "It's not a nice place. And I designed it not to be a nice place."

The prison has no law library, no meaningful job training program and no significant education classes. Mail is severely restricted. A directive states: "Copies or sections of publications, brochures, newsletters, materials printed off the Internet or other printed materials will no longer be allowed or enclosed in incoming correspondence."

Giarratano is allowed to exercise in a concrete area the size of a dog pen. In a recent letter, he wrote: "I am strip searched each time I leave the cell for recreation . ... I am first handcuffed behind the back, legs shackled, placed on a dog leash, escorted by two guards—one holding the leash, the other pressing a laser gun to my ribs and all under the close watch of a guard pointing a shotgun at me from the gun port."

That should be considered soft treatment. Earlier this year, Giarratano was confined to his cell 24 hours a day, except for three showers a week. His offense? He retained a mustache, a major violation of the department of correction's hair grooming regs.

In a letter May 7, Giarratano described his feelings about life in the supermax prison:

"Generally, I am holding up well under the rigors of supermax segregated confinement, probably better than many. Nevertheless, I know that anyone subjected to this type of ordeal —especially for long durations-—does not escape unscathed. I know, in my own experiences here and from past experiences with long-term isolated-segregated lockdowns, i.e., my years on the row, the tremendous amount of mental concentration it requires just to keep one's head above water. There are times, even now, when I'm not so sure of my own grip on reality. The social isolation, greatly restricted environmental and intellectual stimulation, forced idleness, constantly confined to small space day after day, being subjected to a constant denial of one's innate humanity and dignity—constantly being treated like an object and not as a human being—the total lack of personal privacy, the constant light bulb (24 hours a day) and living under the constant threat of officially sanctioned violence will, I suppose, take its toll on anyone. More and more, I find myself having to turn inward just to maintain my balance in this madness; and even then, I must remain on guard for hallucinations, feelings of suffocation, paranoia, fear, and even rage."

In the same letter, Giarratano included an excerpt from a Supreme Court decision involving the sensory-deprivation isolation of inmates in locked-down cells: "A considerable number of prisoners fell, after even a short confinement, into a semifatuous condition, from which it was next to impossible to arouse them, and others became violently insane; others still, committed suicide, while those who stood the ordeal better were not generally reformed, and in most cases did not recover sufficient mental activity to be of any subsequent service to the community."

Giarratano has told me that one of the forces that keeps him from despair, or suicide, is the correspondence he has with supporters who have not forgotten him.

In the spring of 1999, many of them were among the more than 200 friends who gathered at a dinner in Charlottesville, Va., to honor Giarratano's heroic resistance against Virginia's courts and the correction department's efforts to crush his spirit.

The dinner, at a Doubletree Hotel banquet room, was on May 1, the same day that the mayor of Charlottesville, Va., in a move that no one could recall ever happening anywhere else involving a prisoner, declared May 1 "Joseph Giarratano Day." The proclamation was meant to honor a man many Virginians on both sides of the death penalty issue believe is innocent.

Among those speaking at the dinner was retired federal Judge Robert Merhige. He had followed the Giarratano case closely while sitting on the Fourth U.S. Circuit 'Court of Appeals. In a 15-minute speech, he aligned himself with all those in the audience who continued to work to win Giarratano's freedom. Merhige also condemned the 21-day rule.

I sent the printed program of the dinner to Giarratano. It came back in return mail, undelivered because of the no printed-material rule. Later, Giarratano wrote to say that the dinner for him, along with the mayor's proclamation, was "a humbling experience for me. I'm told the honor came down to a choice between me and a U.S. Supreme Court Justice! That had to be Rehnquist or Scalia—only way they could have decided on me!"

from The Baltimore Sun July 23, 2000

11

Settling Conflicts With Love (Yes, Love)

It is the law of love that rules mankind. Had violence, i.e., hate ruled us, we would have become extinct long ago. And yet the tradgedy of it is that the so-called civilized men and nations conduct themselves as if the basis of society was violence.

Gandhi

Conflict, Equality and Marriage
by Richard Driscoll

What can social science research say about equality in marriages? Actually, a great deal. A solid ream of research finds that marriages in which husbands and wives participate equally are the most satisfying. Equal participation usually means that husband and wife share the power about equally, listen to each other and find mutually agreeable solutions to the problems that affect their lives together. The high satisfaction reported in these marriages supports our egalitarian ideals. It is right and proper to respect one another and to work together as equals; this also makes us happy and stabilizes our relationships.

Now for some surprising findings. This same research also discloses that wife-dominated marriages are the least satisfying, while husband-dominated marriages lie somewhere in between. Marriages in which women openly dominate their husbands tend to be more troubled and less fulfilling than those in which men appear to dominate. Men do not find them satisfying, which should be obvious, but women do not find them satisfying either. So something about women dominating men feels unnatural, or at least uncomfortable, and leads to marital distress and dissatisfaction, even more than when men dominate.

How much should we be concerned with women dominating men? We live in what many consider to be a patriarchal society, where men hold the positions of power in politics and industry and are expected to be dominant in their families as well. But take a closer look at what actually happens in intimate conflict.

Men the Weaker Sex?
A researcher at the University of Washington, John Gottman, observed husbands and wives arguing and measured physiological stress. He found that men tend to be more stressed by marital arguments, compared with women, who are more comfortable with emotional confrontation. Men are more easily overwhelmed by emotional conflict than are women, reacting more

strongly to less provocation. A typical man is seriously troubled whenever his wife criticizes him, while a woman can usually handle criticism, unless her mate becomes truly contemptuous. Contrary to popular expectations, men are markedly more intimidated by angry women than women are by angry men. Men tend to become confused during such confrontations, moreso than women, losing track of what is said and where the argument is going. "In the sea of conflict," observes Gottman, "men sink and women swim."

Contrary to stereotype, women are found to be freer and more open than men in expressing their anger. Gottman observes that wives introduce complaints more than husbands, initiating most arguments. Once on a roll, wives tend to justify their positions further and introduce additional complaints, thus expanding arguments, while husbands try to reduce tension.

Gottman concludes that women are more willing to initiate conflict, more willing to escalate conflict, better able to handle it when it occurs and quicker to recover from it. Men, in contrast, seek to avoid conflict, try to contain it when it occurs, are less able to withstand conflict and take longer to recover from it. In short, women are generally more comfortable with personal conflict and are more confrontational, while men, who are more stressed by conflict, tend to placate. concede or withdraw. How strong are these findings? Women dominate in marital arguments about twice as often as men dominate. And the same pattern is observed by various researchers, among different social groups, across geographic locations, from generation to generation.

In the most lopsided altercations, only one partner argues, while the other endures in silence, immobilized by the barrage waiting to escape. Would it surprise you that most of those silenced in marital squabbles are men? In those oneway arguments, in which only one person argues, it is the women, by a ratio of six to one, who demand and scold and the men who are being scolded. If you are not convinced, do your own research. Poll a dozen of your acquaintances. Ask, "Who said most in arguments and had the last word in your family: your mother or your father?" And ask, "Who argues harder and usually has his or her way in your own relationship?"

Women's Emotional Power.

Many women do not feel powerful in relationships, and might presume therefore that men must possess the real power. It has even been argued that the man whose wife is scolding him has the real power, as he is controlling her by not doing what she wants. But the man who is being scolded and is not getting his way could hardly feel more powerful than the woman who is scolding him and not getting her way. All else being equal, would you not prefer to scold someone at whom you are angry rather than be scolded yourself?

It has also been argued that women dominate in arguments just to be heard, because they have the real power. But such thinking totally reverses the way real power works. The one who has the real power ordinarily dominates the arguments, not the subordinate. The drill sergeant dominates the recruit because the sergeant has the real power, and the recruit takes it instead of arguing back because he is being stripped of his power. The boss scolds the gofer but not the other way around, because the boss owns the company and the gofer is expendable. Indeed, dominance in verbal confrontation is an obvious way of gaining power, holding power, showing power and forwarding one's own agenda. The one who fails to hold his or her own either does not have the power or is fast on the way to losing it. Power comes in many forms, of course. Men typically have more physical power than women, and the men who are in charge at work have more authority there, or formal power. It is in the realm of personal arguments that women have the advantage: Women seem to have more of what we might call emotional power, which counts in personal relationships.

These observations are flattering neither to men nor to women. We expect men to be stronger and more independent than they appear here, and we expect women to be softer and gentler. Men ordinarily hide their weaknesses and present themselves as in charge, wanting to seem strong even when they typically lose the arguments or withdraw to avoid losing. Women typically have little respect for men who fold in arguments. And women who see themselves as mistreated underdogs, fighting for a fair break, do not want to acknowledge that they usually defeat their opposites

275

in personal confrontations. So as men and women, we collude to conceal how we are and to show ourselves instead as we wish to be seen.

Traditionally, a man was expected to commit himself to the support of his wife and children. In return, so far as he upheld his responsibilities, he was honored as the head of the family. In exchange for supporting his wife, doing what she and the children need from him, often deferring to her when she is upset with him and usually losing when he tries to argue against her, he was honored as the head the family.

Today we seek equality. Yet we cannot merely proclaim equality and then congratulate ourselves on our high ideals while marriage after marriage unravels amid continuing emotional conflagrations. Women have too much emotional firepower, and men are far too overwhelmed by it for equality to emerge on its own.

John Gottman looked in on his couples again, three years later, to chart their progress. He found that stress reactions among men appear to be most predictive. Marriages in which men were highly stressed in arguments tended to deteriorate over three years, while those in which men were calmer had increasing satisfaction. Indeed, Gottman found that his stress measures can predict 80 percent or more of the subsequent changes in marital satisfaction. A man comfortable in conflict suggests a bright, rosy future together, while high stress means foul weather ahead.

Where do we go from here? To strengthen marriages, the research suggests, we must uphold men. John Gottman is training women to be gentler in presenting personal complaints, so they do not overwhelm their husbands. Howard Markman at the University of Denver is coaching married couples to repeat back what the partner is saying when an argument heats up, to slow the pace so that the men can process the conversation. In my own practice, I use a stress reduction training I call mental shielding, to condition men to brush off the hostility instead of taking accusations so personally. Each of these interventions shows promising benefits.

America magazine, October 17, 1998

Reflective Listening
by Neil Katz and John W. Lawyer

Most people believe that listening is the easiest of the communication skills and that it comes to us naturally without the need for particular attention or training.

In fact, high-quality listening is an acquired skill that can be very sophisticated in practice and powerful in impact, particularly in stressful and conflictual situations. At best, we are only partially successful in its use. Extensive research has demonstrated that in this culture the average listening efficiency (defined as the ability to listen, understand, and retain information) is about 25%: One study reports that 60% of all misunderstandings in business can be traced to poor oral communications (speaking and listening) as opposed to only 1% for written communications (Nichols and Stevens, 1957, p. ix).

An important distinction to explore is the difference between hearing and listening. Hearing does not necessarily connote understanding the meaning of the information the speaker intended to convey. John Drakeford, in his book *The Awesome Power of the Listening Ear,* helps us understand the distinction:

Hearing is a word used to describe the physiological sensory processes by which auditory sensations are received by the ears and transmitted to the brain. Listening, on the other hand, refers to a more complex psychological procedure involving interpreting and understanding the significance of the sensory experience. (Drakeford,1967, p.17)

It is also easy to underestimate the importance of *listening*. In actuality, listening takes up more of our waking hours than any other activity. On the average, we spend between 70% and 80% of our waking moments communicating with others. Of that time, we spend 9% in writing, 16% in reading, 30% in talking, and 45% in listening (Nichols and Stevens, 1957, p. ix).

Listening is central to building and maintaining inter-personal relationships. The quality and effectiveness of our relationships with others, at home or on the job, significantly depend on our ability to listen.

Listening is at the heart of the communication process and is the core, fundamental competency for effective conflict resolution. Listening is critical for school administrators whose success relies on clear, successful communication and the creative, constructive handling of differences. Listening is the key to obtaining and maintaining rapport with another, particularly when that individual is experiencing strong emotion. Listening builds trust and credibility quickly and powerfully because people with strong emotion need and want to be heard and understood. Listening enables understanding in a nonjudgmental, supportive, and respectful manner. In listening, the focus is on the speaker's perspective.

Reflective Listening

Listening is a three-step communication process by which a person gathers information, processes that information, and then forms a hypothesis about what the other person means. Reflective listening is a four-step communications process in which a person gathers information, processes that information, forms a hypothesis about what the other person means, and then tests the hypothesis with the other person (see Figure 2.1). Listening becomes reflective listening when the fourth step is added.

The purposes of reflective listening are these: (1) To understand what the other person is saying, (2) To help the other clarify his or her thoughts and feelings, (3) To let the speaker know you have heard and understood, (4) To enable the other to clear out strong emotion and allow higher order thinking to take place.

Reflective listening is a core skill in communication and conflict resolution. It involves paying respectful attention to the content and feelings expressed in another's communication, hearing and understanding, and then letting the other know your perception of what you heard. In reflective listening you respond actively to another while keeping the focus of your attention totally on the other person. In reflective listening you do not offer your perspective but carefully keep the focus on the other's need or problem.

The process consists of two moments: (1) Hearing and understanding what the other person is communicating through words and body language and (2) Reflecting (saying to the other) succinctly the thoughts and feelings you heard through your own words, tone of voice, body posture, and gestures, so that the other knows he or she is being heard and understood

Reflective listening is a process of testing your hypothesis or "checking" to verify that you are hearing accurately. In order for this process to be effective, you must be able to perceive accurately what the other is experiencing and communicating; understand the communication at both the content and feeling level; accept the other's feelings; and, if there is a problem, commit to be present to the other while he or she works through that problem and arrives at a solution. When you can answer the question "What is going on with this person right now?" and have that verified, then you are listening reflectively with precision.

Important to reflective listening is testing or checking your hypothesis and verifying that your perception of small segments of another's communication is accurate. Each small segment captures a thought, feeling, or meaning or several thoughts, feelings, or meanings that fit together with a theme or are connected in some way. In reflective listening, you will ordinarily listen to a "bite-size piece" of another's communication and express or state the essence of it to the other in your own words. The checking of another's communication allows you to digest a workable amount of content and feelings. Breaking the conversation down in this way allows both parties in a communication to focus their cognitive abilities on manageable segments of a whole communication.

Your expression or statement to the other provides a check to ensure that you are hearing accurately and clearly and to let the other know that you are understanding what he or she is communicating. Your reflection (statement or expression of this essence of a specific chunk of communication) to the other is heard by the other at the unconscious level. If it fits with the speaker's model of the world at that moment, he or she will continue the conversation without a break or say "Yes" or "Exactly" and then continue with the communication. If the reflection is somewhat "off target," the speaker will become conscious of the mismatch at the conscious level, experience an interruption, and make the necessary correction. For example, "No, that's not quite right. I think it's more like irritation." If the reflection is completely off target, it diverts the conversation and takes the focus off the speaker.

In using reflective listening skills, you will often literally "break in" to the other's communication. This is experienced as interruptive only if your reflection misses the essence of the other's communication. If your reflection is accurate, the intervention is experienced as facilitative.

When to Reflective-Listen

Reflective listening is facilitated when the following conditions are present:

• The other person has the stronger need to be heard and the greater emotional energy.

• You have, and choose to take, the time to listen.

• You can remain reasonably separate and objective and not become personally involved in what the other is saying or react with a defensive response.

• You trust the resourcefulness of the other person to be responsible for his or her own life.

Reactive Responses

Reactive responses in listening situations are statements that interfere with the other's ability to express dear meaning. They are likely to take the focus off the other. Because a key element of listening is enabling the other to focus on his or her thoughts and feelings, a reactive response is inhibiting. The communication process is often frustrated and blocked when the listener allows reactive responses, which are particularly inappropriate when the other has a strong need or a problem or is experiencing strong emotion about an issue: Reactive responses tend to

• Serve the need of the responder and not the speaker

• Have a "high risk" of taking the focus off the speaker

• Tend to make the speaker feel judged, stupid, or unimportant

All reactive responses tend to take the focus off the other-those marked with an asterisk are never useful. The following are illustrations of the examples of typical reactive responses:

Solving

1. OrderingTelling the other person to do something

• You must do this by Friday.

- You can't do it that way.
- I expect you to do this.
- Stop it.

2. *Threatening*

Telling the other person what negative consequences will occur if he or she does something; sometimes alluding to the use of force.

- You had better do this, or else!
- If you don't do it, then . . .
- You'd better not try that . . .
- I warn you, if you do that . . .

3. *Moralizing*

Telling the other person why he or she *should* or *ought to* do something.

- You really should do this by Friday.
- You ought to try.
- You ought to do this; it's your duty.
- This is something I really urge you to do.

4. *Advising*

Telling the other person how to solve his or her problem.

- Let me suggest . . .
- It would be best for you if . . .
- If I were you, I'd . . .
- The best solution is . . .

5. *Questioning*

Trying to find reasons, facts, motives, causes, or information that will help you solve the other person's problem (closed-ended questions).

- Why did you do that?
- What have you done to solve it?
- Have you consulted anyone?
- Who has influenced you?

6. *Problem Solving*

Engaging the other in a problem-solving process prematurely (facilitating a problem-solving process with another is often appropriate after listening first).

- Let's solve this problem now . . .
- We have to be rational about this . . .

- Maybe if we brainstorm some alternatives now . . .
- Let's set aside these feelings and address the real issues . . .

Evaluating/judging

7. *Agreeing/Disagreeing*

Making a judgment of another's communication by agreeing or disagreeing with him or her.

- I agree . . . (I disagree . . .)
- Yes.
- You're absolutely right.
- You're all wrong on that point.

8. *Diagnosing*

Telling the other person what his or her motives are or analyzing the "whys" behind what he or she is doing or saying (communicating that you have figured out, or diagnosed, the other).

- You're saying this because you are angry.
- What you really need is . . .
- You have problems with authority.
- You want to look good.

9. *Criticizing/Blaming*

Making the other person feel stupid, outcast, or foolish (stereotyping or categorizing).

- You're out of line.
- You didn't do it right.
- You are a fuzzy thinker.
- It's your fault.

10. *Praising*

Offering a positive evaluation or judgment (often manipulative and/or condescending, sometimes sarcastic).

- You usually have such good judgment.
- You have so much potential.
- You've made quite a bit of progress.

Note: Praising has a powerful and important role in building autonomy when appropriately offered. Praising is a reactive response only when a judgment is made about the other's behavior. The syntax of "You must be feeling good about" reinforces productive behavior and is useful.

Withdrawing

11. Logical Arguing

Trying to divert the other person from his or her feelings with facts, arguments, logic, information, or expert opinions that happen to agree with your own.

- The facts are in favor of . . .
- Let me give you the facts.
- Here is the right way.

12. Understanding

Trying to let the person know you understand by telling him or her directly (saying the words "I understand").

- I understand.
- I understand totally what you are saying.
- I understand just how you're feeling.
- I understand just what you're thinking.

13. Reassuring

Trying to make the other person feel better; trying to either talk the other out of his or her feelings (making the feelings go away) or deny the strength of the feelings.

- Things will get better.
- It's always darkest before the dawn.
- Every cloud has a silver lining.
- It's not that bad.

14. Diverting-

Trying to get the other person away from the problem or getting away from it yourself. Trying to change the focus by kidding, offering other things to do, or pushing the problem away.

- Think about the positive side.
- Try not to worry about it until you've tried it.
- Let's have lunch and forget about it.
- That reminds me of the time when . . .

All the reactive responses have the potential of taking the focus off the other person's agenda and increasing their emotional energy in ways that inhibit effective problem solving. Reactive responses need to be identified in intense listening situations and avoided. You need to reflectively listen to others instead.

Reactive Response Dialogue

Here is a hypothetical dialogue to help illuminate some of

the potential negative effects of reactive responses. The dialogue illustrates the use of each example reactive response where a reflective listening response would be more appropriate.

A school principal (Kevin) and one of the teachers (Emily) are having a discussion in his office after school. Emily has had a terrible day. One of her daughters called to say that she got sick at school and missed her final exams, her fifth-grade students were disruptive in class in anticipation of the school vacation, and one of her students' parents had called her blaming her for something she had not done. To top it off, her social studies curriculum team got into a big argument, and two members who had not been working effectively threatened to quit, even though the work wasn't done. Emily was the accountable person for the curriculum report due in three days.

Emily initiates the discussion:

Emily: *You* won't believe the day I've had. It's one of the worst days I've had here. And that curriculum committee is too much. I'll never get the report done.

Kevin: (*Ordering—Commanding the other to do something*) Now Emily, just pull yourself together. Tell your colleagues to shape up and finish the report. The assistant super intendent is waiting for it.

Emily: *I* know. But there's no way we can get it done.

Kevin: (*Threatening—Using the specter of negative consequences to get the other to do something*) If you don't get it done by Friday, it's you who is going to be in trouble. The assistant superintendent is not a patient person.

Emily: At this point I really don't care.

Kevin: (*Moralizing—Telling the other why she ought to do something*) Don't care! Why Emily, you surprise me. If we all took that attitude this school system would be in a terrible mess. We're part of a team here, and you just need to pick up the pieces for the others on your committee.

Emily: Well, there's no way I can do this task alone by Friday, and the others are hardly speaking to one another.

Kevin: (*Advising—Telling the other how to solve the problem*) Now Emily, I've tried to tell you not to take any nonsense from these teachers. If I were you, I'd crack the whip and tell them to grow up and act their age.

Emily: If I said that, then they would all turn against me. They already think I'm riding them too hard.

Kevin: (*Questioning-Through close-ended questions, eliciting reasons, motives, or facts to allow listener to solve other's problem quickly or put blame on speaker*) Why do you think you're so soft on them? Is it because they are so much older than you? Are you intimidated by people who have been here longer than you have?

Emily: That's nonsense. It's not their age or anything personal. They just won't do the work to get the task done.

Kevin: (*Problem Solving-Solving problem prematurely, cutting short the necessary exploration of the problem*) Let's solve this right now. Tomorrow morning, go in and demand they give you the report within 24 hours.

Emily: I don't know if that will work at this point. They're not even talking to each other right now.

Kevin: (*Agreeing/Disagreeing-Agreeing/disagreeing with other's conclusions or assessment*) You're absolutely wrong to let them carry on like this.

Emily: Well, I really don't know what else to do.

Kevin: (*Diagnosing-Telling other what her motives are or analyzing the "whys" behind behavior or words*) You're just down in the dumps because your husband got laid off. I'm sure you're depressed and worried and you're bringing those attitudes into your work here. You're so negative these days.

Emily: That's not true! I come to work eager to work with my students and colleagues. It's just that these bozos aren't holding up their end and are acting like two-year-olds!

Kevin: (*Criticizing/Blaming-Stereotyping or categorizing the person as a way to diminish her concerns*) I think it really might be your fault. You're such a naive idealist, always thinking the world is fair and everyone will do their share. I don't know who fed you that baloney.

Emily: Oh, that's just great. We should all go around and pick up for the slackers. I should do all the work and they should all get the credit.

Kevin: (*Praising-Offering a nonspecific, positive judgment that is often condescending and manipulative and sometimes sarcastic*) Well, that's *the way* it is sometimes. You've always been one who's willing to go the extra mile for the good of the school. It sure would be good to have you come through again for us.

Emily: Well, I'll try, but I don't think it will work this time. And I'm angry about always having to cover up for them.

Kevin: (*Logical Arguing-Trying to divert the other from her feelings with facts or information to agree with your solution*) Let's look at the facts here. These teachers are making damn good money to meet their responsibilities, and one of those responsibilities is to do committee work. You certainly have the right to demand more from them.

Emily: Maybe you do have a point. But with everything going on in my life right now, I sure didn't need this problem with the curriculum committee.

Kevin: (*Understanding-Using the proper words but not giving evidence of understanding*) I understand just how you feel.

Emily: I don't think you do. You don't have to work with them on this project. I'll never get it done on time doing it all myself.

Kevin: (*Reassuring-Trying to make the other feel better by denying the strength of her feelings*) Don't worry. You'll get it done one way or another and this crisis will pass. Maybe the others will surprise you and come through.

Emily: I doubt it-and I'm still worried and frustrated.

Kevin: (*Diverting-Trying to get you and the other away from the problem by changing the focus*) Let's forget it and go to the lounge for coffee. I can tell you about the new boat I just bought.

Even though reactive responses are usually well intentioned and are habitual in most of us, we need to recognize that they have damaging costs: They take the focus off the other's thoughts and feelings and do not enable them to become more resourceful. In addition, they send subtle messages to the other person. They say, "You are not OK as you are." Reactive responses need to be recognized and avoided, especially in times when one or more of the parties have high energy and a high need to be listened to and understood. On these occasions, use reflective listening instead of reactive responses to help clarify thoughts, work constructively with feelings, and move toward problem solving if necessary.

from "Resolving Conflict Successfully"
Corwin Press
Thousand Oaks CA 1994

Sensing
by Dudley Weeks

Running throughout the techniques of the *conflict part-nership* method are three skills that may seem too obvious, or perhaps too common sense, to mention. But since these foundation skills are often overlooked in the midst of the conflict management process, they deserve attention at the very beginning of our discussion of techniques. The three skills are sensing, sorting, and a difficult toname skill we will term "shifting."

Technique #3: Sensing

Sensing utilizes your ears and eyes to take into your brain the communications given by your conflict partner. In other words, it's the way you listen and see. Many conflicts are dealt with poorly because the conflict partners fail to listen accurately to what is being said, or fail to see the nonverbal communication given by the other party.

Furthermore, some people even fail to listen to and see their own communications accurately. The tension caused by the conflict can lead a person to say something they don't intend to say, or to say it in a way they know will confuse or threaten the other party, or worsen the conflict. Listening to yourself, seeing the way what you say affects your conflict partner, and sensing your own physical reaction to the behavior of the other party are all important foundation skills. If you are doing a good job of sensing yourself, a sudden increase in heartbeat, or sweating, or whatever signal tells you that you are losing control of yourself, should lead you to pause to recollect your composure.

There are ways to sharpen our sensing skills, and suggestions will be given in just a moment. But first let's look at an example of how a poor use of the sensing skill can make effective conflict management almost impossible. Our example is a story involving the Barnes family.

During the past year the family has experienced a growing number of conflicts. Things have become so disruptive that unhappiness fills the lives of the family members, both at home and away from home. On this particular evening, Bob (father),

Ruth (mother), Pat (22 year old daughter), Chip (15 year old son), and Gail (12 year old daughter) are in the living room doing what they do most every night—watching TV and getting on each other's nerves. Suddenly, Chip gets up and changes the TV channel right in the middle of Gail's favorite show.

Gail: Hey!What'd you do that for? Turn it back!

Bob: I don't know what's happening to this family. All we do these days is fight.

Gail: Turn it back to Channel 4, Chip! Dad, make him turn it back!

Pat: We don't have to watch TV, you know. This family could enjoy talking with each other, if we just...

Ruth: I'm dreading having to start on those income tax returns tomorrow.

(Gail gets up and switches channels)

Chip: I want to watch the soccer match! Turn it back, Gail, or I'll *make* you turn it back!

Gail: Oh, I'm scared to death! Big, mean Chip thinks he's so tough! You sissy. You can't even make the football team.

Chip: Dad?! Make her-

Bob: Both of you shut up!!

Pat: Let's just turn the TV off and try to talk about what's happening to this family. Ever since I moved back home last year I've watched all of us get more and more...

(Chip gets up and switches back to the soccer channel)

Gail: Dad?! Please help me! Why am I always the one who has to give in!

Ruth: Maybe I should get a professional to do the returns this year. I hate doing tax returns.

Bob: We can't afford a professional.

Ruth: Well then you do 'em for a change! I'm getting sick and tired of doing all the work around here! Ever since you got laid off I've had to *carry* this family! (Bob stiffens, then gradually begins to slump down in his chair)

Ruth: I do the shopping. I do the cooking. I beat my fingers to death on that typewriter at work. And what do you do, man-of-the house? Nothing, that's what!

Chip: Don't touch that button, Gail! So help me I'll...

Bob: I couldn't help getting laid off. I'm trying every day to find a job. You know that.

Pat: Mom, you know Dad is trying to get a job. It's not his fault.

Bob: And I help with the housework whenever you let me. You're just sore because we can't add a swimming pool to the house so you can get a tan and convince yourself you're not almost 50 years old!

Pat: C'mon, Dad. That's not fair. You're *both* being unfair. And can't we turn that damn TV off?! How can we discuss things when that TV is...

Ruth: You're one to talk, Pat! Married one year and divorced! You brought shame to the entire family! (Gail changes the channel and Chip shoves her down on the sofa.

Gail: I hope you get zits so bad your cute little Betsy gets sick every time she looks at you! Dad? Mom? He *hit* me! Aren't you going to do something?

Bob: Can't you two keep it down?! This place is a circus! (Gail starts crying and runs up to her room.)

Ruth: I'm *not* doing those tax returns this year!

Bob: Then don't do 'em, for God's sake!

Chip: Can't you keep the noise down? I'm trying to watch TV!

(Pat surveys the carnage and slowly walks outside into the thunder and lightning to find a little tranquility.)

Except for Pat, nobody did very much "sensing." Each person was rigidly locked into what he or she wanted to do or say and never really listened to, or observed, the other conflict parties. If effective sensing had been practiced, there is a much better chance that (1) Pat's repeated suggestions and attempts at mediation would have been supported, (2) Gail's obvious feeling of being the family outcast would have been dealt with, (3) Bob's vulnerability to his unfortunate work situation, and Ruth's vulnerability to her age, would not have been exploited, and (4) Chip's selfish behavior would have been disciplined rather than ignored. All of these steps would have aided the conflict management process. Without any real attempts at sensing, the evening's events did indeed become a circus. The sources of conflict within the family were never addressed. Instead, many *symptoms* of the deeper conflicts were allowed to take center stage.

Now let's take the same situation and show how effective sensing might have nudged the Barnes family a little closer to a worthwhile conflict management process. Once again, the evening begins with Chip changing the TV channel.

Gail: Hey! Wha'd you do that for? Turn it back!

Bob: I don't know what's happening to this family. All we do these days is fight.

Pat: Maybe we should take some time tonight and talk about it. We can forego the TV for something this important, can't we?

Ruth: I'm dreading doing the income tax returns again this year. Let's get a professional to do them.

Bob: We can't afford a professional.

Ruth: Well then you do 'em for a change! I'm getting sick and tired of-

Pat.: Mom! Dad! Please! Income tax returns aren't causing our conflicts around here. Let's turn off the TV and have a quiet discussion.

Ruth: Well. . .we do need to get our lives straightened out. I've been so unhappy lately.

Pat: Everybody agree to turn the TV off and have a discussion?

Chip: I want to watch soccer.

Gail:. I want to watch my show.

Pat: Believe me, you'll be able to watch TV with more pleasure in the future if we get this family in a better mood.

Gail: But there's only 10 minutes left in the show!

Pat: Okay, but if you get to finish it, will you agree to take part in the discussion.

Gail: Sure.

Chip: (going to the TV) Well, I'm going to watch soccer!

Bob: No, Chip. Let Gail finish her show. You get the TV tomorrow night at this time.

Chip: But

Pat: While Gail finishes, let's be thinking about some ideas for how we can improve things around here.

(Everybody is relatively quiet while Gail finishes her show, then Pat turns off the TV.)

Ruth: I've thought of something. We ought to have weekly meetings to discuss our family problems.

Chip: Now that's what I call boring!

Pat: Chip, don't you have some things you'd like done differently around here!

Chip: Well, sure, but

Pat: Then a weekly meeting would give you a chance to be heard. Gail? What do you think about a meeting?

Gail:. Yeah, I like it. Maybe people would listen to me for a change if we all had our turn in a meeting.

Ruth: Let's have our first meeting right now. I want to say that I need more help around here. Ever since Bob got laid off, it's been tough.

Bob: It's not my fault I got laid off.

Ruth: I know, Bob, I'm not saying it is. But maybe you could do more of the housework now that you're home most of the time. That would really help.

Bob: Yeah, I guess it would. Okay. You tell me what to do and I'll do it. . .but I may not do it as well as you'd like.

Ruth: Do you have a gripe, Bob?

Bob: Well. . .I wish you wouldn't bring up my being laid off as often as you do. It's bad enough without being reminded of it daily.

Ruth: I didn't realize I mentioned it so much.

Bob: Well, you do.

Ruth: Okay. I'll stop bringing it up.

Chip: Can I watch soccer now?

Gail: You're hopeless, Chip.

The problems and conflicts the Barnes family experiences cannot be solved by one night's discussion. But at least a process has been started, primarily because the family members used basic skills of sensing to listen to and observe the needs and concerns of each other. Sensing skills cannot solve conflicts all by themselves, but they lay a good foundation for the more specific techniques of conflict partnership that will be discussed later.

Some people may be quite adept at sensing, while others

may need to improve their sensing skills. There are several simple ways to improve these skills.

One way is to work on concentration. If you're at a party where several people are talking at once, practice concentrating on what one person is saying while literally shutting out the other voices around you. Picture yourself moving closer to the person whose words you are concentrating on, or picture a movie in which the rest of the crowd is out of focus and only you and the person you're listening to are in focus. You can also improve your concentration skills by picking out one sound from among the many you may hear on a street corner, in a forest, or in your office, or wherever you happen to be. In your mind, try to increase the volume and clarity of that one sound and reduce the other sounds. And as you are concentrating, don't allow yourself to get tense. Try to relax everything but those senses you need to hear or see clearly the object of your concentration. Picture the strength required to operate the rest of your body shifting over to add strength to your sensing skills.

Concentration is only one part of sensing. Another important ingredient is clarifying. Although we will deal in greater depth with this technique later in the chapter, a brief mention of its importance is appropriate at this point. In the midst of conflict, even though you may have your sensing skills operating at full throttle, many statements are so influenced by the emotions and interests of both the speaker and listener that frequent clarification is needed. The person who uses sensing skills effectively will make sure she or he has heard or sensed clearly the communications of the conflict partner. "I heard you saying that you. . ." is a good clarifying comment that gives the other party a chance both to be sure of what they want to convey and to straighten you out if you have heard or sensed incorrectly.

from "Conflict Partnerships"
by Dudley Weeks

Everyday Love
by Sidney Harris

What we commonly call "love" is a lot of little things rather than one big thing. The big thing may bowl us over at first, but it is the repetitive regularity of the little things that keep love alive and afloat.

The defect with romantic films and stories is that they portray the big thing, which incitca the initial feeling, but cannot alone sustain it. Love alone withers without constant watering—and this "watering" is less an emotion than an action and a concern.

When we are young, and yearning for a grand passion to transform our lives, we have such a lofty conception of love that we never think of it in terms of the simple kindnesses of ordinary acts, but as a great abstract idea or feeling, unconnected to reality.

As one of my favorite authors, Paul Tournier, the doctor-preacher-teacher, said in one of his books, "To love is to will the good for another." And the good for another is not necessarily heroic devotion and self-sacrifice, but many small matters that add up over the days and years.

Love is having to say you're sorry time and again, because any two persons living together are bound to step on one another's toes from day to day.

Dr. Tournier takes it even further into particulars:

"Love means writing with enough care so that our correspondent can read it without spending time deciphering it; that is, it may mean taking the time to save him time.

"To love is to pay one's bills: it is to keep things in order, so that the mate's work will he made easier.

"It means arriving somewhere on time: it means giving our full attention to the one who is talking to you. To miss what he or she says can mean that we are more interested in what we are telling ourselves inwardly than in what we are being told.

"To love is to try to speak in his or her own language, even if we have mastered it but poorly, rather than forcing the other to speak ours."

Some of these injunctions may sound trivial, or merely good manners, but what is genuine love but good manners raised to the nth degree?

Love begins as an emotion, but unless it is steadily ratified by acts of the will, it becomes a dead letter as soon as the emotion subsides, and leaves little in its place. This is why the great romantics often have the most tragic, disillusioned or unfulfilled love lives, marked by the heroic gesture, but deficient in the human touch.

Syndicated column, Chicago Sun Times
May 8 1983

Resolving Conflicts Nonviolently
by Colman McCarthy

When speaking before audiences about nonviolent conflict resolution, I ask two questions. How many of you have ever
been hit in any physical way anytime in your life by a total stranger?
A few isolated hands go up. Second question: how many of you
have ever been hit in any physical way anytime in your life by
someone you know or by a member of your family?

Nearly all hands go up.

Yet most of us are conditioned to fear the street criminal,
even though for many people there is more to fear walking in the
house at night than walking out.

In the same convoluted way, Americans are conditioned
to fear international criminals—what have lately been called "rogue
nations"—even though since 1945 we are the ones who have dispatched soldiers to bomb or threaten to bomb people in China
(1945-46), Korea (1950-53), China (1950-53), Guatemala (1954),
Indonesia (1958), Cuba (1959-60), Guatemala (1960), Congo
(1964), Peru (1965), Laos (1964-73), Vietnam (1961-73), Cambodia (1969-70), Guatemala (1967-69), Grenada (1983), Libya
(1986), El Salvador (1980s), Nicaragua (1980s), Panama (1989),
Iraq (1991-2000), Sudan (1998), Afghanistan (1998), and Yugoslavia (1999).

Whether it's across a living room or across a border, conflicts will be settled either through violent force or through nonviolent force. Conflict, by definition, means only this: we need to
change our way of dealing with each other; the old way no longer
works. Conflict is a neutral term, neither positive nor negative. If
someone says, "I like to avoid conflict," get them a one-way ticket
to Mars, Pluto, or Neptune. On earth, this third-rate planet revolv-
ing around a second-rate sun, we have conflict. It's almost always
a signal to get another way of dealing with a disagreement.

Since 1982, 1 have been teaching high school, college,
and law students the methods of nonviolent conflict resolution. I

have learned two realities from having taught some 5,000 students: first, nonviolence is teachable; and second, the young are hungry to learn the skills.

No nation has so vast a literature on nonviolence as America. Yet, judging from our history of wars, our high rates of homicide, spouse and child abuse, abortions, the killing of animals for food, our death row executions, it's as if the art of resolving conflicts nonviolently were as hard to learn as astrophysics in Urdu.

It isn't that hard. The following steps are among the well-tested methods of decreasing or ending violence--whether the disputes are among or within nations, companies, school kids, or families:

Define the conflict. If defined objectively, rather than subjectively, which is how most of us do it, conflict means only this: We need a new way of doing things, the old way has failed.

Sociologists report that in as many as seventy-five percent of husband-wife fights, the combatants are battling over different issues. The husband may be enraged over what his wife said or did that morning. The wife is out of control over what her husband said or did ten weeks ago. They can't settle their conflict because they don't know what it's about. It's this to him, that to her.

This dynamic is seen among warring nations, not only battling couples. In 1991, Iraqi President Saddam Hussein and President George Bush, leaders of two governments long accustomed to solving conflicts by killing people, defined their dispute differently. For Hussein, it was a property issue: Land under Kuwait's control really belonged to Iraq. Bush defined it several ways. First, it was oil. Then it was the threat to the industrial world. Finally, it was that old standby: stopping naked aggression.

Here were two politicians, as self-righteous and self deluded as a warring husband and wife, unwilling to define the essence of the conflict. If two sides can define what they are fighting about, the chances increase that misperceptions will be clarified.

It's not you against me, it's you and me against the problem. The problem is the problem. Most people and nations go into battle convinced, I'm right, you're wrong; I'm good, you're evil; I'm wise, you're foolish; I'm going to win, you're going to lose. Even if one side does win, the first reaction of the loser is, I want a rematch: I'll come back with meaner words, harder fists and bigger bombs. Then you'll learn, then you'll be good and then we'll have peace forever.

This is an illusion, but few can give it up. By focusing on the problem, and not the person with the problem, a climate of cooperation, not competition, is enhanced.

List the relationship's many shared concerns and needs, as against one shared separation. In Ernest Hemingway's novel, *A Farewell To Arms*, the most soulful of his stories (as against his usual chest-thumping books), a character is described in a hauntingly beautiful phrase: "He was strong in the broken places." All of us have been, are being, or will be broken by life. If we are strong in the broken places, chances for mending increase. They'll increase if the strengths of the relationship—the shared concerns and needs—are given more attention than the lone unshared separation.

When people have fought, don't ask what happened. This is an irrelevant question. They will answer with their version of what happened, almost always self-justifying. The better question is, "What did you do?" This elicits facts, not opinions. Misperceptions are clarified, not prolonged.

Skilled trial layers, whether in civil or criminal cases, don't ask people on the stand what happened. Instead, it's "What did you do?" Juries decide or are told to decide on the relevance of factual information.

Work on active listening, not passive hearing. Conflicts escalate when partners try to talk more than listen and then only listen as a timeout for verbal rearming. Listening well is an act of caring. If you are a good listener, you have many friends. If you are a poor listener, you have many acquaintances. Anatomically, we are made to listen more than speak, which is why we have two ears and one mouth.

Choose a place to resolve the conflict, not the battleground itself. Armies tend to sign peace treaties far from the war zones. Too many emotions are there.

In some schools around the country where progressive faculties are teaching, peace rooms are in place. Anyone who was fighting—in the schoolyard, the halls, the bus—automatically knows to go to the peace room at the time set, say every Friday morning from nine to noon. Who will be there? Mediators: classmates who have been trained in the essentials of nonviolent conflict resolution. Principals and psychologists in schools that have peace rooms see the results in lower rates of violence.

Start with what's doable. Restoration of peace can't be done quickly. If it took a long time for the dispute to begin, it will take time to end it.

Work on one small doable rather than many large undoables. Almost always, it's a laughably small wound that causes the first hurt in a relationship. But then, ignoring the smallness takes on a size of its own. Ignoring the problem becomes larger than the original problem.

Develop forgiveness skills. Many people of large minds are willing to say after the conflict, "I'm going to bury the hatchet." To themselves, they add: "But I'm going to mark exactly where I bury it, just in case I need to dig it up for the next fight."

Forgiveness looks forward, vengeance looks backward. Again, it's anatomy: we have eyes in the front of our heads, not the back.

Purify our hearts. This is merely an elegant way of telling ourselves, "I need to get my own messy life in order before I can instruct others how to live."

The United States—President Clinton, Secretary of State Madeleine K. Albright, Defense Secretary William S. Cohen and others—have been busy preaching to Saddam Hussein about Iraq's weapons of mass destruction, while the United States has the largest arsenal of such weapons in the history of the planet.

Why not send in the heralded United Nations inspection team to tell the world where America's weapons of mass destruction are located—and how many, and how much money was spent on them that could have gone to schools, health care, and road repair?

Purifying America's heart would involve facing the unpleasant reality that the Rev. Martin Luther King Jr. spoke of April 4,1967, in his antiwar speech at Riverside Church in New York:

"The greatest purveyor of violence in the world today [is] my own government .... A nation that continues year after year to spend more money on military defense than on programs of social uplift is approaching spiritual death."

Do these nine steps of nonviolent conflict resolution always work? No. Sometimes the conflict partners are so emotionally wounded or ideologically hidebound that nothing can stop the violence. But large numbers of conflicts can be resolved without killing or wounding the other side, provided the strategies for peacemaking are known. If they aren't known, start to teach them: in the world's schools, in religious institutions. They all claim to want peace.

Gandhi routinely said, don't bring your opponents to their knees, bring them to their senses. Nonviolence means prevention before the crisis. Violence says the opposite: intervention after—intervention with fists, guns, bombs, and armies.

With 28,000 high schools in the United States, 78,000 elementary schools and 3,000 colleges, few other opportunities for decreasing violence are greater than peace education: systematically teaching the literature of peace and techniques of conflict resolution, in every grade in every school.

Wishful thinking—yes, let us hope for peace—won't do it. Serious thinking will.

from Fellowship Magazine November-December 2000

12

Nonviolence Towards Animals

Nine billion animals are killed and eaten each year in the United States alone—and they are bred, raised, transported, and killed at a staggering rate of 285 animals every second.

Interview with Paul Shapiro

Q. *What does it mean to be in favor of animal rights?*

A. To be in favor of animal rights is to acknowledge that animals feel pain and that we should avoid causing them pain. The animal rights movement contends that animals are not mere commodities to be used by humans, but rather our moral equals who have the right to live free of abuse and exploitation. Hence, as it is unethical to exploit humans, regardless of what interest may be served by their exploitation, it is also unethical to harm or exploit animals for any purpose (whether it be for food, clothing, entertainment, or science). Discrimination based on species membership (speciesism) is no less of an injustice than discrimination based on other irrelevant characteristics (e.g., race, gender, class, or sexual preference). All of these prejudices are based on perceived inferiority, thereby attempting to justify the ruthless domination of an entire group.

Q. *Obviously humans should have rights, but aren't animals inferior to us and thus not deserving of rights?*

A. Many arguments are used to justify speciesism, or placing animals in an inferior position to humans. Most of these arguments are based on the fact that humans are rational and more intelligent than other animals. These two facts, however, are morally irrelevant. Many animals are more rational and intelligent than human infants and even some seriously retarded human adults. This does not mean that human infants or seriously retarded adults should not have rights. It does mean, however, that these two criterion are morally insufficient characteristics to justify human supremacy.

The only morally relevant characteristic that is needed to warrant the granting of rights is the capacity to feel pain and suffering. In other words, if an individual can suffer, we have a moral obligation to do what we can to avoid inflicting suffering unto him or her.

Q. *Exactly what rights should animals have?*

A. As humans and other animals are not exactly the same, it makes sense that they should not have the same exact rights. For example, all humans should have the right to vote. However, animals are incapable of understanding the concept of democracy or voting and therefore do not need this right. Similarly, fowl have a strong biological need to flap their wings and fly, whereas humans do not. Therefore, humans do not need this right, while fowl do.

Generally speaking however, animals should have the right to live, to avoid pain, to pursue happiness, to live on a healthy planet, and to be free from exploitation, regardless of what human interest may be served by their pain or exploitation.

Q. *How can you prove that animals feel pain?*

A. The same question could be posed with regard to whether it is possible to know if other humans feel pain. If you have never experienced someone else's suffering, how can you know if it's real? Aside from the evolutionary usefulness of pain, there are many ways to conclude that others suffer. Science tells us that if a being possesses both a central nervous system and a brain, it can be deduced that he or she is not only capable of suffering, but is also aware of that pain. Almost all animals possess both central nervous systems and brains. Also, common sense tells us that when we kick dogs, they yelp. When we brand horses, they scream and display facial contortions indicating a state of agony. Animals are not mere machines who respond with artificial cries for help. On the contrary, they are fully capable of suffering and have rich emotional lives.

Q. *If the animals are raised to be eaten or otherwise used, isn't that okay?*

A. Two hundred years ago in the United States, humans

raised other humans for the purpose of making them into slaves. The fact that these humans were raised to be slaves did not justify their slavery. For the same reason, raising animals for the purpose of torturing and/or killing them does not justify their exploitation.

Q. *But animal exploitation is legal.*

A. In the United Sates, it was once legal to own human slaves. At one point in Germany, it was legal to torment and kill Jews. The legality of something does not determine its morality.

Q. *Didn't God give human beings dominion over other animals?*

A. First, we must recognize that there are hundreds of religions around the world, some of which command us to abstain from harming other animals. However, it is true that in the Judeo-Christian Bible there is a passage which states that humans have "dominion" over other animals. Even if we accept Judeo-Christianity as the only true religion and the Bible as the literal word of God, in its original context, the word "dominion" is defined as "humane stewardship." Torturing and killing billions of animals on a yearly basis for largely unnecessary purposes (e.g., palate preference, clothing, or entertainment) hardly seems to fit this definition.

Q. *Other animals eat each other. Why can't we eat them?*

A. Predators in the wild kill other animals out of *necessity*. Without doing it, they would not survive. Humans, on the other hand, kill other animals by *choice*. The human body has no need for animal flesh whatsoever. In fact, it has even been proven consistently that a vegan (pure vegetarian) diet is far healthier than a diet rich in animal products. Eating animals is not necessary for human survival. Rather, it is a matter of morality: Is it acceptable to inflict unconscionable suffering and death unto countless animals for something that is indisputably unnecessary

Q. Humans are the fittest animal on earth. Why shouldn't we use our strength to our benefit?

A. The argument that "might makes right" has been used by many (including Hitler) to justify several forms of cruelty and domination throughout history. Just as rationality and intelligence are insufficient characteristics to justify human supremacy, so is strength.

Q. What about vivisection that would lead to medical break- throughs for humans?

A. First, the premise of vivisection is inherently flawed. Humans and other animals are so biologically different that most of the time, the effects of one substance on an animal subject will be totally different from the results on a human subject. More im- portantly however, there is such a thing as "ill gotten gains." If we were to force unwilling human subjects into a painful experiment that could possibly help other humans, would it be acceptable? Note that this is exactly what Nazis did to their victims.

As humans are the moral equals of other animals, maiming and ultimately killing an unwilling human in hopes that other humans may benefit is the moral equivalent of maiming and ulti- mately killing an animal with the hope that her or his suffering might help some humans.

Q. Where do you draw the line? Insects? Plants? Bacteria?

A. If the only morally relevant characteristic is the capac- ity to suffer, than the vast majority of animals would qualify for the granting of rights. There are some animals (such as extremely small insects) who we are not completely certain are capable of suffering. It is up to each individual to decide where she or he feels the line should be drawn exactly.However, it is indisputable that all of the animals we institutionally exploit are capable of suffer- ing and therefore deserve the right to be free. Also, because of their lack of a central nervous system or brain, it is certain that plants and bacteria do not suffer.

Q. Wouldn't the economy be crippled if we abolished animal exploitation?

A. The profitability of something is not relevant to its morality. Many institutions were extremely profitable, yet inherently unethical. For example, the abolition of slavery and child labor most certainly harmed the economy. After the Emancipation Proclamation, the South had to rebuild its economy through a reconstruction period. Does this mean that the abolition of slavery or child labor should not have occurred? Also, the chance of animal exploitation being abolished all at once is basically nonexistent. Rather, as consumer demand gradually decreases for animal products, the meat industry will gradually fade out. With its demise will come the expansion of the vegetarian food market, and therefore many job openings in that market.

Q. It's impossible to live completely cruelty free. Almost everything we do causes someone suffering. Why try at all?

A. True, it is very hard to eliminate all forms of cruelty in our lives. However, that doesn't justify an "open season" for blatant animal abuse. By adopting a vegan diet, boycotting companies that test on animals, and boycotting shows that exploit animals for entertainment, we can drastically reduce the amount of suffering we cause in our daily lives.

While we can't completely eliminate 100 percent of the suffering we cause, by taking these simple steps to respect animal rights, we can seriously reduce the suffering we cause, and even rid the world of various forms of institutionalized animal abuse.

Paul Shapiro, a peace studies graduate of George Washington University 2001 is the co-director o Compassion Over Killing, a Washington non-profit

Am I Blue?
by Alice Walker

For about three years my companion and I rented a small house in the country that stood on the edge of a large meadow that appeared to run from the end of our deck straight into the mountains. The mountains, however, were quite far away, and between us and them there was, in fact, a town. It was one of the many pleasant aspects of the house that you never really were aware of this.

It was a house of many windows, low, wide, nearly floor to ceiling in the living room, which faced the meadow, and it was from one of these that I first saw our closest neighbor, a large white horse, cropping grass, flipping its mane, and ambling about—not over the entire meadow, which stretched well out of sight of the house, but over the five or so fenced-in acres that were next to the twenty-odd that we had rented. I soon learned that the horse, whose name was Blue, belonged to a man who lived in another town, but was boarded by our neighbor next door. Occasionally, one of the children, usually a stocky teen-ager, but sometimes a much younger girl or boy, could be seen riding Blue. They would appear in the meadow, climb up on his back, ride furiously for ten or fifteen minutes, then get off, slap Blue on the flanks, and not be seen again for a month or more.

There were many apple trees in our yard, and one by the fence that Blue could almost reach. We were soon in the habit of feeding him apples, which he relished, especially because by the middle of summer the meadow grasses-so green and succulent since January-had dried out from lack of rain, and Blue stumbled about munching the dried stalks half-heartedly. Sometimes he would stand very still just by the apple tree, and when one of us came out he would whinny, snort loudly, or stamp the ground. This meant, of course: I want an apple.

It was quite wonderful to pick a few apples, or collect those that had fallen to the ground overnight, and patiently hold them, one by one, up to his large, toothy mouth. I remained as thrilled as a child by his flexible dark lips, huge, cube-like teeth that crunched the apples, core and all, with such finality, and his high, broad-breasted enormity; beside which, I felt small indeed. When I was a child, I used to ride horses, and was especially friendly with one named Nan until the day I was riding and my brother deliberately spooked her and I was thrown, head first, against the trunk of a tree. When I came to, I was in bed and my mother was bending worriedly over me; we silently agreed that perhaps horseback riding was not the safest sport for me. Since then I have walked, and prefer walking to horseback riding—but I had forgotten the depth of feeling one could see in horses' eyes.

I was therefore unprepared for the expression in Blue's. Blue was lonely. Blue was horribly lonely and bored. I was not shocked that this should be the case; five acres to tramp by yourself, endlessly, even in the most beautiful of meadows—and his was—cannot provide many interesting events, and once rainy season turned to dry that was about it. No, I was shocked that I had forgotten that human animals and nonhuman animals can communicate quite well; if we are brought up around animals as children we take this for granted. By the time we are adults we no longer remember. However, the animals have not changed. They are in fact *completed* creations (at least they seem to be, so much more than we) who are not likely *to* change; it is their nature to express themselves. What else are they going to express? And they do. And, generally speaking, they are ignored.

After giving Blue the apples, I would wander back to the house, aware that he was observing me. Were more apples not forthcoming then? Was that to be his sole entertainment for the day? My partner's small son had decided he wanted to learn how to piece a quilt; we worked in silence on our respective squares as I thought . . .

Well, about slavery: about white children, who were raised by black people, who knew their first all-accepting love from black women, and then, when they were twelve or so, were told they must "forget" the deep levels of communication between themselves and "mammy" that they knew. Later they would be able to relate quite calmly, "My old mammy was sold to another good family." "My old mammy was --- ---." Fill in the blank. Many more years later a white woman would say: "I can't understand these

Negroes, these blacks. What do they want? They're so different from us."

And about the Indians, considered to be "like animals" by the "settlers" (a very benign euphemism for what they actually were), who did not understand their description as a compliment. And about the thousands of American men who marry Japanese, Korean, Filipina, and other non-English-speaking women and of how happy they report they are, "blissfully," until their brides learn to speak English, at which point the marriages tend to fall apart. What then did the men see, when they looked into the eyes of the women they married, before they could speak English? Apparently only their own reflections.

I thought of society's impatience with the young. "Why are they playing the music so loud?" Perhaps the children have listened to much of the music of oppressed people their parents danced to before they were born, with its passionate but soft cries for acceptance and love, and they have wondered why their parents failed to hear.

I do not know how long Blue had inhabited his five beautiful, boring acres before we moved into our house; a year after we had arrived and had also traveled to other valleys, other cities, other worlds, she was still there.

But then, in our second year at the house, something happened in Blue's life. One morning, looking out the window at the fog that lay like a ribbon over the meadow, I saw another horse, a brown one, at the other end of Blue's field. Blue appeared to be afraid of it, and for several days made no attempt to go near. We went away for a week. When we returned, Blue had decided to make friends and the two horses ambled or galloped along together, and Blue did not come nearly as often to the fence underneath the apple tree.

When he did, bringing his new friend with him, there was a different look in his eyes. A look of independence, of self-possession, of inalienable horseness. His friend eventually became pregnant. For months and months there was, it seemed to me, a mutual feeling between me and the horses of justice, of peace. I fed apples to them both. The look in Blue's eyes was one of unabashed "this is itness."

It did not, however, last forever. One day, after a visit to the city, I went out to give Blue some apples. He stood waiting, or so I thought, though not beneath the tree. When I shook the tree and jumped back from the shower of apples, he made no move. I carried some over to him. He managed to half-crunch one. The rest he let fall to the ground. I dreaded looking into his eyes because I had of course noticed that Brown, his partner, had gone—but I did look. If I had been born into slavery, and my partner had been sold or killed, my eyes would have looked like that. The children next door explained that Blue's partner had been "put with him" (the same expression that old people used, I had noticed, when speaking of an ancestor during slavery who had been impregnated by her owner) so that they could mate and she conceive. Since that was accomplished, she had been taken back by her owner, who lived somewhere else.

Will she be back? I asked.

They didn't know.

Blue was like a crazed person. Blue was, to me, a crazed person. He galloped furiously, as, if he were being ridden, around and around his beautiful five acres. He whinnied until he couldn't. He tore at the ground with his hooves. He butted himself against his single shade tree. He looked always and always toward the road down which his partner had gone. And then, occasionally, when he came up for apples, or I took apples to him, he looked at me. It was a look so piercing, so full of grief, a look *so human*, I almost laughed (I felt too sad to cry) to think there are people who do not know that animals suffer. People like me who have forgotten, and daily forget, all that animals try to tell us.

"Everything you do to us will happen to you; we are your teachers, as you are ours. We are one lesson" is essentially it, I think. There are those who never once have even considered animals' rights: those who have been taught that animals actually want to be used and abused by us, as small children "love" to be frightened, or women "love" to be mutilated and raped . . . . They are the great-grandchildren of those who honestly thought, because someone taught them this: "Women can't think," and "niggers can't faint." But most disturbing of all, in Blue's large brown eyes was a new look, more painful than the look of despair: the

310

look of disgust with human beings, with life; the look of hatred. And it was odd what the look of hatred did. It gave him, for the first time, the look of a beast. And what that meant was that he had put up a barrier within to protect himself from further violence; all the apples in the world wouldn't change that fact.

And so Blue remained, a beautiful part of our landscape, very peaceful to look at from the window, white against the grass. Once a friend came to visit and said, looking out on the soothing view: "And it would have to be a *white* horse; the very image of freedom." And I thought, yes, the animals are forced to become for us merely "images" of what they once so beautifully expressed. And we are used to drinking milk from containers showing "contented" cows, whose real lives we want to hear nothing about, eating eggs and drumsticks from "happy" hens, and munching hamburgers advertised by bulls of integrity who seem to command their fate.

As we talked of freedom and justice one day for all, we sat down to steaks. I am eating misery, I thought, as I took the first bite. And spit it out.

from "Living By the Word" 1986

The Light in Their Eyes
by Laura Moretti

I've been active on behalf of animals for 31 years. And I've seen a lot in all that time. A lot of blood. A lot of killing. Misery and suffering. I've seen it on film, in pictures, and I've seen a lot of it in my very presence.

When I was nine and living in Bolivia, I witnessed the lethal strangulation of a dog on the street on the outskirts of the city, while passersby gave no second notice. And I felt as absolutely and utterly helpless as that poor, betrayed animal in his violent death throes. There wasn't anything I could do—not for that dying black mongrel dog and the light he took with him, and not for me, that shock-awakened child.

Nothing prepared me for the unexpected crushing weight of empathy and sorrow and outrage, for that connectedness that mercilessly consumed me, and took me prisoner in a fleeting yet lethal moment and for a lifetime.

My eyes were opened. My eyes, my ears, my mind, my senses, my heart and soul. My life would never be the same; not my perspective, not my beliefs or my religion, not my goals or my dreams. I had been, I realized only years later, transformed back into that from which we have all come: a human being.

So who is this animal who claims to be my kin? Who once brainwashed me into believing I belonged to a superior species, who said that I was entitled to—no, let me rephrase that—that I was supposed to wear and eat and use and be entertained by the suffering of these lesser-feeling, lesser-brained, lesser-deserving lesser-beings? Has it never heard the screams of a black mongrel dog dying on a lone dirt road while not even the one person in the whole wide world who cared could help him? Has it never heard such a sound, a sound I heard only once but have never forgotten?

And so, for three decades, I have fought to quiet those screams, to mitigate that suffering, to reduce the killing, to attempt to bring back some of those long-lost human souls. And there are times when I think maybe I have succeeded, maybe I've eased one life's suffering, stopped the taking of another, and aided the passage, opened the eyes, raised the awareness, of a fellow, well, kin.

The older I get, the more often I assess the worthiness of my life. I've saved lives, more than I will ever know. I will be able to leave here having made this place more peaceful than I found it some 30 years ago. I have made a difference. Yes, I can rest now.

Or can I?

It is the present and I am on a crowded freeway in late afternoon; the sun melts over the valley and shines right into the faces of half a dozen young calves on their way to auction. There is no screaming, no strangulation, no lone dirt road upon which they are suffering, but I feel the familiar pressing weight of empathy. And I can see it there in their eyes: Fear, that which separates feeling, living, breathing, sentient animals from other forms of life. The will to live, the knowing.

Young black calves, their noses pressed to the slats of the livestock trailer, jockey for position, taking turns pushing against the metal gate from which there is no escape. Black calves with jet black eyes. And the light in their eyes that reflects back to me commands my attention, has mesmerized me: they are utterly innocent, they are indescribably precious, they are undeniably alive.

How can they be so ...unseen?

No lone dirt road this, but passersby still take no notice. No immediate killing but it lurks behind the scenes--and it is a monster: the accepted, habitual, conditioned, institutionalized degradation of living, desperately wanting, now suffering, one-day screaming beings.

And so what do I do with this helplessness, the shadow of which has haunted me all my life, for half a dozen black calves on their way to inevitable slaughter?

No, I have not done everything I can. I see that now. I am reminded one more time. I've still got one more mind to open, yet another heart to change. No, two more. Wait ...a hundred. But I am up for it. I have yet again seen the light.

In their eyes.

The Animal's Agenda, March/April 1999
Laura A. Moretti is a contributing writer to The Animals' Agenda.

I'll Have a Grain-Consuming Animal Unit Medium Rare
by Jeremy Rifkin

Children of the industrial world have little relationship to or understanding of the animals they incorporate into their bodies three or more times a week. Youngsters are often shocked on coming upon a beef carcass hanging in a butcher shop. They have grown up to think of meat as "a thing," a piece of material produced by the same processes that provide them with toys, clothes, and other such things.

The rank utilitarianism of the modern era has merged with the rational production processes of industrial technology, transforming cattle into so much manipulative matter whose worth is measured exclusively in market terms. The modern cattle complex, in both its organization and goals, is reflective of the state of mind of the modern age. Like nature itself, cattle have been stripped of their intrinsic value, reduced to a resource and then to a commodity, further reduced into an array of commercial products to be consumed and discarded back into the environment in various stages of entropic decay.

Today, cattle and other livestock are tucked away, out of sight of the public, until they are purchased in the form of prepacked cuts of beef at the local supermarket. Ranchers have sequestered the nation's beef cattle in rural enclaves cordoned off from public view like so many industrial parks. The feedlots are now so highly automated that there is little if any direct contact between the "caretaker" and the animals. Even the daily allotment of food is often managed and maintained by computer. "At this level of detachment," says James Serpell, "the animal becomes a mere cipher, a unit of production, abstracted out of existence in the pursuit of higher yields."

The nation's slaughterhouses, once located in the urban heart of busy midwestern cities like Cincinnati and Chicago, are now to be found on the outskirts of small midwestern towns where the activity inside on the kill floors has little or no impact on the sparsely settled human communities on the outside. Upton Sinclair's description of the hidden nature of slaughterhouses is

314

even more appropriate today than at the turn of the century. In *The jungle* the young worker Jurgis tells of his feelings upon being ushered onto the kill floor for the first time: "(It) was like some horrible crime committed in a dungeon, all unseen and unheeded, buried out of sight and of memory. "

Along with shifting blame and concealment, modern man has attempted to misrepresent the process of slaughtering beef and other livestock, reducing the act of killing to a rational process suggestive of machine production. In a recent issue of the British *Meat Trades Journal*, the editors proposed that the term "butcher" and "slaughter" be replaced with the terms "meat plant" and "meat factory" to accommodate the sensibilities of an increasingly squeamish consuming public. Today the United States Department of Agriculture describes cattle as "grain-consuming animal units," demonstrating forcefully that the mechanistic and utilitarian thinking of the Enlightenment still holds considerable sway over the contemporary use of language.

The beef-packing industry and the consuming public would no doubt be more than a little disturbed if beef were marketed as a "slaughtered animal" or the "partly cremated portions of dead animals." Even the terms "beef," "veal," "pork," "venison," and "mutton" are euphemisms, conjuring up an image of food devoid of any relationship with the animals from which they came. Few people would feel comfortable ordering part of a cow, a small calf, a pig, a deer, or a sheep on a restaurant menu.

Modern culture has distanced itself from the animals it eats in still another important way—the preparation of meat for consumption. In the great halls of medieval castles, large sections of oxen and whole pigs were often roasted on spits in view of the guests. On the Lord's day, an entire lamb might be prepared. In medieval households it was common practice to place the whole animal or a large portion of it on the dining table. Whole roasted birds with their feathers stuck back in to look alive were served up, as were whole rabbits, quarters of calves, and the like.

Beginning in the early modern era, much of the food preparation was removed from public scrutiny and fussed over behind the scenes in the kitchen and scullery. The newly urbanized societies, especially in France and Germany, became increasingly uncomfortable at the sight of whole animals served up at the table. Serving a whole dead animal was too forceful a reminder of killing and death and the thin line that separated humans from their prey; only beasts tear into a whole animal. The new culinary standards began to stress disguise. More and more of the carving was done away from the dining table, in the kitchens by the cooks. Heads were removed from animals, fowl, and fish, and meat was increasingly divided into small portions, filleted out of sight of the diners, and then served to eliminate any identification with the animal that was being eaten.

The ubiquitous hamburger represents the final deconstruction of modern meat. The bovine has been disassembled into indistinguishable matter, and made manipulatable and reshapable by the highly mechanized production process. The steer has been "forced out of its natural state and squeezed and molded" by the same scientific methods that Bacon first employed to deconstruct and reshape the rest of nature. The cow has been dismembered, disemboweled, reconstituted, and flattened into round, orderly, easily packagable units that can be fast-frozen, transported, stacked, grilled, and consumed with a minimum of inconvenience. The process by which cattle are raised, fattened, slaughtered, and packaged is highly rational, utilitarian, and expedient. The entire process is automated, with a minimum of human involvement.

Chances are that the supermarket manager who stocks the grain-fed beef will never personally experience the anguish of the victims of poverty, those millions of families thrown off their land so that it can be used to grow livestock feed for export. Teenagers gobbling down cheeseburgers at a fast-food restaurant will likely be unaware that a wide swath of tropical rain forest had to be felled and burned to bring them their meal. Consumers buying prepackaged cuts of steak will never know of the pain and discomfort experienced by the animals in high-tech automated feedlots.

If credit can be extended to a single person for the success of the hamburger and the fast-food industry, then certainly the distinction is due Ray Kroc, the indefatigable founder of the McDonald's restaurant chain. Kroc revolutionized American eating habits during the postwar era. Today the chain he built boasts 11,000 restaurants in fifty-two countries employing 600,000 people with an annual sales revenue of $17 billion. Over half of the population of the United States lives within a three-minute drive of a McDonald's restaurant.

Every month, tens of thousands of head of cattle have to be fattened, slaughtered, and ground into patties to provide millions of hamburgers to hungry customers. Like a general pinning flags on a war map, Kroc placed a McDonald 's restaurant at every strategic location, McDonaldizing much of the suburban landscape in less than a generation. His entrepreneurial fervor bordered on the messianic, as he himself noted in his own memoirs. Kroc once remarked:

"I speak of faith in McDonald's as if it were a religion. And without meaning any offense to the Holy Trinity, the Koran, or the Torah, that's exactly the way I think of it. I've often said that I believe in God, family, and McDonald's—and in the office, that order is reversed,"

It is interesting to note that church steeples played a prominent role in Kroc's strategic planning. He consciously placed his restaurants near suburban churches, believing that the pure, wholesome image of his restaurant and the neighboring church would shine a: a beacon of light on each other. Not surprisingly, Kroc had early on targeted the suburban churchgoing families as his prime market audience. Even his golden arches, say some social commentators, bore a striking resemblance to pictorial images of the gates of heaven.

from "Beyond Beef"

My Parents Worst Nightmare
by Victoria Paal

It was a bad day for a vegan in the school cafeteria. The lunch options included egg noodles, meatballs, or soggy peas soaking in lukewarm water. I moved to the salad bar but the dressings had cheese or honey in them. I settled for some lettuce.

At my high school, I am aware of two other vegans, both in the senior class with me. I have been vegan for about three years. When I first decided to go vegetarian five years ago, I knew very little about it. Something just seemed wrong about eating an animal. After all, I would never eat my dog. Two years later, after reading about veganism on web sites, I decided it was a good option for me. At that point, I was not very concerned with my health or the environment. I simply felt that it was wrong that dairy cows and hens were killed prematurely and kept on factory farms.

I will never forget the day I told my parents. "Vegan? What's that?" my mom asked. After explaining it, she rolled her eyes. My parent's worst nightmare was to have a liberal daughter. She continued, "It will be too hard. You won't get enough nutrients. It's not a good idea." My dad sat across the table, laughing, and swallowing a mouthful of steak.

Even after discussing the topic, my parents remained adamant that it would be a bad idea. My mother was panicking that I would not be getting three glasses of milk a day. I explained that there were other sources of vitamins and minerals, and my parents eventually realized that this was a decision from which I was not going to back down.

Now, more than three years later, my mom still likes to think it's a typical adolescent phase. When I say I'm not going to eat something because it has whey in it, I know to expect her to roll her eyes. My father still forgets occasionally and will offer me fish at dinner. At the same time, however, they seem to have grown used to my lifestyle. My mom gets excited when she finds a new vegan ice cream, and my father loves to try to find good vegan food at restaurants. They are even beginning to learn what vegan and nonvegan ingredients are.

I, too, have learned a lot over time. Bu reading such books as "Diet For A New America, " I better understand the implications of a meat-based society on human health and the environment. I have also become more socially active and aware. Through working with such animal rights groups as Compassion Over Killing, I have been given the opportunity to participate in protest and rallies. I was also fortunate enough to find a great part-time job at a vegan store near my home.

My school is gradually becoming aware of students' lifestyle choices. When it came time for the rat dissection in biology class, students were offered the alternative of participating in a computer-based interactive virtual dissection of the human body. However, when I took up this offer I was not spared from several teachers' disapproving looks and lectures on how I would learn more by actually dissecting.

Each day is a bit of a battle for a high school vegan. While the familiar arguments and occasionally lettuce lunches can get aggravating, veganism is a choice that pays off in the end. I am able to feel better about myself as a person, knowing that I am doing a small part to protect the animals.

from Animals Agenda Magazine
November 2000

Waking Up to Animal Rights
by William Kunstler

Although I have spent almost a half century in the field of
civil rights and liberties, my efforts have been exclusively limited
to attempting to secure them for human beings. For most of my
professional life, I have been remarkably oblivious to the plight of
animals used in experiments, in food and clothing production, and
for human entertainment. Only recently, I have begun to notice
the weekend antivivisection tables in my Greenwich Village neighborhood, and I have learned from my daughter, who refuses to eat
veal that calves are separated from their mothers as soon as they
are born, and, in order to keep their meat white and tender, are
reared in crates too cramped to permit them to move.

And as I have learned more, I have become more disturbed.
The Draize irritancy tests on the unanesthetized eyes or genitalia
of rabbits, the LD50 acute toxicity tests on rats and mice, the sub-
jection of rhesus monkeys to lethal doses of gamma neutron radia-
tion, and the removal of significant portions of the brains of cats
to document the effect on the senses are but four of the supposedly
"scientific" uses of animals. The situation of farm animals is argu-
ably worse. In addition to keeping veal calves anemic and isolated
in order to enhance the value of their flesh, we take piglets from
their mothers a week after birth and then confine them in
wire-mesh cages the condition of which would put the Marquis
de Sade to shame. Laying hens are jammed together in such a
fashion that there is scarcely room for them to turn around, while
broiler chickens, doomed to exist for less than 2 percent of their
normal life cycle and imprisoned in mammoth flocks in darkened
sheds, are cruelly debeaked in order to prevent the pecking and
cannibalism engendered by such an unnatural environment.

In addition to using animals in experiments and for food,
we use them for purposes of mere fashion or entertainment. Millions of animals lose their lives every year, caught in the deadly
jaws of the steel leghold trap or raised in confined conditions in
wire-mesh cages on "fur farms." so that we can adorn ourselves
with the latest fashions. Wild animals, captured violently and re-

moved from their natural habitats, are crated and transported from city to city so that we can enjoy the circus. The abuses go on and on, and there is, I fear, little justification for any of it.

It may surprise many who are familiar with my work that I have become interested in the plight of animals at a time in which there seems to be more human misery and injustice than ever before. I have given considerable thought to this question, and I have resolved any doubts in favor of speaking against the exploitation of nonhuman animals. It seems to me that there are at least two important reasons for taking animal rights seriously.

First, I cannot help thinking that our exploitation of animals has a direct link to our exploitation of our perennial human victims: African-Americans, poor whites, Latinos, women, lesbians and gays, social activists, Native Americans, and Asians, to name a few disempowered groups. As Tom Regan, Peter Singer, and other philosophers have argued so persuasively, "speciesism," or the use of species to determine membership in the moral community, is no more morally justifiable than using race, sex, or age to determine who has rights and who does not. If we are speciesist and feel that we may exploit nonhumans simply because we are more powerful, and we judge that we will benefit from that exploitation, then discrimination against other disadvantaged groups becomes that much easier.

Second, and perhaps more important, is that it is unjust to *the animals themselves* to deny them their rights, irrespective of any salutary effect that it may have on relations among humans. Like us, animals are individuals with interests. Their value does not depend on their use to us any more than does the inherent value of a human being depend on that person's use to others. Justice for nonhumans requires that we recognize that all sentient beings have inherent worth that does not depend on our humanocentric and patriarchal valuation of that worth.

Lack of progress in ameliorating our treatment of nonhumans is attributable to several causes, many of which may be traced to people's ignorance about the animal abuse that they themselves indirectly support. The ultimate consumer of the veal, pork, chicken, and eggs simply has no more conception of what went on before these neatly packaged farm products arrived at the retail level than the purchasers of Civil War clothing had of the conditions under which enslaved black hands planted and picked the cotton from which its threads were made. We all need to educate ourselves about the ways in which we support animal exploitation in our daily lives.

There is another explanation, however, and that is the subject of this fascinating book by Professor Gary Francione. Francione argues—correctly, in my view—that although most of us are woefully ignorant of the massive animal suffering that we cause indirectly through our consumption of animal products, most of us reject the imposition of "unnecessary" suffering on animals and agree that animals ought to be treated "humanely." Although these sentiments are broadly held, the law has lagged behind, and instead of evolving principles of animal protection that reflect our growing moral awareness, the law has continued to protect virtually every form of animal exploitation.

Francione proposes a thesis to explain why the law has failed to protect animals. Our legal system seeks to resolve human/animal conflicts by balancing human and animal interests. Although this appears to be appropriate in theory, in reality the balancing almost always comes out in favor of the human. The reason is that when we balance human and animal interests, we seek to compare the incomparable. Human interests are protected by claims of right; animals are regarded as *property* under the law and are not regarded as capable of having rights at all. When human interests, supported by claims of right and especially by the right to own and use property, are balanced against the unprotected interests of animals, who are the property of their human owners, the outcome is already determined. Francione explores how laws regulating cruelty to animals and experiments with animals delegate virtually plenary authority to animal owners to determine what level of care or lack thereof is appropriate.

Although much has been written on the technical legal aspects of animal ownership and veterinary malpractice, Francione's book is the first sustained effort to analyze our treatment of animals from a jurisprudential point of view. Despite its theoretical orientation, however, Francione's analysis also reflects his practical experience as a lawyer who has been at the cutting edge of litigating animal rights cases for over a decade. He has seen first-hand that the law is more interested in serving the interests of the powerful than it is in providing justice to the disempowered, and his analysis often draws upon his own cases.

Although Francione's analysis focuses on animals, his conclusions are applicable whenever the law allows sentient beings—human or nonhuman—to be treated solely as means to the ends determined by others. Although there were laws that supposedly protected slaves from abuse by their masters, the law very rarely punished any slave owner—regardless of the severity of the mistreatment—because slaves were regarded as property. Similarly, to the extent that our legal system has treated women or children as property, the interests of members of those groups have invariably been compromised.

We must come to understand that pain is pain, irrespective of the race, sex, or *species* of the victim. The animal rights movement is important precisely because it seeks liberation for all beings. The raising of consciousness about the plight of nonhumans must be accompanied by a correlative elevation about that of the millions of human beings who inhabit the ghettos, the barrios, or the streets of our inner cities. When we decry hens confined in precarious cramped spaces, we cannot be indifferent to the horribly overcrowded jails and penitentiaries of this land. Our concern for experimentation with toxic substances on rats and mice must not make us oblivious to the poisoning of entire urban communities with drugs that turn their residents into zombies, homicidal maniacs, or premature corpses.

We owe it to ourselves and to nonhuman animals to create not merely a body of rules and regulations to govern our conduct but a level of sensibility that makes us care, deeply and constructively, about the entire planet and all of its varied inhabitants. If we can accomplish this, then perhaps, some far-off day, those who follow us down the track of the generations will be able to dwell in relative harmony with all of the creatures of the earth, human and nonhuman.

from the foreword to "Animals, Property and the Law"
by Gary Francione. Temple University Press, 1995

How Language Distances Us From Suffering
by Carol J. Adams

So far feminism has accepted the dominant viewpoint regarding the oppression of animals rather than shed the illuminat-
ing light of its theory on this oppression. Not only is our language
male-centered, it is humancentered as well. When we use the ad-
jective "male," such as in the preceding sentence, we all assume
that it is referring solely to human males. Besides the
human-oriented notions that accompany our use of words such as
male and female, we use the word "animal" as though it did not
refer to human beings, as though we too are not animals. All that
is implied when the words "animal" and "beast" are used as insults
maintains separation between human animals and nonhuman
animals. We have structured our language to avoid the acknowl-
edgment of our biological similarity.

Language distances us further from animals by naming
them as objects, as "its." Should we call a horse, a cow, dog or cat,
or any animal "it"? "It" functions for nonhuman animals as "he"
supposedly functions for human beings, as a generic term whose
meaning is deduced by context. Patriarchal language insists that
the male pronoun is both generic, referring to all human beings,
and specific, referring only to males. Similarly, "it" refers either to
non-animate things or to animate beings whose gender identity is
irrelevant or unknown. But just as the generic "he" erases female
presence, the generic "it" erases the living, breathing nature of the
animals and reifies their object status. The absence of a non-sexist
pronoun allows us to objectify the animal world by considering all
animals as "its." I recommend using [sic] when an animal is called
"it" just as feminist critics have done when "he" is used generi-
cally. Should we even refer to a butchered part of an animal's body
as "it"? Is meat an "it"? Isn't the choice of "it" for meat the final
capitulation to the dominant reality that renders real animals invisible and masks violence? (Due to the lack of a generic pronoun,
I will use "she" in this book to refer to any animal, alive or dead,
whose sex is unknown.)

We also distance ourselves from animals through the use

324

of metaphors or similes that distort the reality of other animals' lives. Our representations of animals make them refer to human beings rather than to themselves: one is sly as a fox, hungry as a bear, pretty as a filly. When we talk about the victimization of humans we use animal metaphors derived from animal sacrifice and animal experimentation: someone is a scapegoat or a guinea pig. Violence undergirds some of our most commonly used metaphors that cannibalize the experiences of animals: beating a dead horse, a bird in the hand, I have a bone to pick with you.

From the leather in our shoes, the soap we use to cleanse our face, the down in the comforter, the meat we eat, and the dairy products we rely on, our world as we now know it is structured around a dependence on the death of the other animals. For many this is neither disturbing nor surprising. The death of the other animals is an accepted part of life, either envisioned as being granted in Genesis 1:26 by a human-oriented God who instructs us that we may dominate the animals or conceptualized as a right because of our superior rationality. For those who hold to this dominant viewpoint in our culture the surprise is not that animals are oppressed (though this is not the term they would use to express human beings' relationship to the other animals), the surprise is that anyone would object to this. Our culture generally accepts animals' oppression and finds nothing ethically or politically disturbing about the exploitation of animals for the benefit of people. Hence our language is structured to convey this acceptance.

We live in a culture that has institutionalized the oppression of animals on at least two levels: in formal structures such as slaughterhouses, meat markets, zoos, laboratories, and circuses, and through our language. That we refer to meat eating rather than to the eating of animals is one example of how our language transmits the dominant culture's approval of this activity.

Meat carries many meanings in our culture. However, no matter what else it does, meat eating signals the primary oppression of animals. Peter Singer observes that "for most humans, especially those in modern urban and suburban communities, the most direct form of contact with nonhuman animals is at meal time: we eat them. This simple fact is the key to our attitudes to other animals, and also the key to what each one of us can do about changing these attitudes." Because animals have been made absent referents it is not often while eating meat that one thinks: "I am now interacting with an animal." We do not see our meat eating as contact with animals because it has been renamed as contact with food.

On an emotional level everyone has some discomfort with the eating of animals. This discomfort is seen when people do not want to be reminded of what they are eating while eating, nor to be informed of the slaughterhouse activities that make meat eating possible; it is also revealed by the personal taboo that each person has toward some form of meat: either because of its form, such as organ meats, or because of its source, such as pig or rabbit, insects or rodents. The intellectual framework of language that enshrouds meat eating protects these emotional responses from being examined. This is nothing new; language has always aided us in sidestepping sticky problems of conceptualization by obfuscating the situation.

While self-interest arising from the enjoyment of meat eating is obviously one reason for its entrenchment, and inertia another, a process of language usage engulfs discussions about meat by constructing the discourse in such a way that these issues need never be addressed. Language distances us from the reality of meat eating, thus reinforcing the symbolic meaning of meat eating—a symbolic meaning that is intrinsically patriarchal and male-oriented. Meat becomes a symbol for what is not seen but is always there—patriarchal control of animals and of language.

Children often try to restore the absent referent. Dr. Alan Long reports of his becoming a vegetarian at eight: "I began to ask about the fate of the animals, and I began to inquire about the sources of my food, and I discovered to my horror that the lamb, the mutton on my plate, was obtained from the lambs I had seen in the fields. I said, in effect, that I liked lambs and I didn't like lamb, and that was the start of it all." Harvard philosophy professor Robert Nozick credits his two-year-old daughter with bringing about his vegetarianism. During a Thanksgiving dinner, she queried: "That turkey wanted to live. Why was it killed?" One three-year-old vegetarian demanded that he and his mother confront the local marketpersons with the literal truth that they were selling "poor dead mommie and baby animals."

Most children, however, are inculcated into a basic aspect of patriarchal language by experiencing simultaneously the masks of language and the relativizing of the death of animals. The failure to consider meat literally becalms vegetarianism as an issue.

Vegetarians face the problem of making their meanings understood within a dominant culture that accepts the legitimacy of meat eating. As the feminist detective in Lynn Meyer's *Paperback Thriller* remarks early in the novel, "I could tell you now that I'm a vegetarian, but let's just leave it at that. I won't go into the reasons. If you don't understand them, there's not much I can say; and if you do, there's no need for me to say anything." But she does go on to explain, and traces her vegetarianism to learning the literal truth about meat eating as a child: "It all goes back to a duckling I had when I was a kid. It grew up to be a duck, and then we killed it and cooked it. And I wouldn't eat it. Couldn't. From that, it was all obvious and logical."

from "The Sexual Politics of Meat: A Feminist-Vegetarian Critical Theory. "
Continuum Publishing Company 1990

Persuading by Example
by Chu Hui Cho

In recent days, we've witnessed the mass media paint the animal rights movement as hostile, intimidating, and in some cases even violent. Indeed, some activists have expressed the viewpoint that intimidation as a means for confronting animal exploitation is not only acceptable, but preferable as well. Is this a good course of action? In other words, will it help to abolish animal exploitation, to free animals from the slavery we force them to endure?

First, it is necessary to establish the fact that freedom for animals will necessitate a revolutionary shift in the attitudes and practices of the majority of society. Clearly, without the financial support of the masses, almost every exploitative industry would collapse. So, it is important to recognize our goal as the conversion of the majority if we are serious about achieving animal liberation. If we use hostility, intimidation, or violence as tactics in our struggle, we will only affect a handful of animal exploiters and will ultimately inflict minimal damage to institutionalized exploitation as a whole.

Not only does hostility not help us achieve long-term goals for the animals, it is counterproductive. Hostility in such forms as name-calling, snide or vicious tones, and shouting at animal abusers does not help us gain favor in public opinion. As activists who are trying to provoke fundamental changes in society, we must present our case in a nonthreatening manner if it is ever to be accepted. Most people react well to calmness and reason. Conversely, most people react poorly when put on the defensive by what they perceive to be violence or hostility.

Think about your conversion to a cruelty-free lifestyle.

Did it come about because you were afraid for your physical safety, or because you realized the rationality of compassion and kindness to others? How would you have reacted to actions like shouting, banging on windows, or pointing fingers? If we verbally attack the opposition at protests, members of the public give their sympathy to them. They see the opposition—not the animals—as the true victims. As mentioned, we must appeal to the public, because without the public's financial support, institutionalized animal exploitation cannot survive. Trying to force the hand of a few animal exploiters by using intimidation or some other form of violence is not enough.

As Martin Luther King, Jr., said, "The true activist seeks to defeat the unjust system, rather than the individuals who are caught in that system. This person believes it is important to get rid of the evil system and not the individual who happens to be misguided, who happens to be misled, who was taught wrong." The "enemy" is not the furrier, the vivisector, or the slaughterhouse worker, but the unjust systems that cast people into these oppressive roles. In the case of animal rights, we are fighting the entire human-centered tradition of animal exploitation and not the individuals involved. We must destroy the ideology that supports animal oppression, not the people who support that ideology.

Violence—physical or verbal—is not an ethical or practical tactic for convincing people of the rightness of our cause. Snide or vicious tones, shouting down, misrepresenting what people say, and name-calling are examples of verbal violence, which is the antithesis of respect and communication. Even though we may be dealing with people who are currently our opponents, they still deserve respectful and ethical treatment. We must never assume that our opponents cannot be converted. "Discover the element of good in your enemy," said King, "and as you seek to hate him, find the center of goodness and place your attention there and you will take a new attitude." The examples of Jerry Vlasak, M.D.; Ray Greek, M.D.; Neal Barnard, M.D.; Howard Lyman; and Robert Cohen show us that animal exploiters *can* be convinced to take the side of justice. Today, these former animal exploiters are some of our movement's greatest spokespersons. Would they have been convinced of the wrongness of animal abuse had they been intimidated by animal rights activists? Again, the answer can be drawn from your own experience. Think about what influences helped you gain the awareness you now have. Was it an arrogant person yelling at you, demeaning you, or calling you names that made you reconsider your position? Most likely you learned about animal rights in a non-threatening manner that did not make you feel personally attacked.

We must use nonviolence to persuade others of the injustice of animal slavery. The outrage we feel at the injustices committed against animals is understandable. But we must channel this anger towards constructive, effective actions that promote long-term changes. We must be militant and demand radical changes without condoning or using violence. As activists, we have a choice to make: will we choose hostility, alienation, and ineffectiveness (thereby ensuring the perpetuation of animal exploitation), or nonviolence, conversion, and progress (thereby working toward a more compassionate and just world)? The answer should be clear.

from Compassion Over Killing Newsletter
October 1999
The writer , a COK activist for three years studied at Bryn Mawr College

Law, Religion and Animals
by Colman McCarthy

Animals, Property and the Law
by Gary L. Francione
Temple University Press

Animal Theology
by Andrew Linzey
University of Illinois Press

In their relations with animals, humans eat, hunt, trap, ride, brand, wear, cage, own, sell, breed, dissect, exploit, tame, capture, torture, sacrifice and kill them. This is for starters and doesn't count the estimated 27 species made extinct every hour of every day. Much of this gore and suffering is legal, with such laws as the 1966 Animal Welfare Act providing a comforting balm. Much of it is also out of sight, with the meat-aisle shopper or the hamburger-chomper unaware of the pain inflicted on animals in factory farms and slaughterhouses. The human-caused violence done to animals has been normalized, either through habit or culture, so that it's only the oddball who tries to see life also from the animal's viewpoint who is considered abnormal. As T.S. Eliot wrote, in a world of fugitives those running in the opposite direction are called mad.

Two of these madmen are Gary Francione and Andrew Linzey, both scholars who write with lucid and reasoned prose and who counter the stereotypical image of animal rightsers as contrarian fanatics spray-painting fur coats or invading research labs. Francione and Linzey, complementary thinkers, cannot be so casually dismissed. In a debate too often marked by accusations and misunderstandings, both authors argue their case with much-needed intellectual calmness. They more than make up for the absence of thoughts, or thoughtfulness, that's at the core of how humans mistreat animals.

Francione is a law professor at Rutgers University and co-director of the Rutgers Animals Rights Law Center. Although he is not a pioneer in the philosophy of animal rights—there are many of these, if you want to include George Bernard Shaw, Henry Salt, Peter Singer and Tom Regan—he is in the first rank of those who examine the issue jurisprudentially.

Francione's central argument is that regulatory laws for animal welfare do little or nothing to establish or protect the interests of animals. "Animal welfare . . .," he writes, "is the view that it is morally acceptable, at least under some circumstances, to kill animals or subject them to suffering as long as precautions are taken to ensure that the animal is treated as 'humanely' as possible. That is, an animal welfare position generally holds that there is no animal interest that cannot be overridden if the consequences of the overriding are sufficiently 'beneficial' to human beings."

In 11 chapters ranging from animal experimentation to litigation involving the Animal Welfare Act, Francione prefers the explanatory tone over the argumentative. It's a plus. In my own experiences of teaching nonviolence towards animals, I've found that most students become initially defensive—as if merely to discuss the idea that animals have the same life force and will to live as humans is a personal attack on one's carnivorous eating habits. It isn't an attack, it's a questioning—of a kind that Francione engages in when he asks, is it moral to pass laws that treat animals as property? "It is my tentative conclusion," he writes, "that animal rights (as we commonly understand the notion of 'rights) are extremely difficult to achieve within a system in which animals are regarded as property..."

If legislatures and courts aren't likely to end the killing and abuse allowed under animal welfare laws, it's equally hard to envision that religion will intercede. I've listened to a bellyful of sermons over the years, plus digested the books of Billy Graham, Jerry Falwell, a few popes and assorted divines, but I can't recall any of the clergy calling on the faithful to stop the violence to animals. Except one: the Rev. Andrew Linzey, an Anglican priest and teacher. I met him in 1986 during one of his visits to Washington when he spoke on religion and animals to my high school class. Since then, I've read several of his 14 books, including *Christianity and Animals Rights* and *Song of Creation*, an anthology edited with Tom Regan.

The far-ranging Linzey is at ease in analyzing the views of theologians who insisted that animals lack moral status, including Thomas Aquinas and Francis De Sales, the latter saying that hunting helps in "developing our spiritual life." "From a theological perspective," Linzey writes, "a major weakness in Aquinas stems from what appears to be most derived in his thought from Hellenistic sources. Two axioms from Aristotle are taken over almost without question. The first is that humans alone have a rational capacity . . . The second is that animals have no other purpose save that of serving human beings..."

Debunking Aquinas—to be a doubting Thomist—is not for the intellectually timid. Linzey isn't. Because so few other theologians want to think about the links between religion and violence to animals, this English priest has the field mostly to himself. Linzey is a broad-minded defender of animals. He provides a refreshing moment when chiding those, members of the animals rights movement who don't hesitate to blast away at furriers, lab scientists or the meat industry. Moral absolutism leads to "self righteousness. Some people enjoy a good moral condemnation the way others enjoy a good dinner. When we reach strongly held principles that are implicitly critical of the actions of our fellow human beings, then we always need to look at ourselves and take stock . . . Western society is so bound up with the use and abuse of animals in so many fields of human endeavor that it is impossible for anyone to claim that they are not party, directly or indirectly, to this exploitation either through the products they buy, the food they eat, or the taxes they pay."

In the war on animals, politicians and the clergy are on the edges of the battle zones, offering laws and blessings in support of the carnage. Francione and Linzey arrive on the scene well-armed with reasoned arguments that animals are our neighbors, not our subjects. That's anything but a new idea, but each author, speaking the language of his profession, says it in a convincingly new way.

The Washington Post, Oct. 1, 1995